SOLUTIONS
For
SPECIFIC LEARNING DIFFICULTIES

IDENTIFICATION GUIDE
by Jan Poustie et al
B.Ed. (Dunelm), Cert. Ed., R.S.A. Diploma SpLD, A.M.B.D.A.

This book was written to help both professionals and non-professionals find out the reasons why some individuals are failing to succeed and to provide information on where to turn to for help in overcoming their difficulties.

(The pages of this book have been laid out with an irregular right hand margin and without hyphenation to aid those with visual difficulties.)

SOLUTIONS
For
Specific Learning Difficulties

THE IDENTIFICATION GUIDE

FOREWORD

The Identification Guide will be a valuable resource for parents, teachers and other professionals, as it clearly presents the indicators that can be observed in a range of specific learning difficulties.

Specialists in particular areas have been consulted and their advice, based on knowledge and experience, will certainly increase the understanding of the readers, making them more aware of the nature of the difficulties they are observing.

There is comprehensive information on where appropriate help, advice and diagnosis can be obtained. This, in itself, will relieve many anxieties - to take a book from a shelf and find a possible solution to problems will, hopefully, ensure that children get the right help at the right time.

Violet Brand

Jan Poustie *the creator of Solutions, runs a private practice where she teaches, assesses and advises on Specific Learning Difficulties. Jan also designs teaching materials for both Sp.L.D. and non-Sp.L.D. children.*

She has taught for over 22 years a variety of subjects up to and including HNC level. Her teaching experience includes playgroup, primary, secondary and Further Education establishments. She has extensive experience in the field of special needs (including having been Head of a Special Needs Department).

Besides her professional interest in Sp.L.D. she also has considerable personal experience of this field of which not the least part is her own dyspraxia and dyscalculia, hence her very strong interest in both these fields.

She holds the RSA Diploma Sp.L.D. and Prof. Mahesh Sharma's Diagnosis and Remediation of Learning Problems in Mathematics Certificate. She is also a founder member of the Taunton Patoss group.

ISBN 1 901544 00 1

A NEXT GENERATION Publication.
First Published in Great Britain in 1997
Copyright © Jan Poustie 1997

Layout and origination by Pam Brooks. Cover designed by Michael Ewing
Printed by Kampress, Bridgwater, Somerset.

Published by NEXT GENERATION. 17 Medway Close. Taunton. Somerset. TA1 2NS.

A word from the Author _____

Whilst reading through this book you may realise that it is likely that you (the parent/adult/professional) and/or your child are affected by the conditions that come within the SpLD Profile. For some of you it might explain much of what has happened in the past and what is happening now and for some that may seem quite devastating and be a very traumatic experience. If this is the case it is important to remember that there has been no change in you and/or your child since you picked up this book - just a change in your perception. There is a network of help, support, advice, assessment and intervention available to you which this book will help you to find and access. The information that you gain from this book is not the end of your hopes, dreams and aspirations but it may be the first step towards the realisation of them.

Please start at Chapter 1 to get an overview of the Specific Learning Difficulties Profile - after that you can either read each chapter in order or start at the chapter which interests you most.

This book has been designed for individuals to 'find' the elements of the picture and then know to whom to go for diagnosis and help and support. It is not the isolated indicator that you need to look for in a condition but the whole picture. (For that reason no index has been included in this book as each condition needs to be viewed as a 'whole'.) As you are referred from chapter to chapter the picture will emerge. You will usually 'know' when the full picture has emerged as it will 'feel right and complete'. (Many who read this book may have one or two, of the indicators of one or two of the conditions mentioned within it but this does not mean that they have the conditions. (It's a bit like if you sneeze it does not mean that you have flu!)

You may find it helpful to have a piece of paper handy to write down the chapter numbers as you are referred to them. Once you have read all the relevant chapters you must then decide which of the difficulties is causing the most problems and arrange a referral for that area first but remember it can take months before you (or the child/adult) is seen. Please do not wait until a diagnosis has been made before contacting your relevant local help and support groups - they exist just for you, whether you are a parent, teenager, adult or professional. (They will not think that you have wasted their time if the diagnosis shows that that you, or the child/adult, does not have the condition in the end.)

I wanted to design the book that was needed in the past, when I was the child, and is needed now by professionals, adults and parents. I hope that I have succeeded and that you find it of assistance both to yourself and in helping those around you.

Best wishes

JAN
Jan

Acknowledgements

This book has only been made possible through the cooperation of many agencies and professionals to whom I am greatly indebted. The generosity of my colleagues has been exceptional. They have given their time (a precious commodity for all of them) plus they have given me advice and the benefit of their expertise. Many grateful thanks go to: **Prof. Mahesh Sharma** (Dean of Professional Programme in Education at Cambridge College, Mass, USA and Director of the Teaching and Learning Center of Mathematics, Wesley, Mass, USA), **Keith Holland** (Behavioural Optometrist), **Violet Brand** (International speaker on dyslexia), **Dr Ian McKinlay** (Senior lecturer in Community Child Health, Royal Manchester Children's Hospital), **Rosemary Sasson** (Specialist in the educational and medical aspects of handwriting), **Dr Peter Gardner** (Chartered Educational psychologist and co-founder of Appleford School), **Carol Orton** (Befriender co-ordinator British Dyslexia Association) **Dr Josephine Marriage** (Paediatric Audiological Scientist, Addenbrooks Hospital, Cambridge), **Christine Stache** (Head Occupational Therapist, Musgrove Park Hospital, Taunton), **Michèle Lee** (Chartered Physiotherapist in paediatrics), **Dr Pullaperuma** (Consultant Paediatrician with an interest in children with autistic spectrum disorder, Musgrove Park Hospital, Taunton), **Veronica M. Connery** (Paediatric Speech & Language Therapist), **Denise Caferelli-Dees** (Audiological scientist and speech pathologist, Southampton University Audiology Dept.), **Mary Nash-Wortham** (Speech Therapist), **Dr Hamstra-Bletz** (Social scientist), **Dr Steve Chinn** (Principal, Mark College), **Richard Ashcroft** (Headmaster, Mark College), **Madeleine Portwood** (Specialist Senior Educational Psychologist), **Patricia Clayton** (Irlen Diagnostician), **Colin Allen** (Deputy Chief Inspector for Prisons), **John Stevenson** (Prison Inspectorate's Education Consultant), **Cynthia Klein** (Dyspel Project Director), **Dr Christopher Green** (Specialist Paediatrician, Head of Child Development Unit, Royal Alexandra Hospital for Children, Sydney, Australia and clinical lecturer at the University of Sidney), **Dr Ginny Stacey** (Support Tutor for Dyslexic Students at Oxford Brookes University) and to many others (too numerous to name) who have pointed me in the right direction to find essential information.

I am very grateful for the cooperation and assistance (including that of allowing me to quote from their publications) that I have recieved from the following agencies and organisations and their staff:
AFASIC, The Dyspraxia Foundation, The AD/HD Family Support Group UK, The Dyslexia Institute, the British Dyslexia Association, The National

Autistic Society, The College of Speech & Language Therapists, The Handwriting Interest Group and various departments of OFSTED. The Department of Education and Employment, the Special Educational Needs Tribunal and the Schools Curriculum and Assessment Authority.

Many thanks go to the various organisations that gave me permission to quote from their publications. "Crown copyright is produced with the permission of the controller of Her Majesty's Stationary Office." OFSTED allowed me to quote from their report entitled "The Implementation of the Code of Practice for pupils with special educational needs, pub. by HMSO 1996 (ISBN 01135 00807). The American Psychiatric Association allowed me to quote from the Diagnostic and Statistical Manual of Mental Disorders, Fourth Edition. Washing, DC. American Psychiatric Association, 1994.

Also many thanks to my friends and colleagues who have supported and encouraged me all along the way and especially to Mary Coyle, Hilary Finn and Stephanie Smith who have not only been my companions at many a conference and lecture but have been generous in their advice. Thanks too to Hugh Bellamy (RSA Dip SpLD course tutor) for allowing me the freedom of reading his many books, the benefit of his knowledge and for opening my eyes to wider horizons.

That this book ever reached the printing stage has been due to my friend Pam Brooks who 'foolishly' volunteered to originate the text and has managed to not only cope with me continuously revising each chapter but also with a software program that decided to crash every few minutes. My thanks go to both her and her family for supporting me in this endeavour.

Finally thanks to my family -my husband for tolerating the upheaval in our lives that the writing of this book has sometimes caused and my lovely daughters for whom I needed to find out the information upon which this book is based.

The views expressed by the authoress are her own and do not necessarily represent those who have contributed to, or assisted with the writing of this book

Jan Poustie

Specific Learning Difficulties ———————

SPECIFIC LANGUAGE IMPAIRMENT: (also known as dysphasia): A continuum of difficulties experienced by children and young people who have not reached expected competence in communication skills in their first language, and whose teaching and learning is consequently affected. Often this group is defined by exclusion: 'They are not autistic; the impairment is not the result of a physical, intellectual or hearing impairment....' (Norma Corkish, AFASIC Chief Executive)

DYSLEXIA: difficulties with the acquisition of spelling and/or reading skills. Can also be used an umbrella term for several of the conditions found within the SpLD Profile.

DYSCALCULIA: difficulties in understanding, processing and using numerical/mathematical information that are not caused by another condition within the SpLD Profile.

DYSPRAXIA: (also known as Developmental Co-ordination Disorder). There are various forms of it which all relate to difficulties in motor planning and organisation.

CENTRAL AUDITORY PROCESSING DISORDER: a dysfunction of the processing of the auditory input.

ATTENTION DEFICIT DISORDER: difficulties in concentrating and focusing attention, also affects behaviour. Has several forms. In the UK it is called Attention Deficit Hyperactivity Disorder, ADHD or Attention Deficits and Behaviour Inhibition Disorder in the USA.

AUTISTIC SPECTRUM DISORDER: Difficulties in social interaction, social communication and in imagination based activities/behaviour.

Individuals will have a sub set of wide-ranging difficulties (e.g. visual, auditory, memory, perceptual, planning, processing, behavioural and communication difficulties). No two individuals will be alike and some will have more than one condition.

"Dyslexia is not curable, but the worst of it is avoidable PROVIDING a dyslexic child is allowed to learn according to his / her natural way. This means that early recognition and appropriate teaching methods are vital ; they reduce the severity of the dyslexia. Avoidance of inappropriate early learning is the nearest thing to a 'cure for dyslexia'."
Ginny Stacey (A Taste of Dyslexia) VIDEO

CONTENTS

('Gaining Provision' is based upon an article that was originally published in Solutions for Specific Learning Difficulties Issue 3. Chapter 7 contains information on occulomotor dyspraxia. It, along with Chapter 12, also provides information on dysfunctions which are not learning difficulties in themselves but can accompany the conditions that come within the SpLD Profile.)

Chapter 1

THE SPECIFIC LEARNING DIFFICULTIES PROFILE

Those of us who are interested in the field of Specific Learning Difficulties (SpLD) are recognising that a number of conditions are found in individuals who have a 'Specific Learning Difficulty Profile'. It is believed by many that these conditions are related to each other primarily through the area of language. All individuals affected by Specific Learning Difficulties are likely to have a combination of language-based difficulties (dysphasia). These difficulties can be apparent in any, or all, of the areas of written, spoken, heard language plus that of body language. The appropriate use of language, information processing, understanding and acquiring the areas of language can all be affected.

A simple way of looking at this is to think of the M1 as being the learning and use of language in all its forms with each small aspect of language being a service station. Each person with a SpLD Profile can stop at some of the service stations but are prevented by all sort of barriers from adequately accessing others. They have no control over these barriers but were born with them. They can be taught to go round, overcome etc. the barriers (to a greater or lesser degree). This can only occur once it is realised which ones they are having difficulties in accessing and the appropriate strategies have been learnt.

Various names are used to identify each of the conditions within the SpLD Profile and each condition has its own set of characteristics by which it can be recognised. Many of these conditions go under several names influenced by changes brought about by research and by the influence of name changes in other countries notably the USA. The names that parents know and the names that the various conditions are called by professionals can be very different, and names can vary between professionals. (It is a bit like a flower being known by both its Latin name and the various local names for it.) It does not really matter which name is used as long as all of us know what each of us means.

There is still some confusion amongst some people as to the meaning of various terms e.g. Specific Learning Difficulties and dyslexia. Most professionals accept the term 'dyslexia', or 'Specific Learning Difficulties in literacy' but some feel that the term 'dyslexia' is meaningless simply because the definition has not remained constant over the years but has, instead, continuously evolved as a result of on-going research. This seems a great pity as one can then become locked into disagreements about 'what is dyslexia' and there is then the risk that defining 'dyslexia' can become more important than meeting the need of the individual in question.

At one point during the twentieth century the term for some of the conditions found within the SpLD Profile was 'minimal brain dysfunction'. Then terms such as 'dyslexia' were used. Now many professionals and some of the agencies dealing with these difficulties are moving away from the 'dys' terms and prefer to use 'A Specific Learning Difficulty in literacy etc..)

This evolution of terms and their definitions can cause problems for those involved within this field as it means that the various conditions that come within the Specific Learning Difficulty Profile are regarded in different ways:

❑ **Dyslexia** is accepted by most people as a term which relates to difficulties in reading, spelling and written language but some do not realise that its definition has gradually been broadened to cover other areas. Thus the British Dyslexia Association in 1996 describe dyslexia as:
"A complex neurological condition which is constitutional in origin. The symptoms may affect many areas of learning and function, and may be described as a specific difficulty in reading, spelling and written language. One or more of these areas may be affected. Numeracy, notational skills (music), motor function and organisational skills may also be involved. However, it is particularly related to mastering written language, although oral language may be affected to some degree." [1] This definition makes dyslexia into an 'umbrella term' which covers many of the conditions which come within the Profile.

❏ **Dyspraxia** is regarded by some professionals as being a SpLD in its own right whilst others regard it as the 'motor form' of dyslexia. Other people may regard it in the same way as Dr Ian McKinlay namely as a "motor learning difficulty which may, or may not, be associated with a Specific Learning Difficulty (e.g. dyslexia) and quite often is".

❏ Some people believe that Specific Learning Difficulties is the same as dyslexia others believe that it is not.

❏ Some conditions are still not accepted by some people e.g. dyslexia. (Fortunately the belief, that was common in the earlier part of the twentieth century, that it is 'a non-existent problem invented by over anxious middle-class parents' is held by very few people now.)

It is only to be expected that differences as to what is and what is not a SpLD can cause problems for both parents and professionals and this in turn can cause disagreement between parties. Two particular areas of conflict relate to dyspraxia and dyslexia:

1. In the dyslexia field it is generally accepted that the individual with SpLD will not 'grow out' of his dyslexia and will be affected by it all his life. (He can be taught strategies to overcome many of his difficulties but they will return when he is under stress, ill etc..) However, Dr Ian McKinlay states of dyspraxia that "Most people do grow out of it but some do not". If we accept that dyspraxia is part of dyslexia then conflict arises. However, the study of dyspraxia is still relatively new and so there is only limited research into adult dyspraxia. (It is relatively easy in the modern world for adults not to be involved in practical activities that show up a weakness in the area of motor planning, organisation and control.) No doubt research in the future will clarify this point.

2. Research into dyslexia has shown that it is a condition which is approximately 80% inherited but not all those working in the field of dyspraxia believe it to be a largely inherited condition. Again, the conflict arises if we accept the definition of dyslexia as an 'umbrella term' which includes dyspraxia. However, if we look at families who have several members affected by the conditions that are found as part of the Specific Learning Difficulty Profile an interesting picture emerges. This picture seems to indicate a degree of inheritance of not only dyslexia (as in literacy) and dyspraxia but also of several of the other conditions that are found within the Profile. Thus we can sometimes see in three generations of one family various combinations in the family members e.g.:

• Dyspraxia based handwriting difficulties + Dyscalculia
• Dyspraxia based handwriting difficulties + Dyslexia (as in literacy)
• Undifferentiated Attention Deficit Disorder + Dyspraxia + Dyscalculia
• Low-level Speech/Language Impairment + Dyspraxia + Dyscalculia
• Dyslexia (as in literacy + Occulomotor dyspraxia + Oppositional Defiant Disorder

All the time that research is being conducted we can expect to continue to further refine definitions and it is only research that will answer many of our questions and resolve these disagreements. In the meantime we all have to work within the knowledge that is available at present. As more and more research is conducted we will find out more about each of the conditions. As certain patterns of difficulty emerge we will start naming others as in the case of Central Auditory Processing Disorder. So, those of us involved in this field (either by desire, or, because it is part of our job and/or our family) will need to accept an ever-changing world where definitions become more and more refined. We need to be aware of the areas of disagreement and accept that differences will continue to exist for some time until more research is done. In the meantime instead of feeling that we are in a 'quicksand' of ever shifting meanings we need to greet this ever-widening pool of knowledge as something which can only improve our situation and that of the individuals in our care. It is the acceptance that there is a difficulty which is specific to a particular area of learning and which has a set of recognisable characteristics which is important not the terms that we use.

For the majority of us arguing about just what the term Specific Learning Difficulties means, which of the conditions in this book are SpLD's and which ones are associated conditions is not an important issue. What is important, however, is that we all learn to identify all the different conditions within the Specific Learning Difficulties Profile. In this way we can help the individuals within it to overcome their difficulties - *in brief for most of us it is important to concentrate on finding Solutions!*

References
1. Crisfield J. (editor) (1996) The Dyslexia Handbook pub. by British Dyslexia Association, Reading.

Chapter 2

WHAT IS SPECIFIC LANGUAGE IMPAIRMENT
(Dysphasia)

Edited by Jan Poustie
(This article includes extracts from the AFASIC
Glossary Sheets which can be obtained from AFASIC,
347 Central Markets, Smithfield, London EC1A 9NH)

As many as 500,000 children have a speech and
language impairment. "It is estimated that 1 in 1,000
school-age children will have severe long-term
impairments, whilst up to 250,000 will experience some degree
of difficulty at some time."[1] "For some of these it is a 'delay' in
language but for others with a **language disorder** the difficulty is more
complex. These children do not stammer or lisp. Their language
impairment is **specific** or **primary** (not the result of any other disability)
and is sometimes referred to as dysphasia."[2] As both language delay
and dysphasia can have a considerable effect upon the individual's life
both types of impairment require appropriate provision.

Specific language impairment
(This is the most commonly used term but two other terms can also be
used: 'developmental language delay' and 'developmental language
disorder'.) "Dysphasic individuals will "have difficulties with talking
(expressive language), understanding (receptive language) or both."[3]
Some may have a discrepancy between verbal and non-verbal skills or
between expressive and receptive language. Late onset of speech can
also occur. Speech and language therapists divide the areas of difficulty
into:
◆ **Speech apparatus** - the mouth, tongue, nose, breathing etc. and how
they are coordinated and operated by muscles (see Verbal Dyspraxia
Chapter 5)
◆ **Phonology** - the sounds that make up the language
◆ **Syntax** or **grammar** - the way that words and parts of words
combine in phrases and sentences
◆ **Semantics** - the meaning of words, bits of words and phrases and
sentences
◆ **Pragmatics** - how we use language in different situations and how
we convey feelings

◆ **Intonation** and **stress** (prosody) - the rhythm and 'music' of the way we speak.

A child can have difficulties with phonology, syntax, semantics and pragmatics which are comprehensive (receptive) and/or expressive.[4] Individuals can be affected by various difficulties e.g.

Expressive language difficulties - this may affect any or all of:
◆ morphology (the way words change e.g. sleep, sleeping, slept)
◆ syntax
◆ semantics
◆ pragmatics
◆ phonology

"Bloom and Lahey classified disorders according to the area of language presenting the problem:" [5]

❑ **Content**: difficulties with content of language relate to its meaning. Can cause limited vocabulary, difficulty expressing abstract concepts or categorisation problems and word finding difficulties. (The latter causes individuals to have problems with accessing the word that they want to say from their memory

❑ **Form**: difficulties with developing surface aspects of language (the sounds, word forms and grammar). Individuals may have difficulties with word order, structuring sentences or expressing what they know and understand. "They will perform better on non-verbal tests than on language tests. They may have difficulties with word endings, plurals, possessives, verb tenses and prepositions.

❑ **Use**: language is used inappropriately or out of context. Sometimes called **Semantic-pragmatic disorder**. They may seem to have very good verbal comprehension and age appropriate sentence structure, but may have difficulty receiving or interpreting conversational cues. They often lack verbal fluency and may overuse a limited or concrete vocabulary, and frequently fail to appreciate a need for clarification or the needs of others in conversation. (Wilg and Semel 1980). "Rapin identified the following characteristics:
◆ fluent, well formed sentences
◆ verbose with adequate speech articulation
◆ literal interpretations often alongside a good vocabulary
◆ uses scripts in situations (i.e. say the same thing each time that they are presented with a similar situation)
◆ they say more than they are capable of understanding

◆ turn-taking and topic maintenance (problems with knowing what is being talked about)
◆ going round the point, being unclear what they are saying [6]
They often show signs of limited social development and play as do individuals who are affected by either semantic or pragmatic disorders. Many of those individuals affected by Semantic-pragmatic Disorder will also be affected by Autistic Spectrum Disorder. (See Chapter 10).
semantic disorders:
Two types of disorder- Receptive Language Disorder and Higher Level **Language Disorder**. *Characterised by difficulties with:*
1. knowing the possible meanings of a word but unable to work out how it is being used in a particular sentence.
2. words that refer to emotions (e.g. sad) or status (e.g. important)
3. when a phrase does not keep its literal meaning (e.g. when 'cut it out' is used for 'stop it')

Pragmatic disorders:
1. Difficulties in using language in its social context e.g. taking turns when talking, and keep the conversation going by small words at appropriate times e.g. yes, uh huh.
2. Can be unaware of what their partner wants or needs to know.
3. Difficulties with inference, innuendo, irony, sarcasm and inflexion.

Phonological Disorder
It can be associated with articulatory dyspraxia, dyslexia and frequent ear infections such as 'glue ear'. Individuals will have difficulties in saying a number of sounds which can be grouped according to certain features such as the place in the mouth where the sound is produced or how it is produced e.g.
fronting: sound should be produced at the back of the mouth e.g. 'car' but is produced further forward in the mouth so becomes 'tar' or 'par'.
backing: opposite of fronting so 'pen' becomes 'ten' or 'ken'
stopping of fricatives: when longer fricative sounds (f, v,s,z,sh,th) are pronounced as short plosive sounds (p,b,t,d,k) so 'sun' becomes 'tun'.
cluster reduction: one of the two or three consonants which occur together in a word are omitted e.g. 'black' becomes 'back' .
The above difficulties may not occur on every occasion and may only occur in certain places in the word e.g. the beginning of words. These difficulties can make the speech unintelligible and can cause both the individual and the person they are speaking to a great deal of frustration. Speech is closely linked to spelling and reading. Individuals with a phonological disorder are likely to have problems

with both activities.[7] Some of these individuals will find it very difficult to learn phonics and will need very specialised tuition to help them overcome these difficulties.[8]

Receptive Language difficulties

This problem in understanding what is said may have an auditory difficulty called Central Auditory Processing Disorder as the root cause of this problem. 'Glue ear' can also cause difficulties as can a hearing impairment. Individuals have to have acquired various auditory skills if they are to recognise words and understand what they mean in a sentence. Some of the skills which are involved in language comprehension are:

4. Ability to pay attention to the sounds of speech.
5. Ability to distinguish between speech sounds (auditory discrimination).
6. Ability to process language.
7. Ability to remember the sequence of the sounds (auditory sequential memory).
8. Knowledge of sentence structure.
9. Knowledge of word meanings.
10. Ability to make sense of language in and out of context.

The speaker may become very frustrated because the individual is 'not paying attention', is misbehaving or has decided to give up trying. Children can be told off for doing the exact opposite of the teacher's instruction (See Chapter 8) Such individuals can be so busy translating the first sentence that they fail to listen to the next one. Others need extra time to absorb the sentence and so will often repeat back the sentence whilst processing it (echolia).

It is not always easy to assess as the individual can obtain cues from the speaker, the environment etc.. Research has shown that difficulties in understanding are more widespread than was previously thought. Even children whose difficulties appear to be limited to expressive language may have subtle but significant receptive language difficulties. [9]

Higher Level Language Disorder (HLLD)

(HLLD has similarities to semantic-pragmatic disorder. Depending upon the focus of the diagnosis an individual may be diagnosed as having one or the other of these disorders.) Individuals with this condition will develop language which is structurally normal and have some understanding, but will have problems with:

◆ understanding more complex statements, questions and instructions, they often 'get hold of the wrong end of the stick'
◆ expressing more advanced concepts e.g. 'I ought to have .....

9

◆ word finding
◆ the more sophisticated aspects of language e.g. 'You must go home now' is rude, but 'You must try these biscuits' is polite.
◆ humour which depends on language
◆ inference - they have to have things 'spelled out' to them
◆ literal interpretation e.g. the child told to 'pull your socks up' (meaning try harder) bends down and pulls up her socks.

Many people with HLLD are of normal or above normal intelligence with good cognitive (thinking skills) and literacy skills. They often learn coping or masking strategies which hide their problems, Diagnosis is made via various assessment tools e.g. CELF-R (see Chapter 12) close observation and knowledge of the person and use of a checklist as above.

Often there is early language delay or disorder which seems largely to resolve, leaving the difficulties defined above. People with HLLD often have difficulty with social skills and forming relationships with others."[10]

Some other speech and language based difficulties are:
◆ **Temporal language**
If a pupil is weak in this area she will have difficulties in processing information related to position in speech, written language or auditory processing. (Spatial difficulties will make this difficulty worse). So, the pupil will find instructions which contain several comments on position e.g. left, right, back, front, up and down, points of the compass etc. very difficult to process and act upon. Temporal language difficulties are likely to cause problems for pupils in most practical subjects.
◆ **Paraphasia**: confuses a word for one of similar pronunciation e.g. splinter for slipper'
◆ **Word labelling difficulties**: have problems with remembering the names of items e.g. might go up to the washing machine and say 'What is this called?'.

As a result of a speech/language impairment the individual may become frustrated, have temper tantrums/arguments, and emotional and behavioural difficulties. For some individuals there will be problems with relationships (both social and work/school based) and in using the telephone. Alongside the difficulties we are also likely to see low self-esteem and a lack of confidence.

"Language is the basis of learning and social interaction, children {with speech and language impairment} will fall further and further behind their peers if help is not given early and in an appropriate way. Research findings show that though difficulties with understanding and speaking may apparently resolve, reading skills may be poor at seven years of age and beyond." [11]

Checklists developed by AFASIC are available from LDA [12] which help teachers confirm - or otherwise- any fears they have. As language skills develop very rapidly in the early years much is gained if difficulties are identified as early as possible - 2-3 years of age is not too early. If the difficulties are not tackled in the early years, and the child struggles through primary schooling, the difficulties are seriously compounded by secondary age."[13] Even those with low-level difficulties will have problems in a mainstream secondary school/college/university (e.g. understanding homework/assignment instructions given out in a hurry at the end of a lesson/lecture, following instructions for tasks, listening to the teacher/lecturer).

Those with moderate/severe difficulties in a mainstream school "are unlikely to be able to master the necessary conceptual understanding and complex social interactions expected in such a setting. As a result they are likely to become confused, disorientated, suffer emotional stress and succumb to serious bullying. Special schooling is then likely to be the only way to provide effective help." [14]

Assessment of the difficulties is via a speech therapist with the referral to them being made by the teacher (in consultation with the parents) or by the parents themselves. Those with severe difficulties will need a special school or language unit/language class where the speech and language therapist and teacher work closely together. ("There are about 400 such units throughout the country, but few as yet are available for secondary aged pupils." [15]) For the less severe individuals programmes devised by a speech and language therapist on at least a termly basis is recommended (plus advice from paediatric occupational/physio therapists may also be needed if co-ordination if affected).

Difficulties can be addressed if individuals are "taught appropriate skills in a structured setting:
• A planned approach needs to be used to teaching speaking and

listening skills as to reading and writing for all pupils.
• Activities should encourage the development of turn-taking, rhythms and rhyme and the building up of self-esteem and confidence [16]
• Where a child has difficulty in learning the order of a task, it helps to structure the sequence of skills and to simplify each step.
• The use of computers and a combination of sight, sound, touch or movement can be valuable. [17]
• Small group work (4-8 pupils) is essential to achieve national curriculum attainment targets successfully.
• Social skills and the use of social or functional language needs to be developed." [18]

Relating work to the child's interests/family will make it more effective. As with all conditions within the Specific Learning Difficulty Profile as each area is improved a re-evaluation needs to take place of what needs to be concentrated upon next (see Chapter 11 - The Code of Practice.) As it is speech and language that is affected it may not be obvious that many of these individuals are the equal of their peers of similar academic ability and so they may be placed in inappropriate lower sets in secondary school. (Many will be able to do the same work as their peers as long as they are allowed extra time.) It is important that all teachers are aware of speech/language impairment, that they be trained to be able to recognise it and help those affected by it to reach their potential.

Parents need to be actively involved plus need empathy and support (the child is at home longer than they are at school). They can often be confused because there is no clear diagnosis or 'label'. There are schemes which are designed for parents to participate in helping the child overcome his problems [19] whilst others can be used under the direction of a teacher/therapist. [20] Even if the parents are not involved in such a way they should always be kept informed of the child's difficulties and the progress being made (See Chapter 13 - Code of Practice section).

Legislation
"The legal position relating to speech and language therapy can be confusing, as both health and education authorities have responsibilities and duties to provide. Health authorities have a **general** duty of care to provide for all children and young people,

irrespective of age and whether or not a child has a Statement of Educational Need. [21] In practice provision is severely limited by the resources available. Education authorities have a **specific** duty to provide for children and young people with a Statement of Educational Need. In 1989, in R v Lancashire County Council ex parte CM, the Court of Appeal ruled that where a child 'requires speech therapy to enable him to communicate so that he may be fully understood by others' such therapy is an educational provision. In such cases, education authorities have a duty to arrange provision of speech and language therapy for a child with a Statement of Special Educational Need, either by ensuring the health authority provides and funds it or by purchasing the therapy themselves from a health authority or elsewhere. In addition, reference to such therapy should appear in Sections 2 & 3 of a Statement {which deal with special education needs - learning difficulties and special educational provision} and not Sections 5 & 6 of the Statement {which deal with non-educational needs and non-educational provision}. That the health authority is providing and funding does not determine where it appears on the Statement. This Ruling stands irrespective of the 1993/1996 Education Acts and Code of Practice." [22]

Some of the individuals with **Specific Language Impairment** are also affected by other conditions that are found within the Specific Learning Difficulty Profile. Each condition will have its own set of difficulties. Thus individuals can have difficulties in:
▲ Making the movements which produce speech e.g. the mouth, tongue, nose, breathing etc. and how they are co-ordinated and operated by muscles. (**Articulatory dyspraxia** see Chapter 5). In its most severe form they understand what is said to them but cannot use words to make themselves understood. For others the most noticeable difficulties may be in swallowing and saying some sounds.
▲ The development of language because of focusing attention difficulties (**Attention Deficit Disorder** see Chapter 9). These can also cause the individual to:
•Interrupt a lot.
•Not think before she speaks.
▲ The development of language due to listening difficulties (**Central Auditory Processing Disorder** see Chapter 8).
▲ Reading (**Dyslexia** see Chapter 3). These individuals are likely to have problems with short-term memory which prevent them from using complex sentences (especially in written work) and may also have sequencing problems and so find it difficult to put words in the

right order (in speech and in written work).

▲ In relating to the outside world (**Autistic Spectrum Disorders** see Chapter 10)

An individual's difficulties in putting his thoughts down on paper are made much worse if there is also a difficulty in controlling the pen (see **Dysgraphia** - Chapter 6 and **Dyspraxia** - Chapter 5) and both dysgraphia and dyslexia will be made worse if there are also vision difficulties (see Chapter 7) such as (**Occulomotor dyspraxia** see Chapter 5.)

There is a need for professionals from all the disciplines, parents/adults and teachers to be aware of the effects of Specific Language Impairment upon the individual in the school/workplace, social and home environments. This information can be gained from the many lectures and courses organised by AFASIC. However, as language is the basis of all academic work it would also seem appropriate that all teachers/lecturers should be trained in recognising and providing for Specific Language Impairment via either inservice training or as part of their initial teacher training.

© Jan Poustie

Recommended reading

The AFASIC language checklists (pub. Learning Development Aids)
Childhood speech, language & listening problems - what every parent should know
by Patricia McAleer Hamaguchi (pub. John Wiley & Sons Inc.)

References

1 Norma Corkish, Chief Executive, AFASIC (Croner 'Teacher's Briefing', Issue No 26, 20)

2 & 3. AFASIC leaflet 'Talking isn't always child's play'.

4. Information from AFASIC Glossary Sheet 1.

5. AFASIC Glossary Sheet 15

6. Information from AFASIC Glossary Sheet 5

7. Information from AFASIC Glossary Sheet 8

8. A useful tool when working with this group of individuals is the Edith Norrie Lettercase (See Solutions Product and Resource Guide pub. Next Generation)

9. Information from AFASIC Glossary Sheet 22

10. Information from AFASIC Glossary Sheet 13

11. Norma Corkish, Chief Executive, AFASIC (Croner 'Teacher's Briefing', Issue No 26, 20)

12. For further information on this checklist contact Learning Development Aids or see Solutions for Specific Learning Difficulties Resource Guide (pub. Next Generation)

13-15. Norma Corkish, Chief Executive, AFASIC (Croner 'Teacher's Briefing', Issue No 26, 20)

16. Editor: Local music groups such as Saturday morning schools may provide music experience classes which can be invaluable here. Suzuki teaching methods can also help to improve listening skills (but the child can become frustrated at his slow progress if only the Suzuki method is used.)

17. Editor: The combination teaching style is called 'multisensory' when all four senses are used simultaneously.

18. Norma Corkish, Chief Executive, AFASIC (Croner 'Teacher's Briefing', Issue No 26,20)

19. e.g. Early Communication Skills (see Solutions Resources Guide)

20. e.g. Listening skills Keystage 1 &2 (see Solutions Resources Guide)

21. see Code of Practice sections in Chapters 11 and 13

22. Norma Corkish, Chief Executive, AFASIC (Croner 'Teacher's Briefing', Issue No 26, 20) For details of Statements see Chapter 11.

Chapter 3

RECOGNISING
DYSLEXIA

The British Dyslexia Association define Dyslexia as "a specific learning difficulty in learning, in one or more of reading, spelling and written language. It may be accompanied by difficulty in number work, short-term memory, sequencing, auditory and/or visual perception and motor skills. It is particularly related to mastering and using written language, alphabetic, numeric and musical notation. In addition, oral language is often affected to some degree." [1]

Medically - Our knowledge in this area has increased dramatically over the course of the this century. From the world of genetics we know that dyslexia is approximately 80% inherited. Researchers such as Galaburda and Frith have shown us that the brain structure of the dyslexic individual is not damaged but different. (It is this difference which can give the individual skills as well as difficulties. In the struggle to attain literacy these skills can be forgotten but the imaginative and creative professional will use the them to help '*him*' learn to spell, read etc..

'Him' - If we look in most of the books we will find that the numbers of diagnosed dyslexics in the male population is greater than in that of the female (four males for every one female). However, some professionals believe that there are more females affected than has been thought. [2]   It certainly seems to be the case that some females who learn to read, but fail to master spelling and/or planning and organisation skills, are not being recognised early (if it all). They may well not be noticed until secondary school where they can fail to live up to the expectations of staff and parents. These girls may also have number difficulties which are not apparent at transfer to secondary school but which prevent them from learning higher mathematics concepts. (*See Chapter 4.*)

Is there such a thing as a 'typical dyslexic'? No, but what tends to happen is that a certain profile is recognised by professionals and so a particular type of dyslexic tends to be diagnosed at a young age. Such a pupil is likely to be a boy who has difficulties in acquiring literacy skills (and possibly number/language/music skills too). He is likely to come from a family which has at least one family member with a weakness in spelling, reading, writing, number and possibly dyspraxic difficulties too. *(See Chapter 5.)* He may well be very good at practical skills that do not involve writing. The girls that are likely to be diagnosed at a young age often fit the same profile.

If only it was that simple, to say, "Look for the above and that's it you have found all your dyslexics." Unfortunately, nothing is ever that easy and this is where the difficulties and delays in diagnosis and referral occur. The tendency is to wait - "Let's see what he/she is like next year." "Well, there is a new baby in the family/parental separation/moved house etc. etc.." "You need to make him sit down and read with you," "He isn't very interested in reading yet but it will come" are familiar statements given to worried and anxious parents who because of the genetic factor may well lack the language skills/self confidence to explain their concerns.

Why aren't all dyslexics recognised? No two individuals will look the same as there are many aspects to dyslexia but there is a core of indicators that we can use to spot them. "Two factors are invariably present in dyslexia: a poor short term memory and low self esteem unless effective intervention takes place."[3] We can expect to see many errors in both reading and spelling. Dr Bève Hornsby in her book 'Overcoming Dyslexia' lists thirteen spelling and twenty-five reading difficulties and is a very good source of information on this aspect. Likely errors are:
Reading/spelling: missing/adding in words/letters; transposing words/letters (changing the position of a word or a letter e.g. saying 'lots' for 'lost'.); reads/spells words back to front.
Reading: repeat phrases/words when reading even though it was read correctly the first time; reverses words/letters; misreads the first word in a sentence; struggle with a word even though it may have been read correctly seconds before; lose place when reading; dislike/avoid reading, missing out lines of text.
Spelling: have difficulties in learning spellings unless taught using specialist teaching methods e.g. Fernald method, onset and rime etc.[4]
Writing: write letters/numerals back to front and upside down

which causes many confusions between letters/numerals e.g. *bdpq*, *hy, 69, 25, un, mw,* and *ij*.

'How else can these individuals be spotted?'

Many of them are likely to have most of items 1-16:

1. A difference between their oral and written ability (but this may not be the case if they also have language dysfunctioning). *(See Chapter 2.)*

2. A difference between the knowledge that they possess and their ability to communicate it on paper and/or read about it (they learn through conversation, by doing and watching television).

3. Confusion as to which is left and right.

4. Difficulties in understanding, following or duplicating a sequence e.g. tying shoelaces, following an instruction; learning tables/months of the year/ seasons/days of the week/which meal comes next etc..

5. Work erratically (one minute he can do it and the next he can't) Adults may feel that he is lazy and/or careless. The individual's standard of work/behaviour may be much worse at the end of the week/term. A child's homework standard (where parents are helping them to cope) may be higher than their classroom standard.

6. Has a reading age below that of his peers (of the same chronological age AND ABILITY). For example a non-dyslexic child with an IQ of 130 is expected to have a reading age that is four years above his chronological age.

7. Is under stress which can be shown in many different ways, stomach aches, headaches, irritable bowel syndrome, irritability, aggression, tempter tantrums all of which are less noticeable when not at school. (Or, the child can become totally passive in a school situation and make little attempt to strive as the whole task is just too hard. Adults may avoid careers which need literacy skills or struggle be under stress due to the literacy to cope with the literacy aspects of.)

8. Written work can have words missed out, sentences that barely make sense and incorrect use of tenses and prepositions. *(See Chapters 2 & 6.)* Often they will use only a very small vocabulary (because that it all that they can hope to spell. Writing can be very untidy and poorly presented. *(See Chapter 6.)*

Their written work can follow one of the following three types of pattern:

* • they work very slowly and very neatly, produce less work than you would expect for their ability,
* • slowly and very untidily with hardly any work to show for an hour's effort,
* • they work fast, very untidily and will often pour out their thoughts in a tangled mess.

9. Poor short term memory, but often able to remember what they did on holiday last year.

10. Unable to make a start - e.g. to get ready to go out, to write a story.

11. Untidy bedrooms/desks - (or exceptionally tidy ones and almost an obsession with tidiness as they cannot cope if it is untidy). Either of these traits in adulthood can make it very difficult for their families to cope with them - lost keys for adults can be a daily frustration!

12. Poor ability to read the time accurately and/or poor time sense (e.g. not knowing what the next meal is , getting to places on time, knowing how long they have been waiting, knowing how much time they have left in which to complete work. One of the big stresses for the dyslexic mother can be actually collecting her children on time from school.

13. Difficulties in processing their thoughts.

14. Difficulties in copying accurately from a worksheet and/or the board.

15. Difficulties in proof reading their work - they cannot 'see' their mistakes even if their work is read out to them.

16. Likelihood of having any of the following: allergies, hay fever, asthma and eczema.

Important points to note in relation to items 1,2 & 6
1 & 2: may not be apparent to the teacher if the child is shy or fears looking different from his peers
6: The child's reading age can be artificially high if the parent has given the child considerable help/the child is very bright. (It is very important that parental comments are taken into account in these areas.) Most dyslexics will have difficulties in breaking words down into their parts and the more severe dyslexic is likely to have great problems in blending sounds together to form words, even words

like c-a-t will be difficult for them.

Vision & hearing
Sometimes the individual's difficulties are not due to dyslexia but are because they cannot see and/or hear properly.
- **Vision:** may be short/long sighted, etc. A referral to an optometrist can be made via the school doctor or local GP. The optometrist may make a further referral to an orthoptist.
- **Hearing:** may not be able to hear certain sounds etc. Schools can refer via the Local Authority's Hearing Impaired Service, parents can refer via their local GP who then contacts the local NHS Audiology Department.

Indicators of other conditions which may be present
- **Visual or perceptual difficulties**: Any of the following may be present - find written material (e.g. words/music/ number/ maps) unpleasant to look at, avoid reading tasks, slow at reading and writing, complain of headaches/nausea when doing academic work. *(See Chapters 5, 7 & 12.)*
- **Listening/receptive language difficulties**: Any of the following may be present - have difficulties in following instructions, do not seem to concentrate on listening tasks, omission of vowels/parts of consonant blends in reading/spelling, mispronounces words, difficulties in sounding out words and/or blending sounds. *(See Chapters 2, 8 & 9)*
- **Listening/attention difficulties**: misbehave when the teacher is talking, complain that they cannot hear the television. *(See Chapters 8 & 9.)*
- **Autistic Spectrum Disorder traits**: Any of the following may be present before the age of 30 months -language disorder (Semantic/Pragmatic or Higher Level Language Disorder: *See Chapter 2)*, repetitive behaviours, poor social skills, resistant to learning new skills, physical over activity, lacks fear in dangerous situations, lacks eye contact, dislikes changes in routine, over-attachment to particular objects. *(See Chapter 10.)*
- **Number/mathematics**: Can have difficulties in remembering their tables, write numbers upside down or back to front, learning the language *(see Chapter 2)*, concepts of mathematics, learning to tell the time, unable to follow correctly the sequence needed for a particular mathematical operation. *(See*

Chapter 4.) Difficulties in estimating length, knowing whether lines are parallel to each other, in controlling/using mathematical tools e.g. compass, protractor. *(See Chapter 5.)*

• **Specific Language Impairment**: Any of the following can be present: difficulties with the speech apparatus, the sounds that make up language, grammar, word finding, word meanings and the appropriate use of language. Can have difficulties in saying some sounds, in using grammar correctly, word finding, the appropriate use of language, vocabulary, using correct tenses/prepositions, stressing the correct parts of words and using intonation correctly, difficulties in learning phonics. Any of these difficulties can be present in speech and/or written work. *(See Chapters 2 & 5.)*

What can teachers/special needs assistants/therapists do about it once they have recognised it?

• Arrange for an assessment by the necessary specialists.
• Seek advice from providers of specialist information e.g. Local Education Authority 'Special Educational Needs Support Team' (SENST) and/or appropriate organisations *(see Chapter 15)*
• Implement the recommendations in the specialist's report (even if it may come from a non-LEA source).
• Realise that both the child/adult and his family are likely to be under considerable stress because of the dyslexia.
• Talk to the child/adult about his dyslexia, tell him that you accept that he has a difficulty. Discuss with him his best way of learning - he may know more than you about how he learns or he may be locked in a rut of learning in one particular way (even though it may not suit him) because that is the way that he has learnt to cope with his difficulty.
• Be prepared to change the way in which you teach, even if you are a very good teacher/special educational needs assistant/therapist the dyslexic may not be able to learn via your normal methods. He cannot alter the way he learns or overcome his difficulties unless you help him to do so. You will find life much easier (and much less frustrating) if you adapt rather than if you try to force this very round peg into an exceptionally square hole! [5]
•The majority of dyslexics will have difficulties in learning to read

via traditional 'Look & Say' methods. Some very bright individuals may learn to read by this method (often with a great deal of parental/teacher/school assistant support) but are unlikely to progress at the appropriate rate for their intellectual ability. Most will need a heavily structured cumulative phonologically based programme [6][7] which uses multisensory teaching techniques. [8] The more that this programme is tailored to their <u>exact needs</u> the more effective it will be.

- Be prepared to learn more about the conditions which come within the Specific Learning Difficulties Profile. A child with several conditions (especially behavioural ones e.g. dyspraxia and ADHD) can make the teachers life very difficult in the classroom through no fault of his own. If the teacher trains he will be able to turn the situation around. Training agencies offer courses for a wide range of professionals and some also offer them for interested parents. Teachers can also ask for training via their local authority. [9]

Who assesses for it? Holders of specialist qualifications such as teachers and Educational Psychologists (private or LEA employed). Specialist teachers and a few Special Educational Needs School Assistants hold appropriate qualifications in Specific Learning Difficulties/Dyslexia such as the Kingston University Diploma and the RSA Dip SpLD or RSA Cert SpLD (though this is not as high a qualification). A list of appropriate qualifications can be obtained from the British Dyslexia Association[10]. These specialist teachers will either work privately or for the Local Education Authority (LEA). Some schools have appropriately qualified staff, others will need to refer the child to their LEA's Special Educational Needs Support Team. The Dyslexia Institutes *(see Chapter 15)* offer assessment for both children and adults.

How is a Specific Learning Difficulty in Literacy assessed? By a full assessment of the individual's functioning which should include an assessment of verbal and non-verbal ability and the sub-skills needed to read, understand, write and spell e.g. phonological awareness, visual and auditory skills and memory.

Reading, writing and spelling should also be assessed - this is usually done by using a combination of standardised tests and miscue analysis (the latter is when the errors made are used to diagnose the difficulties).

Various tests exist which give an overview of the individuals functioning. They identify the areas of sub-skill dysfunctioning which are causing the individuals to have difficulties in learning. One of these is the _Cops1_ computer based test which identifies the cognitive deficits which are known to be associated with dyslexia. It identifies pupils who are likely to have noticeable difficulties in acquiring literacy skills as a result of these deficits. It is fun to do and pupils do not realise that they are being assessed. This test can be used with children as young as four years old and can be administered by non-teaching staff. As specialists in this field know that the earlier the intervention the more successful the outcome many of us would like to see tests such as the Cops1 in all schools so that provision can occur in Reception classes for any 'at risk' children. The _Bangor Test of Dyslexia_ (a very easy test to administer) identifies high scoring individuals as being dyslexic plus it recommends further assessment if an individual is borderline. The _Aston Index_ identifies literacy difficulties and many areas of sub-skill dysfunctioning. Its results are plotted onto charts which enable the overall literacy functioning of the individual to be seen. Only Educational Psychologists can use the _Wechsler_ and _British Ability Scales_ (BAS) tests which consist of a variety of sub-tests which can be used to assess sub-skill functioning, intellectual ability, mathematical functioning etc.. Some tests that are still in use now are very old e.g. the various Schonell tests were designed over forty years ago and so some of the vocabulary has become dated. Some tests have more than one form so that they may be used with an individual more frequently than once a year e.g. _New Reading Analysis._

Assessment of intellectual ability: Sometimes the _British Picture Vocabulary Scale_ (BPVS) is used to produce a verbal intellectual ability score _(see comment on this test in Chapter 11)_. The _Ravens Matrices_ are sometimes used to provide a non-verbal intellectual score as is the _Goodenough Draw-a-man Test_ (sub-test 3 of the Aston

Index) but the latter is rather unreliable for this purpose. An Educational Psychologist uses the Wechsler/BAS tests but usually at least eight of the sub-tests need to be used. (*See Chapter 11*) **Speech & Language:** Vocabulary is assessed in various ways. Some assessors use tests such as the *BPVS* or part of the *Aston Index.* Educational Psychologists may use sub-tests of the *Wechsler/BAS* tests. The *AFASIC* checklist may also be used to identify 4-10 year olds for referral to speech and language therapists. The *Dyslexia Screening Test* (DST) sub-tests 10 & 11 (verbal and semantic fluency) may also be used. [11] (*See Chapter 2*)

Phonological awareness, visual and auditory skills and memory: (12) Teachers may use sub-tests of the Aston Index to assess these whilst Educational Psychologists will again use tests such as the Wechsler/BAS tests. The *Schonell Single Word Recognition Test* is still used by some as a tool for finding sound patterns which are not known whilst the *Gill Cotterell Checklist* (part of her *Phonic Reference File*) enables the assessor to check present knowledge of sound blends plus keep a record of them as they are taught and learnt. Newer materials such as the comprehensive *Test of Phonological Awareness* which is part of *'Sound Linkage'* [13] and the *Phonological Assessment Battery* enable an assessment of a range of phonological skills to be made. The Phonemic Segmentation sub-test of *The DST* [14] and the assessment tests in Lynette Bradley's *Assessing Reading Difficulties* [15] are also useful tools. **Reading:** A wide range of tests are in use but most of them are conducted orally. The *Wechsler/BAS* have reading sub-tests. The *Aston Index* includes the *Schonell Single Word Recognition Test.* Much of an individual's reading in the school or workplace takes place silently. The *Schonell Silent Reading Test* can be used to assess the 'reading processing' time of an individual. It enables one to compare the pupil's speed at this task with others of his age and gives a guide as to how much extra time he needs to complete work.

Reading and comprehension: There are also specialised combined reading and comprehension tests such as the *New Reading Analysis (formerly known as the Macmillan Reading Analysis).* This test requires that the individual reads a story aloud and then answer oral questions on the text. The three versions of this test mean that it can be used on a termly or six monthly basis to assess how effective one's teaching is without the individual becoming too familiar with the test. A low comprehension score compared with the reading score can indicate receptive language difficulties *(see Chapters 2 & 8)* especially if the teacher can confirm that there are no problems with written comprehension.

Spelling and writing: There are various spelling tests, commonly used ones are by *Vernon*, *Burt* or *Schonell.* (The latter is available separately or as part of the Aston Index.) *(See Chapter 6 for writing tests in common use.)*

Other Assessments: Since as previously mentioned other conditions may also be present the assessor should always look for their indicators and refer the individual to the other specialists mentioned in this book as appropriate.

The 'gifts' of dyslexia
It is easy for an individual to see only the 'difficulties' aspect of dyslexia but we all need to remember that there can be good aspects too. Before 1870 (when schooling became compulsory) most people had never been taught to read therefore it was not the essential skill for life that it is now. Different qualities were praised in people - the ability to 'think quickly' and get on with practical tasks and build things, the ability to create (e.g. in drawings, pottery and ideas) and the ability to see the 'whole' of a concept. These qualities are often among those that individuals affected by dyslexia possess and they are just as important qualities to have now as they have always been. It is not surprising that in some areas of employment such as architecture, individuals who are dyslexic are highly sought after. In such cases the employer is not put off by poor literacy skills, it is the 'gifts' of dyslexia he seeks. All of us need to remember that the 'gifts' are there in many individuals. It is important to identify these 'gifts' and to provide opportunities for them to flourish without the restrictions that difficulties in literacy can cause.

Footnotes

1. *British Dyslexia Association Early Help, Better Future video*
2. See *Dyslexia the pattern of difficulties* by T. R. Miles (pub. Whurr Publishers Ltd.)
3. *The Dyslexia Handbook 1996* (pub. British Dyslexia Association)
4.. See '*Solutions for Specific Learning Difficulties: Resources Guide* (pub. Next Generation)
5. *Teaching for the two-sided mind* by Linda Verlee Williams (pub. Simon & Schuster) and *The Learning Revolution* by Dryden & Vos (pub. Accelerated Learning Systems Ltd.) provide plenty of ideas.
6.. Both professionals and parents will be safe using any of the following programmes in which everything is all set out for you. Any spelling programme will automatically teach reading: '*Spelling made Easy*' books by Violet Brand (pub. Egon), '*Beat Dyslexia*' books by Stone, Franks & Nicholson (pub. LDA) and *Toe by Toe* by Cowling & Cowling or the *Alpha to Omega* teaching programme by Dr Beve Hornsby (pub. Heinemann) plus the *Wordshark* computer program (only available for PC) which is based against it. (These can be bought from your local suppliers or contact Next Generation Tel: 01823 289559 for details of our Direct Buying Service.) The above programmes will also improve spelling. Strategies for teaching spelling are also found in the '*Solutions Resource Guide*' (pub. Next Generation).against it. (These can be bought from your local suppliers or contact Next Generation Tel: 01823 289559 for details of our Direct Buying Service.) The above programmes will also improve spelling. Strategies for teaching spelling are also found in the '*Solutions Resource Guide*' (pub. Next Generation).
7. There is a small subgroup of dyslexics who find a phonologically based programmes exceptionally difficult and so non-phonological strategies e.g. 'Fernald' may need to be used instead. For further information see '*Solutions for Specific Learning Difficulties: Resources Guide*' and '*Solutions Forum*'.
8. Multisensory methods are the most effective ones you can use i.e. using the senses of movement (hand and speech), vision, hearing simultaneously. For further information on effective strategies see the '*Solutions for Specific Learning Difficulties Resources Guide*' by Jan Poustie & '*Solutions Forum*' edited by Jan Poustie (pub. Next Generation)
9. e.g. The Dyslexia Institute (see Chapter 15), The Hornsby International Dyslexia Centre, Tel: 0181 874 1844 and Helen Arkell Dyslexia Centre, Tel: 01251 2400. The '*Solutions for Specific Learning Difficulties: Resources Guide*' lists agencies which provide lectures (for both professionals and non-professionals) and training for specialised qualifications throughout the UK.
10. See Chapter 15 for their address.
11. & 14. Note: Some practitioners have found that some parts of The Dyslexia Screening Test do not fit with their definition of dyslexia.
12. Reading and spelling error analysis can give an indication as to whether auditory channel and/or visual channel deficits are present. See *Developmental Dyslexia* by Thomson (pub. Whurr Publishers Ltd.)
13. *Sound Linkage* by Peter Hatcher (pub. Whurr Publishers Ltd.)
15. Published by NFER.
Written by Jan Poustie with the co-operation of the British Dyslexia Association, The Dyslexia Institute and Hugh Bellamy.
© **Jan Poustie**

Chapter 4

IDENTIFYING MATHEMATICAL DIFFICULTIES

The identification of mathematical difficulties is not a simple task because there are many aspects to the learning of mathematics. In order to decide the cause of an individual's mathematical difficulties each of these aspects will need to be explored so that the individual's weaknesses and strengths can be assessed. Only once such an assessment is made can appropriate and adequate provision be given. If this is not done provision is likely to be very much a 'hit and miss affair' which if one is lucky may achieve something but may well be a complete waste of time.

Two of the most important aspects of mathematics are its sequential nature (which is based upon a foundation of early skills and knowledge[1]) and the fact that all of mathematical knowledge interrelates to its other parts and as such no topic can be seen in isolation. Each new topic has to be related to those areas already covered and to those which will be introduced in the future.

Therefore, in order to teach mathematics the teacher needs to be aware of where mathematically the individual has been, where he is now, where he will be going shortly and where he will be going in the far future. He also has to be aware of what information has been internalised by the individual i.e. what has been accepted as making sense, understood as a concept and can be used by the learner in any situation. If the teacher lacks this awareness it will be more difficult for the individual to place the new information into his 'schema' of mathematics. (This 'schema' is the system by which the individual has organised, arranged and connected each piece of mathematical information.)

Each teacher will also have his own way of teaching mathematics which is often based upon his own way of learning it. There are two extremes of learning style:

The qualitative learner.
This learner is sometimes called a global learner or a 'grasshopper'. He needs to see the whole of a concept first and then learns by 'jumping in

27

a disordered manner' from one part of the whole to another. Such learners rely on their intuition to learn and understand. They can easily miss out a vital part of the 'whole' because of this disordered manner of working. However, the advantage of such a learning style is that they may be able to see the 'whole' of a concept in a way that other people cannot see it or make unusual connections between pieces of information. Such learners can find that school teaching techniques are in conflict with their learning style. Their preferred choice of learning style may be that of open learning where they have more control over the learning process.

The quantitative learner.
This learner must take the concept a step at a time in an ordered sequential manner just like an 'inchworm'. He cannot see the whole until he has built up all the parts. He prefers teacher directed learning to open learning methods and so is likely to find that school is not in conflict with his learning style.

Most people's learning style [2] is somewhere on an imaginary line between the two extremes. Few people are actually at the extremes but as much of teaching is done in a sequential manner it is often those who are closest to the 'grasshopper' learning style that are at the greatest disadvantage in our educational system. Some individuals are able to adopt the learning style of their teacher and this gradually replaces (to a varying extent) their natural learning style. However, others are totally unable to adopt another style and perhaps this is more common in those who are qualitative (grasshopper) learners. Ideally concepts should be introduced via the learners natural style and then reinforced, revised etc. via the opposite style.

At present there is a great interest in dyscalculia. The term 'dyscalculia' is currently being used in two different ways i.e.:

1. used <u>loosely</u> to refer to all kinds of learning problems in mathematics

2. used to refer to a <u>specific</u> learning difficulty in mathematics where the individual has a difficulty in processing numerical/mathematical information with deficits in various aspects of the subject causing difficulties in some, or, all areas of it. (*This is the correct use of the term and all references to dyscalculia in this book relate to this meaning*).

Some regard dyscalculia as the cause of all mathematical difficulties. However, this is not the case. Each learner has his own set of difficulties differences which will affect his ability to learn by the methods used by the teacher and very few individuals will actually have dyscalculia. The learner's differences/difficulties vary tremendously from those which are easily resolved to those that require a great deal of provision. If we look at all the circumstances that surround, or are part of, the learner we can see any, or all, of the following as being the cause of an individual's mathematical learning difficulties:

1. Limited mathematical experience. This can be due to various factors e.g.
◆ frequent absences from lessons due to illness
◆ working slowly
◆ being withdrawn from maths lessons in order to attend specialist tuition for difficulties caused by conditions such as those found within the SpLD Profile (e.g. for literacy, movement etc.).
◆ not being allowed to progress to the 'problem solving' aspects of mathematics. This can occur when the teacher has an incorrect perception of the individual's mathematical ability which is based upon the fact that they are unable to do simple number work with any accuracy. Teachers are aware that just like a house will collapse if built upon weak foundations so the ability to acquire "higher mathematical knowledge" will collapse if the foundation is not both complete and secure. However, mathematics contains two elements number (arithmetic) and mathematical concepts. The ability to cope with number can be weak but there can still be a fair (if not excellent) ability to understand highly developed mathematical concepts. Once appropriate strategies/equipment are given to the learner to overcome their difficulties in number then they are then able to progress to their correct mathematical level.

2. Inappropriate teaching e.g.
◆ use of a teaching style/method which does not suit the individual
◆ use of inappropriate teaching materials such as pictorial based materials when the individual needs concrete based ones and/or materials unsuitable to the individual's learning style
◆ the teacher lacking enough knowledge of number/mathematics to teach it well. (Mathematics is part of all teacher training courses in the UK and teachers of mathematics in secondary schools and above can be expected to be mathematics specialists. However, most class teachers in primary schools are expected to teach mathematics regardless of whether

they have a particular expertise in this field.)

◆ The teacher failing to notice that the individual does not understand the concept. This can occur when the teacher does not mark the work on a regular enough basis, does not involve individuals in enough discussion about how they work out a sum and when continuous revision is not used as an ongoing strategy. (*All lessons/homework should include some element of revision. Individuals with severe mathematical difficulties will initially need lessons/homework in which only a small amount of time is used for introducing new concepts with the rest of the time being devoted to revision.*) Individuals may appear to know and understand the concept when it is taught but it is not internalised and so does not go into long term memory. Such individuals may do well in class but have poor homework marks in comparison to class work (unless they receive a great deal of support from their parents) and may have poor marks in examinations.

3. A condition found within the Specific Learning Difficulty (SpLD) Profile. This can be a condition which affects the learning of arithmetic/mathematics (e.g. dyslexia) and/or dyscalculia itself. Various conditions are known to have a high incidence of associated mathematical difficulties. Figures vary as to the incidence of arithmetical/mathematical difficulties in the dyslexic population, they range from Prof. Mahesh Sharma's belief that "between 20-25% of dyslexics also have difficulties with arithmetic/mathematics"[3] to that of Chinn & Ashcroft who work with "boys who have been diagnosed as dyslexic and find that upwards of 75% of them are affected by such difficulties.[4] (*See Chapter 3*). Dr Ian McKinlay's research indicates that difficulties in number usually accompany dyspraxia in childhood [5] (*see Chapter 5*).

What are the general indicators that an individual has mathematical learning difficulties?

Some of the most obvious indicators that someone is struggling with mathematical tasks are as follows.

Indicators which are noticeable at school and which will carry on into adulthood

◆ Difficulties in fully understanding new concepts unless they are introduced using concrete apparatus (things that they can touch).

◆ Becoming angry/frustrated with any mathematical task/game.

◆ A dislike of any leisure games that involve numbers and/or spatial concepts e.g. Rummikub™, Dominoes, Draughts and Snakes and Ladders. If spatial skills are weak the individual will find Chess and Othello extremely difficult.

◆ Rarely checking change when shopping.

◆ Finding cooking stressful.

◆ Difficulties in learning to read the time

◆ Frequently pressing the wrong keys on a calculator

◆ Failure to understand and use money.

◆ Difficulties in understanding and using statistical information.

◆ Miscounting of objects and/or misreading of text/numerals. This can cause difficulties when first introduced to number. Individuals may miss out numbers when counting and/or may fail to include all the objects. They can also write one thing but read it back as another. These difficulties can be found as part of dyslexia *(see Chapter 3)* and/or dyscalculia.

◆ Difficulties with understanding fractions and/or algebra.

◆ Individuals having difficulties in planning and organising their lives, their environments and/or a mathematical task.

◆ Difficulties with understanding and using the language of mathematics.

◆ A dislike and/or fear of mathematics.

◆ Have combined attention span and information processing difficulties. If both these difficulties are present then the individual is likely to be slow at, or unable to, recall basic arithmetic facts. Such individuals may rely on inefficient and very basic methods to work out calculations e.g. serial counting. They may:

Work very slowly and still get the answer wrong. This can occur for a wide variety of reasons e.g. loss of confidence, poor planning skills, slow recall of numbers and imperfectly learnt processes etc..

Work erratically. Failure to internalise concepts and methods can cause individuals to be able to make what appear to be 'careless errors' in sums that they were having no difficulties with a few minutes earlier. This is common to several of the conditions within the Profile e.g. dyslexia, dyscalculia and attention deficits. *(See Chapters 3 & 9.)*

Avoid doing mathematics by misbehaving, day dreaming, offering to do jobs outside of the classroom, forgetting their books etc..

Tire easily when doing mathematics. This can be very noticeable at the end of the day/week/term.   A huge amount of effort can be required to cope with the simplest of calculations. Often the only indicator of this is more frequent illness, less work being produced and/or more untidy work as the effort to present work well is just too much. (Some will produce beautifully presented work but there will be hardly any of it.)

Difficulties which will be present in the individual when young but are likely to be more noticeable in adulthood.

◆ Frequently miss appointments because they have been written down incorrectly and/or the amount of time spare before the appointment has been miscalculated.

◆ Frequently mis-dialling on the telephone

◆ Difficulties when travelling e.g. going to the wrong platform, getting on the wrong bus, finding it difficult to read a map and to remember road numbers etc..

◆ Difficulties with working out how much wallpaper/paint etc. is needed for a DIY task.

◆ Preferring to cook meals that cook in one pot/oven rather than those that require various elements that have different cooking times but must all be ready at one time. Preferring to make up a recipe as you go along rather than follow the recipe in a book.

Is dyscalculia likely to be the cause of an individual struggling with mathematical tasks? No, very few people are believed to have dyscalculia with some research figures suggesting that less than 2% of the population are affected. [6] However, as there seems to be a general acceptance in the population that "its okay not to be good at mathematics because you can't be good at everything' and that 'females are usually poorer than men at mathematics' it may well be that many people's difficulties with mathematics are going unrecognised.

How do we recognise dyscalculia? Dyscalculia (sometimes referred to as Developmental Dyscalculia) is "a disorder in the ability to do or learn mathematics i.e. difficulty in number conceptualisation, understanding number relationships, and difficulty in learning algorithms and applying them" (7) which is present at an early age. *[An algorithm is a process or rule for calculation]* "It is characterised by substantially lowered arithmetic achievement, i.e. several years below the appropriate level" (8) as compared with their peers of similar chronological age and intellectual ability. The person may be able to read fluently (or even exceedingly well).

Relatively little research into dyscalculia has been conducted (as compared with research into literacy difficulties). Thus, much is not known about dyscalculia and what is known is based on only a small amount of research. (9) Some research indicates that dyscalculia (like dyslexia) is caused by a difference in the way in which the brain works. It is believed by some professionals that few individuals have only a specific problem with number. Some believe that mathematical and language difficulties occur concurrently.(10) Some believe that difficulties in number/mathematics are part of a language dysfunction e.g. Specific Language Impairment, or, part of other conditions found within the Specific Learning Difficulties Profile e.g. dyslexia.

If an individual has dyscalculia any, or all, of the following types of arithmetic disorder that were identified by Luria in 1966 (11) may be present.

1. Defects of logic

Difficulties in holding and processing information in the mind. (Forgetting where you are in the calculation, failing to carry a number accurately into the next part of the procedure). Luria linked some of these difficulties to spatial problems. (12) The failure to integrate spatial and visualisation skills causes difficulties in understanding calendars and reading clocks and geometry.

2. Defects in planning

Difficulties in planning and failure to check one's answer. (The individual attempts the task before making a preliminary analysis of what it requires and does not check that the answer is right.) Various skills are needed in order to plan so an individual may have difficulties in any, or all of the following.

Understanding the information within the problem. If individuals have difficulties in any of the areas of memory, language, reading and comprehension they are likely to find it difficult to understand information which is presented in a symbolic and/or textual (or oral) manner. Until the information is understood the mathematical problem cannot be solved.

<u>Organisation of the information and planning the steps needed to reach a solution.</u> Individuals may not be able to work out which pieces of information are related and/or the order in which certain operations need to be carried out. One cannot plan if one cannot see the whole of the task. A person with dyscalculia can know exactly what all the signs and numerals mean in the sum and can know how to use them but a 'wall' can appear which seems to stop some of the elements (e.g. signs/numerals) existing during the mathematical operation. Although these elements are 'not seen' by the individual there is an awareness that 'something is wrong' but the individual has no idea what it is. It is as though the whole of the task is not seen accurately and only the fragments can therefore be worked upon.

This fragmentation of the task also applies to the reading of problems. Often the individual is unable to work out which parts of the information given are needed for the sum and which parts of it have been added in to make the sum harder but which are not actually needed for the calculation. Since there is so much self doubt as to whether one is thinking clearly/logically the individual can waste a lot of time going up mental 'dead ends' and may not recognise the correct 'path' when he sees it.

<u>An inability to reliably check work.</u> Checking may achieve nothing for if the answer is checked several times the person may just produce several answers and have no idea as to which one is correct! Thus individuals may:

■ not bother to check at all because they feel that it will not help

■ keep on checking it until the same answer appears twice (this can take ten 'checks', or more, and it can still be wrong)

■ go by the 'feel' of the answer (it 'feels' as though it ought to be right)

■ have no strategies by which they can check the answer because they either can only follow the procedure that they originally used (and which they have failed to internalise correctly) and/or have difficulties in following procedures. (*The calculator may not help as it too involves a procedure. Individual may also have such poor estimation skills that they do not know whether the answer that comes up is likely to be correct anyway.*)

■ cross it all out and leave the answer blank, or, just leave it with an answer that they know is incorrect. *(Doing the task once can be very stressful - sometimes the individual just cannot face doing it again.)*

3. Perseveration of procedures that are no longer appropriate
Perseveration is when an individual continues to use an approach/thought process which may have been appropriate when first introduced to the task (or at the initial stage of it) but which is no longer appropriate. (Such individuals may also be unable to reverse concepts e.g. can count forwards/do addition but have difficulties in doing subtraction/counting backwards. The individual may also not recognise a number if it is given in a different way e.g. may habitually say the phone number 289559 as 28-9,55-9 and may find it very difficult to accept that it is the same number when it is grouped differently e.g. 28-95-59.) Other aspects of perseverating are:

■ writing the same number just after one has written it e.g. 4x2=2,
■ writing a number just because it is the next one in sequence e.g. 6+4=5,
■ applying the rules of one operation incorrectly to another e.g. so the individual treats 24x2 and 24 -2 in the same way.

Perseveration can cause individuals to <u>become 'locked' into a behaviour/process.</u> As some individuals can find internalising procedures extremely difficult they can find it very hard to stop using the time consuming methods/processes that they were originally taught when they were young. They can 'feel safer' when using previously learnt methods/processes or when just carrying on with the one that they first thought of even though they suspect it may not be the best one for the task in hand.

4. Inability to perform simple calculations e.g. + and -
"The person understands the logic of the arithmetic operations but cannot recall the facts automatically."[13]

What other terms have been used for certain characteristics of dyscalculia?

<u>Paraphasic substitutions:</u> This is when one number is substituted for another. It can happen when writing or using a calculator. In the case of

calculators the person can be saying the number that she wants but her hand can still press a different number. This is not a case of inverting/reversing numbers or pressing a button on the calculator that is next to the one that is wanted.

Reversals: Digits are reversed (e.g. 26 written as 56), misordered (e.g. 453 written/read as 435), or inverted e.g. 69. *(This can also be an indicator of several other difficulties/conditions e.g. visual difficulties, autistic spectrum disorder, dyspraxia and dyslexia. See chapters 3, 5, 7 & 10)*

Slowness of responses: Taking longer than normal (as compared with peer group of similar chronological age and intellectual ability) to give a correct answer to an addition/multiplication fact e.g. 1+9=10. *(Note: response time could take longer if any of the following are present: specific language impairment, dyslexia, central auditory processing disorder and/or articulatory dyspraxia. See chapters 2., 3., 5. & 8.)*

Misalignment: Operations performed incorrectly because numbers/symbols are placed incorrectly e.g. the decimal point. (This can also occur as part of near-vision dysfunctioning- *see Chapter 7.)*

What other difficulties are individuals affected by dyscalculia also likely to have? They are likely to have difficulties in:

1. naming, reading, or writing mathematical symbols and terms as compared with one's peers of similar intellectual ability and age.

2. manipulating real or abstract/ representational objects e.g. difficulties in algebra etc..

3. 'seeing' one's errors at the time. This can cause individuals to feel annoyed, stressed, frustrated and upset when they cannot do simple calculations. They can know that the answer _feels wrong_ but are not able to find the error, though two days later it may be utterly obvious!

4. the way that they react to mathematics emotionally. Maths anxiety, and low self esteem resulting from it, is likely to be present. *Anxiety can take several forms e.g. a fear of anything related to numbers, fear when faced by a page of sums (the student's face can visibly turn white) and anxiety over certain aspects of mathematics e.g. fractions.*

5. understanding absolute and relative positions of objects *e.g. 2.3, 23 and* 2^3.

6. understanding new concepts unless concrete apparatus is used to introduce it (*Concrete apparatus is apparatus that the individual can touch and hold.*) Individuals are likely to need such apparatus for a longer time than their peers of similar chronological age and intellectual ability.

7. remembering numbers. Although individuals may be able to produce the correct answer to a simple sum the difficulties that some have in remembering any numbers can make it very difficult to:

■ answer complex and multi-step tasks correctly
■ remember simple number bonds e.g. up to ten and up to twenty
■ remember numbers that are of personal importance e.g. own telephone number

Unlike many of those with dyslexia (as in literacy) individuals affected by dyscalculia may be able to learn their tables by rote learning methods. However, difficulties in remembering isolated numbers may mean that they cannot use their knowledge of tables efficiently in calculations for they may have to 'say their table' from the beginning each time.

8. The individual may say that mathematics does not appear to be logical. The effort to understand, accept and internalise the logic behind a mathematical concept can be very great. If earlier methods of teaching have laid too small (or a faulty) foundation individuals may be unable to easily adapt/transfer the logic to a new level of learning and will fail to understand and/or internalise the new concept.

An example of this can occur when there is a failure to introduce the 'area' method of multiplication [14] alongside the 'repeated addition' method (in which 'lots/groups' are used). A teacher using repeated addition might initially explain the multiplication sum $2 \times 3 = 6$ in the following way:

● 2 apples on a tree (teacher draws it). How many apples are there? 2, there is one lot of apples ($2 \times 1 = 2$)
● Here is another tree with two apples on it. How many apples are there altogether? ($2 \times 2 = 4$)
● Here is another tree with two apples on it. How many apples are there? Count all the apples. There are three lots of apples. ($2 \times 3 = 6$) Some individuals find that this method does not make sense as soon as they are asked to do sums such as $2 \times 0 = 0$ because they have started off

with 2 apples so where have they gone! Even though to the teacher (and maybe to the rest of the class) the explanation that there are no trees for the apples to hang on makes sense it will not help the individual with dyscalculia. However, an explanation using the area method will enable the individual to understand the concept.[15]

9. Unable to solve 'magic squares' (see figure 1) with any ease even those only adding up to numbers less than 10.

Figure 1: a magic square which adds up to 6

This task is hard because there is no obvious starting point and even though the numbers may 'work' vertically they may not work horizontally/diagonally too. The stress of repeatedly working out the calculations when the individual is not at all sure as to whether each calculation is correct anyway can just be too great.

10. Individuals may be less efficient than their peer group of similar age and intellectual ability in <u>mathematical thinking</u> (cognitive) skills e.g. reasoning, problem solving etc.. (A delay in mathematical cognitive skills is found "in approximately 25% of people.)" [16]

11. Mathematical thinking is based upon understanding mathematical concepts. There are various prerequisite skills (sub-skills) which are the foundation for the understanding and implementing of a mathematical operation and some of these may be absent or incomplete. *(Further information on these sub-skills is supplied in Table 1 at the end of this chapter.)* If a sub-skill has not developed then any mathematical process to which it is linked will not be fully understood and internalised properly. This results in the individual appearing to learn a process (e.g. subtraction) but it becomes 'unlearnt' at a moment's notice. Sometimes the individual can become 'locked' into a process and is totally unable to come out of it as in the case of the ten year old who did the following:

$$\require{cancel}\cancel{1}\,\cancel{0}\,\cancel{1}\,\cancel{0}\,\cancel{1}\,\cancel{0}\,\cancel{1}\,\cancel{2}2 \\ \underline{14} \\ \overline{}$$

Many indicators of mathematical learning difficulties cross over the boundaries between the different conditions that are found as part of the SpLD Profile. Thus each indicator can indicate that dyscalculia is present and/or that another condition is present. For convenience information on this group of indicators is listed in Table 2 at the end of this chapter along with more comprehensive information on the general indicators of mathematical learning difficulties.

What are the effects of mathematical learning difficulties on the individual's life?

Numbers are all around us, so individual's affected by moderate to severe number difficulties have to cope with stress and frustration being part of their normal day. As with all the other conditions found within the SpLD Profile one can have good and bad days. Many individuals may struggle at home, at school and in the workplace but for individuals with dyscalculia the situation will be worse as they can exist in a world of total mathematical confusion.

At school:

A working knowledge and understanding of number and mathematics are necessary for many subjects e.g. working out calculations in science, statistics in history, map reading, co-ordinates and graphs in geography, reading tables in English. In all lessons the individual with poor mathematical language will have to translate common day terms said as part of instructions e.g. you have 'quarter of an hour' to finish this task and this should be a 'right angle'. If the child is bright concerns may not be noted until 7+ or even 13+ when the demands of the secondary mathematics curriculum become too much for the pupil's weak mathematical skills.

Everyday tasks:

The individual with dyscalculia may have an inability to remember any numbers for any length of time even those which have great meaning for them. This lack of retention of numbers can make for an interesting life. When individuals are travelling across country they can forget which road they are meant to be following! If individuals are unlucky enough to live in a town where all the roundabout turn offs and intersections signposts do not have place names on them but just use numbers instead they may rarely ever get to their destination at the first attempt. Remembering numbers accurately can pose quite a challenge when using a 'PIN' number and a bankcard to withdraw money from the 'hole in the wall' at the local bank. Failure can result in no money for that weekend! A continuous source of embarrassment can be the individual failing to give their phone number accurately during a telephone conversation despite the fact that they are looking at it at the time. People do regard individuals as being a little odd when they cannot remember their own age, the date of their own wedding anniversary and their children's date of birth etc..

Many everyday tasks involve number, spatial skills and time e.g. setting the video manually, writing appointments at the correct date on the calendar, using clock reading skills to get children to school on time. The individual may fail to get to meetings on time because a totally different date and time were entered into the diary and/or because clock/watch reading skills may be totally unreliable no matter whether digital or analogue systems are used. Sometimes it can help to use a kitchen timer to help know what time one has to leave. However, if the individual's number skills are unreliable then there is no way of being certain that it has been set correctly. Thus the mother with dyscalculia can find it totally humiliating and frustrating when the teacher rings her up to ask her to collect her children as school finished over half an hour ago. Of course she set the kitchen timer but poor number skills mean that it still says that she has a half hour spare before she needs to pick them up.

Fortunately some problems can be solved by passing on the responsibility for the timing of events to others. Thus repeated failures to send birthday cards/presents can be solved by sending them when they are bought even if it is two months before the event. This also solves the problem of the individual losing the present because they put it in a 'safe place' prior to sending it!

Cooking can be very stressful! In order to cook a meal one has to correctly interpret the numerals in the recipe, proportionately increase the ingredients according to the number that one is catering for, measure the ingredients accurately, set the oven/hob at the correct numbers (some knobs have numbers whilst others rely upon spatial skills instead), plan the operations involved and time both the preparation and the cooking so that all the elements of the meal are ready at the same time.

At work:
On a bad day it can become an art to actually obtain the right number when using the phone or calculator. The individual thinks they are

pressing the right number but they are not. A talking calculator helps - at least it tells you what you have done even if you have forgotten the correct operation to do the sum! It is often 'third time lucky', or even 'tenth time lucky' on a very bad day. The likelihood is that the individual's job entails that she use her reasonable (or even exceedingly good) reading skills throughout the day so she cannot even use the "I've forgotten my glasses" trick that the individual with severe literacy difficulties sometimes uses to avoid the task.

How do we assess for mathematical learning difficulties?

If any of the conditions that can be found within the SpLD Profile are found to be present in an individual then their mathematical ability should also be checked and appropriate provision made for any difficulties that they may be having. "One should consider the possibility of assessment for dyscalculia if the individual's performance is significantly below the level expected given their age and intellectual/cognitive ability" and [they have a] "difference in achievement and expected level of performance [of] at least two years."[17]

What should an assessment include?

1. The learning style of the individual e.g. qualitative/grasshopper or quantitative/inchworm [18]
(One of the tests used for this can also show difficulties relating to visual perception and the degree of maths anxiety present.)
2. An assessment of the individual's mathematical level which can be assessed via standardised tests such as the 'Wide Range Achievement Test' and 'The Profile of Mathematical Skills'.[19]
3. Mathematical language level (e.g. vocabulary level) plus word finding/word labelling difficulties which affect the acquisition of language and understanding of instructions etc.
4. The prerequisite skills for learning mathematics.[20]

Some professionals also favour an assessment of times tables knowledge. Such an assessment can show whether the individual can learn information by rote and whether sequencing difficulties are present. It can enable the assessor to see if the individual can use his tables knowledge in the questions that form part of the standardised tests above. In a 1:1 situation the assessor can also see whether the individual has to count from the beginning of the table to get to the answer he requires.

Who assesses for mathematical learning difficulties?

Teachers and educational psychologists will be able to assess the individual's mathematical age and areas of weakness but unless they also know how to assess the particular sub-skill difficulties they will not be able to gain a whole picture of the individual's difficulties and may well not be able to identify the presence of dyscalculia. [21] A sub-skill assessment is part of a Prof. Sharma course but there are few Sharma trained teachers in the UK at present. At the time of printing some private schools offer this type of assessment to pupils other than their own e.g. Edington & Shapwick School (Somerset) Tel: 01278 722012, Appleford School (Wiltshire) Tel: 01980 621020 and Steve Chinn, (Mark College, Somerset) Tel: 01278 641632. Children can participate in one of Sharma's residential courses where they will be assessed by Prof. Sharma and his Certificate students. This is a very thorough assessment the results of which will be given in the form of both an oral and written report (the latter also includes a remediation programme).[22]

Overcoming mathematical difficulties

Even if an individual's number/mathematical difficulties are not caused by dyscalculia the individual may still need specialist mathematics tuition to overcome them. [23] However, the shortage of such specialists for both assessment and teaching may make such provision difficult to obtain.

Individuals need a teacher who both fully understands mathematics in all its complexity and who also understands how to teach it to all of those affected by difficulties in this subject including those with dyscalculia. [24] The individual's maths anxiety needs to be reduced and their self esteem raised. This can only occur if they are able to feel success at some aspect of maths. In order to achieve this the prerequisite skills for learning mathematics need to be brought up to intellectual age. This can only be achieved by playing certain types of mathematics based games. Concrete apparatus such as Cuisenaire rods will also be needed to re-teach concepts. Concepts should be introduced via the individual's natural learning style and reinforced using that style plus the alternative style whilst topics need to be introduced via methods which avoid later confusions.

CONCLUSION

Some people feel that one cannot be good at everything and so there is no need to worry if the individual cannot do maths and, after all, surely literacy is of more importance. Many professionals feel that their departments/schools are very over-stretched in just catering for those with literacy difficulties. However, mathematical difficulties leave individuals open to ridicule and humiliation when they are not able to do a simple task such as adding a couple of figures correctly or make an appointment on time. Without adequate provision such individuals may have great difficulties in reaching their potential because they struggle to acquire, or lack, the qualifications to enter a grammar school and/or university/college. Their difficulties do not go away, under stress and when tired they worsen.

The individual with severe difficulties may exist in a world where they understand little, or no, mathematics. When all is confusion the individual has no hope of explaining their difficulties nor any chance of overcoming them. High intelligence and a good memory may enable some individuals them to survive and even appear good at mathematics during the primary school years. However, once they reach secondary school their standard of mathematics rapidly goes down hill as the demands on memory and non-understood processes become too great. Individuals can be reduced to tears when they know that their mind can soar with reading tasks but suddenly refuse to even float with those based on numeracy.

Although, with age, some of those affected by mathematical difficulties manage to devise coping strategies of their own, many do not. Early provision will help individuals to overcome their difficulties but unless we all learn to recognise such individuals and professionals become trained in the most effective methods which can help them, many will never have the opportunity to test their wings let alone reach the sky.

Table 1

The following indicators may be present if the prerequisite skills are absent or incomplete.

1. Number *(This sub-skill should have been acquired by the age of 6 years. It is needed for all operations)*
•Inability to relate size to quantity/shape when appropriate. The individual may have difficulties in learning that one number has a greater value than another e.g. 5 has a value greater than 3.
•May have difficulties with concepts that relate to more and less. This plus directional confusions/spatial relationships difficulties may make it difficult to use the symbols > and < correctly.
•Is likely to have difficulties with estimating the answer prior to working out the problem. May cope with very small numbers but anything added to the number which makes it more complicated e.g. numbers after the decimal point will confuse the individual.

2. Weight *(This sub-skill should have been acquired by the age of 6 years if concrete tasks are to be carried out or by 10 years if the concept is used in hypothetical situations. It is needed for addition, division and fractions.)*
An inability to see that the reshaping of an item does not affect its weight. The person may be able to accept that two identical items weigh the same (though they may need to use scales for this task as they do not have an innate sense of sameness of weight and so cannot gauge it by comparing the feel of the weight when different objects are held.). However, when one of the objects has changed its shape e.g. by being squashed, lengthened they are unable to see that they are still the same weight unless shown with scales that this is the case. If this sub-skill has not been developed the individual may not be able to accept that a $1/4$ of a room and a $1/4$ of a page are still the same mathematical unit even though they are vastly different in the area which they cover.

3. Length *(This sub-skill should have been acquired by the age of 7 years. It is needed for addition, multiplication and fractions.)*
An inability to see that two lines are the same length. The person may be able to do the task when straight lines are used but is unable to visualise in their mind whether the lines are equal when they consist of curves and angles.
4. Area *(This sub-skill should have been acquired by the age of 8 years. It is*

needed for multiplication, division and fractions.)
• Inability to visually match given amounts of area. The individual may not be able to do simple matching tasks e.g. match the identical two squares out of a group squares.
• Inability to visualise the area of each of the separate parts of a shape to construct the whole in their mind. An example of this would be an inability to 'see' that the five single centimetre cubes in the Cuisenaire rod set are the same as the five centimetre long rod until they are placed alongside it.

5. Volume *(This sub-skill should have been acquired by the age of 9 years. It is needed for multiplication, division and fractions)*
• Inability to realise that the changing shape/size of a container of a given amount of liquid/gas etc. does not alter the amount of it. This may be understood in its simplest form but the individual may have difficulties in understanding it in its hypothetical form. When used hypothetically many other factors may need to be integrated and/or may affect the information that has been given to the individual. This can result in each item remaining a fragment of the question with the individual being unable to relate them to the whole.

6. Understand the relationship between variables. *(This sub-skill should have been acquired by the age of 11 years. It is needed for the calculation of interest and principal. The presence of this sub-skill indicates that the individual has the ability to think in the abstract mathematically.)*
An inability to understand the relationship between two, or more, pieces of information. Individuals with this difficulty will have difficulties in solving problems which involve a combination of elements such as speed, time and distance e.g. 2 men dig a 5 metre tunnel in 10 minutes and two women dig a 3 metre tunnel in 4 minutes who digs the fastest.

(Difficulties in these areas will be made worse by poor knowledge of time as can be present in both dyslexia and dyspraxia see chapters 3. & 5.)

7. Classification *(This sub-skill should have been acquired by the age of 12 years. It is needed for subtraction, addition and is essential for fractions.)*
An inability to group and regroup items according to given patterns and an inability to work out a pattern by which items can be grouped for themselves (or when shown by others). Difficulties can be seen as:
• incorrectly interpreting problems presented in words e.g. in a

question such as: 'There are six tall houses and five wide houses how many tall houses are there altogether' the answer may be given as 11. The person does not misread the question and it is not a case of not knowing what the words 'wide' and 'tall' mean. It is as though the person is concentrating so hard on understanding the maths that is within the question that they do not 'see' that 'grouping' a vital element of it. Often there can be an awareness that the answer does not 'feel right' but the person is unable to explain why. This is not a case of a general inability to understand written text as the individual may have superb comprehension of written text when it relates to literacy.

• inability to recognise groups e.g. in sets

• inability to categorise attributes of items e.g. all angles below 90° are acute angles. Sometimes the individual can classify this far but then cannot extend/apply the classification rule so that they are unable to recognise the different types of triangle. (*Where classification has not developed in geometry it may also be a sign of visual perceptual difficulties. which can be found as part of a spatial relationship difficulty. See Chapter 5.*)

It is not a case of individuals lacking classification skills across the board. They may be able to 'see' and use classification patterns in literacy, philosophy etc.. It may be that the individual does not so much have a dysfunction in their classification system but a 'difference' in it. Some individuals can see more readily unusual classification patterns than those which other people usually see. They can also see so many different ways of classifying/relating the items that they do not know which one is needed. This can cause problems when attempting to psychologically test such individuals as they can see so many relationships between several words/concepts but do not know which one the assessor requires.

8. Spatial (*This sub-skill should have been acquired by the age of 12 years. It is needed for all mathematical operations.*)
• Directional confusion and difficulties in carrying out instructions relating to movement and objects from someone facing you (mirror image) are likely to be present. (This skill should have developed by 8 years.) Such individuals will have difficulties in carrying out practical tasks when the instructor is facing her e.g. PE, CDT, art, cooking and science. Part of the difficulty is because the learner has to copy the movements of the instructor by reversing what she sees visually e.g. when you <u>look at</u> the instructor his right hand appears to be on his left side.

• Inability to work out spatial relationships where the original item has been rotated/moved to any extent. *(Being able to do this from any perspective should have developed by 12 years.)* Difficulties in reading maps, reading compass points etc. are likely to be present. The individual may have to turn their body round and/or the compass/map to face the right direction to even be able to attempt the task.

• Difficulties in symbolism (e.g. understanding that an item can represent something else such as the symbol on a map representing a church) may also be present. If this and difficulties in spatial relationships are severe then the individual is likely find it impossible to read the simplest of maps.

• Inability to create a copy of a model. The individual may be able to copy it if she has a 3D model to copy from but can have great difficulties in copying the model from a 2D model e.g. picture/diagram etc. *(Also see dyspraxia- Chapter , dyslexia - Chapter 3 and autistic spectrum disorder- Chapter 10.)*

9. Transivity *(This sub-skill should have been acquired by the age of 12 years. It is needed for multi-step activities, theorems in geometry and deductive reasoning.)*

• Inability to solve problems that contain elements where each one is related to the next and is also related to all previous and future elements e.g. Joan is older than Fred who is younger than Tom. Tom is older than Mary who is younger than Fred. Who is the youngest child?

The individual can get 'lost' in the problem and 'lose' one step of the relationships and so be unable to solve the problem. If there are also difficulties in understanding mathematical language then an explanation of the problem may achieve little unless concrete objects (and then pictures) are used to show the sum. If transivity difficulties are present then much of algebra will not make sense.

Table 2

These are the main indicators of difficulties in learning mathematics which may be found in individuals affected by dyscalculia and/or the other conditions that are found within the SpLD Profile. *(Also see Table 1 for the prerequisite skills which may be absent or delayed.)*

1. Difficulties in learning new mathematical skills. The first concept/process may be learnt but the individual may have great difficulty in acquiring new ones that build upon the first one and that require it to be adapted in some way. Some individuals may 'learn' the new concept/process in a 1:1 situation but are unable to transfer/apply it to other situations e.g. within the classroom or daily life environments. *(This can be present as part of dyscalculia. Also see dyspraxia - Chapter 5 & autistic spectrum disorder - Chapter 10.)*

2. Planning and organisational difficulties. These can be present as part of specific language impairment, dyslexia, dyscalculia, dyspraxia, and attention deficits. *(See chapters 2., 3., 5. & 9.)* There can be difficulties in both planning and starting the task. Individuals may not be able to find a starting point, or have several to choose from. As they do not know the correct starting point they cannot start the task at all. (This behaviour can be misinterpreted by teachers/parents etc. as laziness.)

3. Understanding the language of mathematics. Individuals may know how to do the calculation but may make errors because they do not understand mathematical language. The individual with dyscalculia may lack a mathematical vocabulary appropriate to his age and ability and may also have a similar deficiency in understanding mathematical language both written and oral. If Specific Language Impairment is also present he may also lack an appropriate vocabulary and understanding of language in literacy as well. There may be difficulties in following/understanding instructions, listening and word finding *see Chapter 2. (Note: difficulties relating to word finding and following instructions can be found as part of dyspraxia - see Chapter 5.)* These difficulties could also be caused by Central Auditory Processing Disorder *(see Chapter 8)*. Individuals may be able to cope with the basic four rules of number but are likely to have problems in word based problems.

Sometimes the person may have good to excellent literacy skills. These can 'get in the way' of understanding the language of mathematics because the individual may always first think of the meaning of the word as in the literacy rather than as in number. This sort of difficulty can cause major problems in understanding written problems and when listening to the teacher explaining how to do an operation.

An example of this sort of problem can be found in the use of the word 'by' e.g. "The piece of wood was 5 cms *by* 5 cms, what is its area?" In this case 'by' is requiring the individual to multiply the relevant numbers. However, in literacy 'by 'can be used as a word relating to:
• sequence/a line of items e.g. the animals went into the ark one *'by'* one
• position e.g. the duck went *by* the house
• to a visit' e.g. I'll drop *by* your house tomorrow.
Both sequence and position are concepts that are used in mathematics so the individual may 'try' those first. The individual cannot pay attention to the rest of the teacher's explanation/information in the question etc. until the use of the word is understood.

Problems can also occur because higher level language may not have been introduced at the beginning e.g. 'sum' , 'take away' were used but not the term 'equation' and 'minus'. Such individuals spend a lot of time 'translating' the teacher's vocabulary into their own (and vice-versa) and so can 'miss' vital parts of the explanation.

Individuals can also confuse words. This can have several causes e.g. 'word finding' difficulties, failure to internalise vocabulary and a failure to understand a concept. An example of this is the child who confuses a third for a quarter. A simple concrete example plus explanation does not help the person. The individual can still believe that each item is a 'third' of the whole even when they have:
• physically divided an object into four equal parts
• had it explained that each item is a quarter of the whole
• had both the numerator and the denominator explained
(Such confusion can only be overcome by specialist teaching.)

4. Sequencing: Individuals can have difficulties in recognising and remembering sequences. They may not know the correct sequence of numbers/events (e.g. in counting, saying their tables and the seasons of the year etc..). They can also have difficulties in carrying multi-step mathematical processes e.g. long multiplication. *(Such difficulties can be*

49

seen as part of dyslexia -see Chapter 3 and autistic spectrum disorder -see Chapter 10.)
If individuals have any combination of sequencing, remembering numbers and other memory difficulties present they will find it difficult (if not impossible) to learn their tables. Difficulties with carrying out a sequence as part of a practical task can also be found in those affected by dyspraxia *(see Chapter 5)*.

5. Concentration/attention difficulties. Individuals may:

• not be able to attend to the task long enough to finish it and and/or may have difficulties in starting the task. *(See Attention Deficit Disorders Chapter 9).*

• have difficulties in concentrating on instructions. *(See Attention Deficit Disorders Chapter 9 and Central Auditory Processing Disorder - Chapter 8 & Specific Language Impairment - Chapter 2.)*

• refuse to co-operate with the teacher. This may indicate the presence of Attention Deficit Disorders *(Chapter 9)* and/or traits of autistic spectrum disorder *(Chapter 10)* .

• have concentration difficulties due to visual/perceptual difficulties *(See Chapters 7., 5. & 12.)* and/or stress and tiredness.

6. Difficulties in understanding fractions. There can be difficulties in understanding fractions once the units become smaller than quarters because they have not fully understood the concept of fractions. Previous knowledge of numbers can 'get in the way' of understanding the new concept. Thus individuals can:

• have difficulties in knowing which is the bigger of a pair of fractions because 4 is bigger than 3 but in fractions 1/4 is smaller than 1/3.

• find it illogical that when fractions are multiplied the result is smaller than the original fractions so equations such as $1/2 \times 1/2 = 1/4$ make no sense at all. (The area method of mathematics will enable them to make sense of this.)

• have difficulties in using/understanding the terms used for the parts of the fraction and for the different types of fraction as these terms may not be known well enough.

• be extremely anxious when presented with a task using fractions or even just the sight of a page of fractions.

7. Failure to understand algebra (and this may extend to even the simplest of equations). This can occur when early mathematics teaching did not extend concepts high enough and when the new concept is not related to present and past knowledge. Those with dyscalculia are likely to be the worst affected with this difficulty.

The individual may not understand where the 'letters' used in the equation have come from and it can make no sense at all that 'x' can mean one thing in one sum and something else in another. A failure in understanding the symbols used in algebra mean that there is no chance of being able to solve such tasks. This lack of understanding can be avoided if concrete examples of the use of letters representing known numbers is used early enough e.g. via the use of Cuisenaire rods. This can be done at very early ages - in fact the rods can be used as soon as equations (sums) are first written down. Just showing the individual once the fact that the sum 2+5=7 may be described as: pink rod + yellow rod = black rod and may therefore also be described as the initial letters of those words e.g. p+y=b can be enough to enable individuals to make sense (and reduce their fear) of algebra.

8. Memory. There are many aspects to memory and difficulties in a particular aspect will show itself in a particular way. Difficulties in this area are commonly associated with dyslexia. Individuals may have weaknesses in the memory skills which are needed to retain information in one's head whilst working out a calculation. Such difficulties can also cause the individual to forget all, or part, of the instruction for/explanation of a given task.

• *Auditory memory/processing difficulties.* These cause the individual to have difficulties in quickly recalling numbers, he may be able to cope with written sums but not with oral ones. (*This can be seen as part of specific language impairment, dyslexia, attention deficit disorder and Central Auditory Processing Disorder - see Chapters 2., 3, 9 & 8.*)

• *Visual and symbolic memory* skills are needed to remember what the different signs mean and which way up/round etc. they should be. Individuals may be unable to remember the meanings of the symbols long enough to organise them and put them into the 'plan' of how to solve the question. Difficulties in understanding the use of symbols as representations of a concept etc. may also be present.

Memory difficulties can result in slow working and what seem to be 'careless errors'. Memory difficulties may be present in dyscalculia but they are also associated with dyslexia, attention deficit disorder and autistic spectrum disorder. *(See Chapters 3, 9 and 10.)*

9. Visual-spatial, spatial orientation and/or spatial relationships.
Spatial difficulties can show as difficulties with geometry, shape discrimination, size and length. Such difficulties can affect the ability of the individual to find their place on the board/page and there may be difficulties in learning place value. [25] Spatial difficulties can be seen as part of dyspraxia *(see Chapter 5)*. If both motor co-ordination difficulties and spatial-based difficulties are present individual may appear 'clumsy' and 'careless'. Such individuals may place objects on the edge of desks without realising that they are about to knock them off. They can also have difficulties in handling apparatus and constructing diagrams. Difficulties with visual spatial skills can occur as part of near-vision dysfunctioning and/or perceptual difficulties. *(See Chapter 7. & 12.)*

10. Writing difficulties: The individual may lay out sums/fractions etc. incorrectly and/or present work so badly that various errors occur in the calculation e.g. incorrect following of a sequence of operations, misunderstanding of place value, misreading of the sum. In Chapter 6 the many causes of writing difficulty are described in full - all of which can apply in the writing of mathematical information of which the following are very important:

• expressive language difficulties which are present as part of specific language impairment and are usually seen in dyslexia. *(see Chapters 2. & 3.)*. Such difficulties make it difficult to know how to write the sum down. The individual may also have problems in stating what part of the task they are finding difficult.

• motor co-ordination and control difficulties caused by dyspraxia, stress, anxiety etc. may make it difficult to write the symbols, numerals and diagrams (e.g. geometric shapes, graphs etc.) correctly. *(See Chapters 5. & 6.)*. (Vision/perception difficulties will also cause difficulties in this area. *(See Chapters 7., 9. & 12.)*.

• the person with dyscalculia/dyslexia may not understand the significance of writing a particular part of a sum in a particular way e.g.
-not fully understand why 2^2 cannot be written as 22
-failing to properly understand which is the denominator and which is the numerator in fractions.

11. Reading difficulties due to dyslexia (as in literacy) and/or visual/perceptual dysfunction being present. The individual may either have great difficulties in reading any maths books, or, only be able to read the words in the lower level books and therefore may not progress to the more complex text books. He may find it very tiring to read which will slow his work down. Both slowness in work speed and being unable to read more complex text will result in the individual having less experience of mathematics. *(See Chapters 3., 7. & 12.)*

12. Comprehension of the written and spoken word. Individuals may know how to do the calculation but produce an incorrect answer because they do not understand mathematical language. The individual with dyscalculia may be able to read the words in a mathematical word problem but can struggle to understand the meaning of the words and struggle to write it as a sum. Difficulties in literacy based reading comprehension can also be present if the individual is also affected by dyslexia *(see chapter 3)*. Difficulties in understanding the spoken word can also be part of Specific Language Impairment *(see Chapter 2)*, dyspraxia *(see Chapter 5)* and Central Auditory Processing Disorder *(see Chapter 8)*.

13. Directional confusion. This can cause several types of difficulties which relate to the individual being unsure in which direction to go next in either deciding which part of the sum to work on, or, in constructing the numerals etc.. Such difficulties are commonly associated with dyslexia and visual and/or perceptual difficulties. They can also be present as part of dyspraxia and autistic spectrum disorder. *(See chapters 3., 7., 12. & 10.)*

The individual has to know where he has to start the sum and where he has to put the answer and this varies according to how the sum is laid out and what type of sum it is. Thus in a vertically written subtraction sum the individual has to start at the right hand bottom figure (with the answer going at the bottom) whilst in a long division the starting point is at the left hand side and the answer goes at the top.

Directional confusion relating to construction can cause the individual to reverse/invert numbers and signs e.g. writing 5 for 2 and + for x. The poor writing that can result from this problem can make it difficult to distinguish one operational sign from another e.g. + and x and a 7 from a 1. *(Though putting a bar across the middle of the 7 as is done on the continent can solve the latter difficulty.)*

Directional confusion can cause the individual to have difficulties with visualisation (the ability to 'see in your mind' what it is you want to write). Affected individuals may not be able to 'spell' the equation correctly as they cannot remember what it should look like.

14. Motor co-ordination difficulties in practical tasks. Even though it may be essential for the individual to use concrete apparatus those individuals with dyspraxia are likely to find it difficult to use such apparatus without their peer group teasing them. They are not likely to neatly throw the dice when working out probability tasks and can easily knock everything over when using equipment. *(See dyspraxia - Chapter 5.)*

15. The individual is reluctant , or struggles to look at written/visual information. The individual can find looking at this sort of information painful and tiring if near vision dysfunctioning/visual perceptual/perception difficulties are present. *(See Chapters 7., 5. & 12).*

Further Information

Mathematics for dyslexics - a teaching handbook by Steve Chinn & Richard Ashcroft, 2nd Edition (pub. Whurr)

For UK stockists of Prof Mahesh Sharma publications contact: Next Generation, 17 Medway Close, Taunton TA1 2NS

References

1. Mathematics for dyslexia, a teaching handbook by Chinn & Ashcroft.(Pub.Whurr)

2. Different professionals use different terms e.g. Sharma uses the terms qualitative/quantitative and Chinn uses the terms first used by Bath et al i.e. grasshopper/inchworm.

3. Prof. Sharma at his Certificate Course in UK 1995.

4. Information supplied by Chinn & Ashcroft. The large difference between their figures and Sharma's may be attributed to a variety of factors including that of the population with which they deal e.g. children attend Sharma's centre because of their arithmetic/ mathematical difficulties and some may be undiagnosed dyslexics whereas all of Chinn & Ashcroft's students are dyslexic.

5. Dr Ian McKinlay at the Dyspraxia Trust Professional Conference 1996.

6. Mathematics for dyslexia, a teaching handbook by Chinn &

Ashcroft.(Pub.Whurr)

7. & 8. Math Notebook Vol. 8, Numbers 7, 8, 9 & 10 page 11 by Prof. Mahesh Sharma (see Footnotes 11 & 13 for further details.)

9. & 10. See page 3 of 'Mathematics for dyslexics: a teaching handbook' by Dr Steve Chinn & Richard Ashcroft (pub. Whurr Publishers Ltd.) Both Chinn & Ashcroft are based at Mark College, Somerset.

11. & 12. See page 14 of Math Notebook Vol.8, Numbers 7,8,9 & 10- Dyslexia, dyscalculia, and some remedial perspectives for mathematics learning problems by Mahesh Sharma (pub. The Centre for Teaching/Learning of Mathematics, Office Box 3149, Framingham, Ma 01701, USA).

13. See page 15 of Math Notebook Vol.8, Numbers 7,8,9 & 10- Dyslexia, dyscalculia, and some remedial perspectives for mathematics learning problems by Mahesh Sharma (pub. The Centre for Teaching/Learning of Mathematics, Office Box 3149, Framingham, Ma 01701, USA).

14. & 15. 'The area method of multiplication' is as follows:

The extract below has been reproduced by kind permission of Prof. Mahesh Sharma who owns the copyright for it. It is from p.17 of the Math Notebook -Cuisenaire Rods and Mathematics Teaching Vol 10, numbers 3 & 4 by Mahesh C. Sharma (for publisher see footnotes 11. & 12.) This Notebook goes on to explain how this method can be used for fractions and to explain why 'of' means 'multiplied by'. Once this method is used it becomes obvious that any number multiplied by nought must equal nought!

" Cuisenaire rods are very useful in connecting the two definitions of the multiplication (the repeated addition as a representation of multiplcation and multiplication as the area of a rectangle with the dimensions of the rectangle as the two factors in the product). for example, 3x4 could be represented as: *(See illustration opposite)*

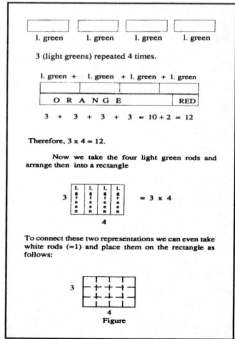

16. & 17. *Prof. Sharma during his Certificate Course in the UK 1995.*
18. *For information on Learning Styles see 'Solutions for Specific Learning Difficulties: Resources Guide', and Chapter 2 of 'Mathematics for dyslexics: a teaching handbook' by Dr Steve Chinn & Richard Ashcroft (pub. Whurr Publishers Ltd.)*
19. *Profile of mathematical skills is available from NFER-Nelson Publishing Co. Ltd., Darville House, 2 Oxford Road East, Windsor, Berkshire SL4 1DF and the Wide Range Achievement Test (WRAT) is available from the Dyslexia Institute, 133 Gresham Rd, Staines, Middlesex. TW18, 2AJ.*
20. *Prof. Sharma's 'The Diagnostic Assessment of Mathematics Potential and Achievement' will identify some of the main areas of sub-skill dysfunctioning which prevents the individual from acquiring mathematical skills.' This test is only available to those who have hold his 'Diagnosis & Remediation of Learning Problems in Mathematics Certificate. At the time of printing this Certificate was held by very few people in the UK.*
21. *Sub-skill assessment is part of Prof. Sharma's courses (see Footnotes 18 & 20)*
22. *Prof. Sharma comes to the UK several times a year to give lectures andusually once or twice a year to run his course. Information on these can be obtained from Mrs Patricia Brazil Tel: 01189 474864 Fax: 01189 461574.*
23. *For further information see 'More Help for Dyslexic Children by Miles & Miles (pub. Methuen Educational Ltd.) Information on this is quoted in Math Notebook Vol.8, Numbers 7,8,9 & 10 (see footnotes 11. & 12. for further details).*
24. *The authoress is dyscalculic. She had to wait until her forties (when she attended one of Sharma's lectures) before she understood why 2x0=0 and why 1/2 x 1/2 =1/4. She is therefore of the opinion that all teachers of mathematics should have a working knowledge of Sharma's techniques no matter what age group they teach.*
25. *"Mathematics for dyslexics: a teaching handbook" by Dr Steve Chinn and Richard Ashcroft (Pub. Whurr)*

Acknowledgements: Dr Steve Chinn & Richard Ashcroft

Chapter 5

THE IDENTIFICATION
OF DYSPRAXIA

*The pupil is referred to as 'she' and the teacher and the educational
psychologist as 'he' for the sake of convenience.*

Dyspraxia is also known as Developmental
Co-ordination Disorder. It is a Specific Learning
Difficulty in gross and fine motor planning which
is not caused by muscle/nerve damage. It is
believed to affect between 5-10% of the
population with "approximately 10,000 children
being affected in the UK. It affects both sexes with three affected
boys for every two affected girls. However, the ratio known to the
professional services is four boys to one girl. This is because boys are
more likely to respond by behaving badly. Girls are more likely to be
anxious or depressed but less conspicuous."[1]

An individual affected by dyspraxia may have both fine and gross
motor control difficulties, or, only one of them. Gross motor control is
related to whole limb/body movements. Fine motor control is related
to hand/finger movements, the organs of speech and eye movements.
Each individual will have a unique array of difficulties which are
likely to affect many aspects of her life. Many individuals will need
help to adopt strategies that will enable them to overcome many of
the difficulties caused by this condition. Some will find that the
difficulties become apparent again when under stress and/or illness.

As there are many types of dyspraxia no one person will show all of
the various indicators. Generally speaking the easiest individuals to
recognise will be those having the common indicators (see Table **1).**
The most difficult individuals to recognise are those who have only
one indicator from Table 1. Such individuals may also have one
indicator from Table 2 and certainly have several, or all, of the other
indicators relevant to a particular sub-group of dyspraxia e.g.:

◆ **Articulatory dyspraxia,** also called verbal dyspraxia *(see Chapter 2).* Affects various aspects of speech e.g. correct breathing for speech, keeping speech understandable in long sentences, controlling the speed, rhythm and volume of speech saying particular sounds e.g. 'th' and 'thr', pronouncing parts of words in the correct order and the swallow reflex. *(See Table 1 section 6 of this chapter.)* The Nuffield Centre Dyspraxia Programme can be used by speech and language therapists to help individuals overcome the difficulties that this form of dyspraxia presents. *(See Further Information section at the end of this chapter.)*

◆ **Occulomotor dyspraxia** (see Chapter 7)

◆ **Ideomotor dyspraxia** (difficulties in doing single motor tasks e.g. picking up a cup)

◆ **Ideational dyspraxia** (difficulties in planning and carrying out a sequence of operations e.g. can pick up shoe polish, duster and shoes but cannot carry out the task of polishing the shoes)

◆ **Constructional dyspraxia** (difficulties in creating a duplicate of a model due to an inability to know how to place things in relation to one another e.g. Lego ™)

◆ **Dressing dyspraxia.** This has two forms. 50% of dyspraxic children have gross motor problems and most of this group are likely to have problems with dressing and undressing at some stage.[2] Dressing difficulties can make trying on clothes in shops, getting ready for school in the morning and changing for PE, swimming and drama particularly stressful. They can struggle to remember the order in which to put the clothes on and how to arrange their body and the clothes to get dressed. As a result clothes can end up inside out and back to front.[3] There is a much less common form which causes the individual to only dress and groom one side of the body.

◆ Writing difficulties can be present as part of dyspraxia which in this book are referred to as graphomotor dyspraxia. Individuals with this difficulty are likely to have difficulties with the manipulation of tools e.g. pen, saw and compass. *(Other conditions/circumstances can also cause writing difficulties see Chapter 6).*

Various difficulties/conditions are seen alongside dyspraxia:

◆ Both numeracy *(see Chapter 4)* and speech/language difficulties *(see Chapter 2)* are usually associated with it.[4]

◆ Behavioural difficulties and the way in which the pupil interacts with her peers *(see Chapters 9 & 10).*

Early recognition is vital if the dyspraxic children are to reach their potential.

As so many areas are affected it is often necessary to obtain a full picture of the individual's strengths and weaknesses. This is via 'a multidisciplinary assessment' which involves several different specialists assessing for different conditions (see Table 5). Severe dyspraxia is very apparent even to the lay person and it is likely to be recognised at the pre-school stage (by professionals such as Health Visitors and doctors) during routine developmental checks. This is especially the case if the child's main difficulties are in motor control e.g. body, limb, hand or speech movements rather than behaviour, vision etc.. However, in some cases the individual has a low-level of several conditions. When the difficulties caused by each condition are added together they can markedly affect the individual's life and create a considerable problem in learning. It is this *'moderate specific'* group which is likely to be in non-specialist schools and which may be missed by both educational and medical professionals.

Recognition of such children may often only be made if professionals ask the parents about the presence of the indicators of dyspraxia (as mentioned in Tables 1 & 2) and then talk to their colleagues in the relevant professions. *(The Checklist of the Movement Assessment Battery for Children (Movement ABC) by Henderson & Sugden can be used by non-specialist teachers to determine the likelihood of dyspraxia being present. The Movement ABC itself can be used by specialist teachers and other specialist professionals to make a diagnosis of dyspraxia. However, neither of these tools can be used to diagnosis articulatory/occulomotor dyspraxia.)*

Delayed development or dyspraxia?

The associated features of dyspraxia (see Table 1) and what appears to be difficulties in motor planning/organisation can be seen in both late developers and in those with dyspraxia. At the playgroup/nursery stage it can be very apparent that a child lacks rhythm and/or appears less co-ordinated than his peers. The latter can be because the child is not given enough opportunities at home to develop co-ordination skills. Unless it is very noticeable compared with their peer group the first course of action is the provision of concentrated practice and exposure to a variety of activities.[5] This avoids unnecessary referrals which result in the physio/occupational therapists when they see the child (some several months later) finding that most if not all of the causes for concern have disappeared.

Some of the associated features that can be spotted early are:

The fact that a dislike of having ones hair/nails touched and or cut is commonly associated with dyspraxia needs to be brought to the attention of all of those who work with young children. All of us who are parents, or who work with young children, know that many children dislike having their hair washed but the reaction of the dyspraxic child to this process often has to be seen to be believed. This dislike can carry on for many years even into the teenage years and adulthood. Textural sensitivity (liking/disliking soft/rough textures to touch or in the mouth) is another indicator that is easily spotted in the early years.

The 'not dyslexic' child

Sometimes low-level and moderately dyspraxic children pass through all the usual early health checks without their condition being recognised. As many teachers are unaware of the indicators of dyspraxia these children can go through the whole educational system without being picked up. ("Though there may be emotional/behavioural problems including signs of anxiety, depression or withdrawal including school refusal or poor attendance attributed to frequent minor illness.") [6] They can quite often be the pupil that the parent has concerns about and so asks for an assessment of dyslexia to be made. The teacher makes a preliminary assessment of the child (e.g spelling and reading) but finds little or no areas of concern in literacy. (Though there may well be a noticeable problem with presentation of work and handwriting which may be put down to carelessness and/or laziness). Consequently the teacher informs the parent that the child is 'not dyslexic' but he does not refer the child for dyspraxia because he does not know the relevant indicators. The child may then struggle throughout her academic life and in the worst scenario may have both teachers and parents nagging her because she is not trying hard enough, or, they may write her off as being 'not that bright'.

TEACHING

Teacher/parent partnership

Having empathy with the pupil and her difficulties is important but by itself it will not be enough to enable her to overcome her difficulties. It is essential that the teacher accepts and recognises the pupil's difficulties. He also needs to:

◆ Make use of the reports made by the various professionals e.g. a paediatric occupational therapist and a paediatric physiotherapist report.

◆ The pupil should not be expected to attain goals at the same rate as her peers of similar intelligence. She should be allowed to progress at her own pace via a structured teaching method which is based upon multisensory methods and which has considerable reinforcement built into it.[7] It is essential that opportunities for praise being given throughout the lesson and practise sessions for each tiny task achieved are provided.

◆ Be prepared to adapt his teaching technique to the pupil's needs including using the appropriate learning style e.g. qualitative, or, quantitative learning[8] and modifying PE activities so that the child with dyspraxia is enabled to participate.

◆ If there is a SpLD in numeracy and/or literacy (e.g. dyscalculia/dyslexia) some tuition in a 1:1 environment is likely to be necessary for the child to achieve her potential.

◆ Accept that the child's fidgeting, clumsiness and overreaction to certain situations are not within her control.

◆ Be aware that the child may be under stress throughout the whole school day although she does not appear to be so and that this occurs even when she has very good relationship with her teachers. This can be caused by the child fearing that she will make errors and/or be clumsy and she is anxious that she may be told off by her teacher (or, if in a group lesson that she will be teased by her peer group.)

◆ "Seat the child appropriately in the classroom i.e. not near a window/door or at the back of the classroom where she can become easily distracted or not hear the instructor or see the blackboard easily."[9]

◆ Teach strategies that will help individuals to overcome difficulties in short term memory, organisational and planning skills. [10]

Transfer from primary to secondary school

Individuals affected by dyspraxia may have poor planning, organisation and time keeping skills plus they find it difficult to relate to their peer group or the rules of lots of different teachers. Although the poor time-keeping skills may have caused a great deal of difficulty for some children many of them were just able to cope with the primary school situation. However, the demands on these skills at secondary school level plus the inconsistent approach of the different subject teachers may overwhelm them.

Even bright children could need considerable support from the Learning Support Department and may become school refusers if they are not handled carefully. They can become more aware of their weaknesses in the secondary school environment as set segments of the day are devoted to different subjects. Thus, they may find it very stressful when a day has nothing but 'motor planning' based subjects e.g. CDT, Art, PE and Cooking. Due to the frequency of maths lessons the child with both dyspraxia and dyscalculia may have no days in the week when they are not under stress.

If stress induced illness or frequent withdrawal from class for teaching/therapy causes them to miss lessons then more stress is created as they try to catch up on work. This can result in them being under so much stress that they can no longer face attending school at the end of the week. In such cases the stress can be reduced by allowing them to attend for some 'short days' (e.g. the first two lessons of the day only) and by either allowing them to attend the learning support department for a particularly stressful lesson, or, providing learning support within the lesson. It is very important that parents and school work together in such situations to help the child overcome her difficulties. It is also important that all those involved with the pupil realise that it may take weeks/months rather than days of such provision before the pupil has settled into her new environment.

Adult dyspraxia

Professionals view the continuation of dyspraxia into adulthood in different ways. Some believe that few individuals experience problems as an adult others believe that it usually continues into adulthood. Research in this area is limited but some evidence shows that dyspraxia does continue into adulthood for a larger group. (Although this may not be obvious because they use coping strategies in both their choice of job and leisure pursuits to avoid problems associated with their dyspraxia.)[11] It is thought that the most noticeable adults in this group are likely to be of above average intelligence and possess resilience and determination.[12] It also seems that the 'clumsiness' of youth is not regarded as one of the main problems by adults. Instead it is often the difficulties that are found alongside dyspraxia that become the dominant difficulties in adulthood e.g. difficulties in overflow movements (e.g. moving arms when it is only necessary to move legs); dancing; keep fit; lack of rhythm; judging speed and distance; weak muscle tone; slow handwriting (failing to finish words off) and drawing; poor pen grip; lack of concentration; disorganisation and maths plus social and emotional problems e.g. low self-esteem, anxiety and difficulties with relationships.[13]

Daily living and dyspraxia

Movement of some sort is needed for most of the tasks we do in our daily lives. Such tasks range from personal hygiene, eating, moving around the school/workplace and maintaining an appropriate posture throughout the day. For the adult the 'final straw' may be the preparation of a meal at the end of the day. Once adults become parents they then had to use their inadequate skills to cope with more demanding tasks relating to childcare. Changing the baby and doing up nappies so that they both stay on and work properly is an art. The rest of the family want variety in their meals and for some reason, yet to be explained, so much of what they want seems to involve much more food preparation than the individual can really cope with without becoming stressed! The area of personal hygiene can be one of the most troublesome areas if both gross motor and fine motor (as in the hand) skills are affected. Hair care and dental hygiene in particular can be poor due to a combination of a number of difficulties that can be found with dyspraxia.

Some difficulties with hair care can be resolved (*see Chapter 6*) though pony tails and bunches which both look alright and stay in - are most probably asking a bit too much!

One area of particular difficulty can be that of dental hygiene because it involves so many factors and skills. There may be difficulties in controlling the brush due to poor fine motor control and/or poor spatial relationship skills. Individuals can also have difficulties in using the correct pressure. All of these difficulties can combine to cause individuals to hurt the inside of their mouths and/or make their gums bleed. Heightened oral sensitivity can cause them to dislike the texture of the brush and/or the feel of it in the mouth. Heightened awareness of taste and/or smell can cause them to dislike the smell/taste of the toothpaste. Difficulties in swallowing can cause them to 'gag' on the saliva/liquid that collects in the mouth whilst brushing. Difficulties in knowing where to put the tongue and/or in controlling it whilst cleaning the teeth can cause problems in co-ordinating these movements plus those of the brush. All of these factors can result in teeth being rarely/poorly cleaned and can make visits to the dentist very stressful especially if individuals are also affected by 'hyperacusis' where they cannot cope with certain levels of sound e.g. dentist's drills. *A strategy that parents can use is to clean the child's teeth using a very soft (baby's/infant) toothbrush and finding a flavour of toothpaste that the child can tolerate (or even just using a wet toothbrush). Dental gum and dental mouthwashes can also be useful in some cases.*

CONCLUSION

In order to reach her potential the child needs a supportive teaching environment where her behaviour is understood and gradually modified as appropriate. It is of equal importance that she both understands the cause of her difficulties and that she is made aware of her skills. She should be enabled to shine in at least one area (leisure or academic) so that the low self-esteem which can spoil her life is reduced. (The depression which can exist alongside low self-esteem can be so destructive that the dyspraxic individual attempts suicide.)

Many teachers confronted by a pile of reports on one child comment that the child is 'the most assessed child they have seen'. Teachers can find it difficult to accept that the pupil needs such a full assessment. Unfortunately, if a full assessment is not made many pieces of the diagnostic 'jigsaw' will be missing and intervention is unlikely to be appropriate to the child's needs and so be less effective. Teachers can also find the sheer volume of the reports too much to take in and that the child's needs are so complex that they cannot meet them.

Parents and teachers can find the diagnosis of dyspraxia traumatising and/or daunting. They are likely to cope better if they both have a 'working knowledge' of dyspraxia which the local Dyspraxia Foundation co-ordinator can provide.[14] As the child's needs are so complex the parents and teachers need to work together to identify key areas for concern and design both a long-term and short-term Individual Education Plan (IEP). Both IEP's are necessary as it is easy to get 'bogged down' in short-term goals and forget that there is a bigger long-term picture. The IEP's also enable both parents and teachers to know what expectations they each have of the child.

When a child has many low-level SpLD's it is easy to underestimate their level of future achievements. Individuals affected by dyspraxia can succeed in school and in the workplace (and can go on academically to further and higher education) but they will need encouragement, support and reinforcement of skills in order to do so. This can be achieved for the child if her dyspraxia (and any other associated Specific Learning Difficulties) is identified, acted upon and all the professionals involved work as a team in partnership with the individual and her parents.

For those whose difficulties continue into adulthood there is a need for a greater awareness of dyspraxia amongst employers. There is also the need for an effective support system whereby adults (with low-level to severe dyspraxia) can receive both training for their job and teaching to overcome their difficulties under a single long-term government funded training initiative. Such individuals will need support from their spouses if they are not always to feel inadequate in motor based tasks which can range from DIY to cleaning the house.

For those affected by dyspraxia the loss of self-esteem and self-confidence in physical tasks can make the individual feel inadequate and less likely to take part in physical leisure pursuits e.g. keep fit classes. Poor presentation of self (via one's appearance and one's handwriting) can give totally the wrong impression about the individual. Eventually with support (or out of sheer determination) individuals can both accept and find ways around their dyspraxia if those around them also accept it. Dyspraxia is part of the adult, in reality a small part but one which can become dominant if we let it. After all in the great scheme of things the odd broken plate, the occasional burnt meal and the habit of sloppy dressing is not really that important it is the person that matters not the clothes that we wear.

References.
1. & 2. Dr Ian McKinlay
3. *The writer has observed a child affected by dyspraxia wearing her jeans back to front without any apparent awareness of the discomfort she must have felt.*
4. Dr Ian McKinlay
5. *Useful sources of information on such activities are: Skipping not tripping by Neralie Cocks, Take Time by Mary Nash-Wortham & Jean Hunt and Graded activities for children with motor difficulties by James P. Russell.*
6. Dr Ian McKinlay
7. *Multisensory teaching methods are those where the senses of movement, vision, speech and hearing are used simultaneously. If they are not used simultaneously then the teaching method is not multisensory and so will be less effective. (The senses of touch and smell can also be used if wished.)*
8. *See Solutions Resources Guide for further information on Learning Styles.*
9. & 10. Michèle Lee
11 *A good source of information on this subject is Perceptual Motor Difficulties by Dorothy Penso.*
12. & 13. *Mary Colley of the Adult Dyspraxia helpline (Tel: 0171 4355443). This helpline offers free help and support to adults with dyspraxia.*
14. *The British Dyslexia Association's local helpline and befriender may also be of use. See Chapter 15 for details of both agencies.*

Acknowledgements: This chapter was written by Jan Poustie in co-operation with Dr Ian McKinlay, Christine Stache, Michèle Lee and Veronica M. Connery.

FURTHER INFORMATION

📖 *Skipping Not Tripping* by Neralie Cocks (pub. Simon & Schuster)
📖 *Praxis makes perfect* published by The Dyspraxia Foundation
📖 *Take time* by Mary Nash-Worththam and Jean Hunt (pub. Robinswood Press)
📖 *Developmental Dyspraxia* - a practical manual for parents and professionals by Madeleine Portwood (pub. Durham County Council) ISBN 1 897585 21 7
📖 *Developmental Motor Speech Disorders* M. Crary (pub. Whurr Publishers Ltd)
📖 *Dyspraxia - A handbook for therapists* by Michèle Lee & Jenny French (pub. the Association of Paediatric Chartered Physiotherapists, available from Carol foster MCSP, Superintendent Physiotherapist, The Children's Hospital, Middleway, Birmingham.)
📖 *Solutions Resources Guide* (pub. Next Generation) provides information on further titles that will be of use.
The Nuffield Centre Dyspraxia Programme. This provides ideas and materials for speech and language therapists to use in their management of children with articulatory dyspraxia. Its materials cover most of the oro-motor, sound production and sound sequencing activities which dyspraxic children will need to practice. For further information contact: 0171 915 1535
Movement Assessment Battery for Children by Henderson & Sugden (pub. The Psychological Corporation Ltd., London). Note this is a very expensive assessment tool but the Checklist can be bought separately.

--- **TABLE 1** ---
Important indicators of dyspraxia and their consequences

1. Poor balancing skills caused by motor planning difficulties which can lead to problems in learning to ride a bike, roller blade etc.. Balancing skills can also be affected by the mechanism in the inner ear failing to register speed, orientation and direction of a movement. Individuals may have travel sickness and dislike swings etc..

2. Difficulties in doing tasks which need good control over fingers (fine motor control) e.g.

Difficulties in dressing oneself. This includes difficulties in learning to cope with any fastenings (e.g. zips, buttons, buckles, shoelaces) and ties which is mainly a fine motor and sequencing difficulty and difficulties with dressing which is a sub-group of dyspraxia.

Other difficulties are: writing, drawing, cutting (may have difficulties in colouring-in shapes without going over the edge of the shape).

Difficulties with handling small objects. They may be able to pick up and move counters at speed with ease but find it difficult to manipulate an object e.g. jigsaw pieces and construction toys. These sorts of difficulty can also be related to poor spatial skills.

Difficulties in using knife, fork and spoon. This is caused by several factors e.g. poor shoulder control means that they will tear food with the knife rather than cut it. Poor eye/hand function results in messy eating with food missing the mouth, poor eye/hand control results in difficulty in controlling the utensils (food can end up on the table/floor and so can the utensils!) (Also see Bilateral integration section of Table 3.)

3. Difficulties relating to spatial awareness and judging distances. These children are not aware that a mug placed on the edge of a table is likely to be knocked over. They can misjudge stairs and so fall down them frequently especially during a 'growth spurt' when they no longer know where the ends of their limbs are. They can knock into people and misjudge gaps. Some affected people with this problem have joint laxity.

4. Fidgeting which may be caused by low muscle tone and "Attention Deficit Hyperactivity Disorder as some of these children have motor problems and vice versa."[1] ('These actions ARE NOT DELIBERATE such children have to exert a tremendous amount of control to only fidget just a little bit, to not fidget at all may be impossible.) Some individuals that come within this category are being defined as having DAMP Syndrome (where there is a combination of disorders of attention, motor coordination and perception) *see Chapter 9)* Autistic spectrum disorder can also be seen as part of this syndrome *see Chapter 10).*

5. Clumsiness - "Many have used clumsiness to describe motor learning difficulties - others use it to describe gaucheness or proneness to accidents."[2] This can also be seen as part of autistic spectrum disorder *see Chapter 10).*

6. Signs of **articulatory dyspraxia**. Sucking, swallowing, and chewing difficulties and which may go on to speech articulation problems.

• Difficulties with the mechanics of swallowing. May have difficulties in closing mouth whilst eating (which can also be linked to poor breath control). May have taken a long time to feed as a baby and some may still eat very slowly at secondary school - the 'first and second sitting' system in schools may not provide her with enough time to eat her lunch and so she may be hungry most of the afternoon. (Packed lunches will need to consist of easily chewed foods which she can eat quickly. May find it difficult to swallow her catarrh when she has a cold.) *Also see Chapter 10.*

• may be slow to learn to use a straw

• can tend to prefer foods which need very little chewing (this can also be related to textural/oral sensitivity)

7. Difficulties in learning to blow her nose (possibly still finding this difficult at secondary school which can be very embarrassing if she has a cold, or, hay fever). *(Atopic conditions such as eczema, hay fever and asthma are believed by some professionals)* e.g. Geschwind to be more common in Sp.L.D. individuals.

8. Lack of co-ordination between the two sides of the body with the individual often avoiding crossing the 'midline'. (The 'midline' is a hypothetical vertical line passing through the middle of the body which runs from the top to the bottom of the body.)

Associated features often seen are:

1. Clinging, dependent behaviour - wanting to be too close to people so that they feel that their personal space is being invaded and needing lots of cuddles.
2. A few individuals find it very pleasurable to have their hair touched.
3. Inappropriate reaction to temperature *(also see Chapter 10)* especially being unable to cope with hot and humid conditions.[3] The individual may also not be able to cope with being cold.
4. Emotional problems - "anxiety, depression & withdrawal being the commonest ones."[4]
5. Behaviour being inappropriate to the situation. This can take several forms they can:
• Have difficulties controlling their emotions
• Be bullied by their peer group and/or bully others. "Most children are teased and tormented at some time but their response varies according to the confidence and competence of the child."[5] *(Also see Chapter 10.)*
6. Have difficulties in playing games due to difficulties in understanding the rules. In such cases these children can be seen to be over-assertive as they insist upon playing games based upon their own rules. Such children will often find it easier to play with pupils younger than themselves and can become isolated when they transfer to secondary school and there are no younger children to play with. *(Also see Chapter 10.)*

References:
1. 2., 4. & 5 Dr Ian McKinlay
3.Dr Sidney Chu in 'Praxis makes perfect'

─────────── **Table 2** ───────────

Sensory Perception Difficulties

1. "Tactile defensiveness, hypersensitivity etc. are associated with a minority of dyspraxics. (The need for reassurance, clinging etc. reflects the majority)." [1] These aspects of dyspraxia can be seen as:
• Over-reaction to certain smells (can feel physically ill by some and feel over-elated by others). *(Also see Chapter 10.)*
• A dislike of being touched (including being tickled) and/or being in crowds. *(Also see Chapter 10.)*
•A dislike of any of the following: having hair cut/combed, dislike

of having teeth brushed, nails being cut and/or the individual can dislike doing any of these for himself. *(Also see Chapters 6 & 10.)*

• Over-reaction to taste and textures. The latter can affect the textures of clothing, towels etc.) and can be present as oral sensitivity with regard to both textures of food and anything else that goes into the mouth. Oral sensitivity can cause problems with maintaining dental hygiene and it along with a sensitivity to sound (i.e. *hyperacusis - see Chapter 8*) can make visits to the dentist exceptionally unpleasant. *(Also see Chapter 10.)*

10. Difficulties in finding things against a busy background e.g. difficulties in finding a certain pair of socks in a drawer full of underwear, difficulties in spotting a word on the page. (In its severest form the pupil will be trying to read the 'white bits' on the page rather than the black letters. Such pupils will need specialist intervention in order to be able to learn to read.)

Some individuals will also have difficulties in settling down to work (which may be associated with Attention Deficit Hyperactivity Disorder). May need a few minutes at the beginning of the lesson to focus and calm down if they have had to rush to a lesson.
References: 1. Dr Ian McKinlay.

Table 3

Paediatric Physiotherapist's report

The physiotherapist largely assesses Gross Motor skills e.g.:

General posture: The following areas will be assessed in relation to general posture: muscle power, symmetry of movements and agility. (If this is poor then you can expect the pupil to have considerable difficulties in maintaining a posture so they will be moving from one position to another even whilst sitting. If the pupil's muscle tone or joints are lax (weak) then the pupil is likely to have difficulties in applying the correct pressure to items e.g. could break a test tube because they are having to hold it very tight in order to control it. "There are several common connective tissue laxity conditions with increased risk of arthritis, poor healing of scars, uterine/rectal prolapse and which can occur alongside coordination problems."[1]) The following areas will be assessed in relation to general posture:

71

Shoulder control: this relates to muscle strength and joint laxity around the shoulder girdle. It is an important factor for hand function and a prerequisite for being able to write.[2]

Pelvic control: This relates to the joint laxity around the hips and is required for activities such as standing on one leg, hopping and kicking a ball.[3]

Proximal stability: The ability to use both shoulder and pelvic control together.

Balance: This involves the trunk muscles which bend, straighten and rotate the body in addition to shoulder and pelvic control. Good balance is important in all positions e.g. sitting, kneeling and standing in order to maintain the position and not be easily taken off it or be knocked over. This may be seen in the playground when children can be knocked over by peers running past them. Children with problems with balance may also find sitting still on a chair difficult and various PE tasks maybe very hard e.g. balancing on a narrow object.

Eye/hand co-ordination: This is the ability of the eyes and hands to work together and is needed for activities such as writing, throwing and catching a ball.[4] It is mainly assessed by a physiotherapist with ball games such as throwing and catching both with two and one hand.

Eye/foot co-ordination: This is the ability of the eyes and feet to work together and is required for walking around obstacles, over rough surfaces or up and down stairs [5] Assessment of this area will include kicking and trapping a kicked ball.

Motor planning: This is the ability to plan the necessary movements that are required to move from one position to another. Children with planning difficulties often show problems with task organisation and writing essays [6]

Short term visual and verbal memory: This is the ability to remember activities that are both shown and asked of the child. These tasks are required for activities such as copying from the blackboard and taking\writing dictation.

Symmetrical integration: This is the ability to move both sides of the body simultaneously in identical patterns of movement such as jumping forwards [7] Difficulties in this area are likely to result in problems in learning to swim.

Bilateral integration: This is the ability to move both sides of the body simultaneously in opposing patterns of movement such as jumping sideways. This is particularly important in assessing whether the child has difficulty with activities such as using a knife and fork.[8] *In addition the following areas (some of which will formally recognised by an educational psychologist) will also be assessed:*

11. Directional awareness: to ensure the child understands forwards, backwards, sideways and diagonally.

12. Right and left side domination: e.g. whether the child uses the right, or, left hand/foot/eye most of the time. If the dominance is 'unfixed' the child might use her right hand one minute and her left the next. "If the dominance is not established until late (e.g. after seven years for writing) then this can cause difficulties with practical tasks."[9]

13. Body perception and proprioception: *(also see Table 4).* This includes boy image, body scheme and body awareness.

14. The ability to cross midline. *(See Table 1.)*

15. Kinaesthetic awareness: The ability of the brain to know the position and movements of parts of the body.[10]

16. Rhythm and timing: This is taken into account in all activities.

17. Auditory and visual motor sequencing: e.g. clapping out a tune or copying movements when shown to the child.

18. Sensory: recognition of when pupil is being touched and the pupil being able to recognise an object by touch alone.

19. Distractibility and concentration skills.

References:

1. & 9. Dr Ian McKinlay
2.- 8. & 10. Lee M. & French J.:Dyspraxia - A Handbook for Therapists (pub. APCP Publications, 1994)

─────────── TABLE 4 ───────────

PAEDIATRIC OCCUPATIONAL
THERAPIST'S ASSESSMENT

(Those marked with "p" may be assessed by a paediatric physiotherapist.)

Motor

Motor proficiency (p)

Weakness in upper limb co-ordination is likely to cause problems in controlling bats/racquets in PE, apparatus in science and CDT lessons, in handwriting, art and in playing musical instruments.

Visual-motor integration

Visual-motor control difficulties cause problems with relating to where you have to place the apparatus/parts of the body in order to carry out the task correctly. Poor hand/eye co-ordination will cause difficulties in using small apparatus e.g. needle and thread, science equipment, paint brush, pen and compass.

Motor planning difficulties (p)

A weakness in this area will make it difficult for the pupil to organise her body so that she can move into a position to do a task e.g. getting into a position to catch a ball. There can also be dressing/undressing skills difficulties and left/right confusion. The latter can cause difficulties in knowing which way to write (e.g. start from the left of the page and travel towards the right of the page) and incorrect letter constructions.

Eye movements

Problems in controlling eye movements can be part of what is called by some visual (or occulomotor) dyspraxia or near-vision dysfunctioning. Near-vision may not be caused by dyspraxia but will affect the quality and quantity of written work and learning to read. They will also affect any work where any fine control of objects is required e.g. threading needles, accurately measuring on analogue scales. When visual difficulties are present individuals will need to keep their place by using their finger/pencil etc. when reading. The control needed for this task combined with the visual difficulties can be too great a task for some individuals who have both difficulties. *(See Chapter 7, for perceptual difficulties that can affect reading skills see Chapter 12.)*

Muscle tone and strength (p)

Tremor can be apparent in some individuals. It can have a variety of causes one of which is a difficulty in regulating the amount of pressure that they use to control an object this can lead to 'tremor' of the hand. Sometimes this is not apparent when the individual is not joining the letters but becomes very apparent when he is asked to join them. In such cases it is the increased effort that heightens the difficulty. This is one of many factors which may cause the individual to press very hard. Knuckles will whiten when writing and the imprint of the writing can be seen on the next page (or pages) of a notepad. This will result in the individual finding writing both painful and tiring. The pupil may write her letters so small that they give an impression of neatness (and inaccuracies of construction are not spotted at a glance) but she cannot control the pen enough to make the letters any larger. Poor control of pressure can cause the individual to grip the object so hard that they can break the object that they are holding (e.g. a glass test tube) or lose control of it, as in making a pot on a potter's wheel. Poor muscle tone can be shown by poor posture i.e. slouching over the desk and round shoulders. Such individuals will tire more easily because they are working harder to stay upright.

If the individual's shoulder girdle is weak she will have difficulties in activities which involve shoulder actions. These include writing on paper and writing on the blackboard. Other difficulties are playing instruments that need to be supported and/or held at shoulder height (e.g. instruments in a marching band, violins and flutes). PE can be particularly difficult with regard to any activities where the shoulders are the controlling force (netball) and/or have to take the body weight (climbing ropes, press ups). This difficulty is also likely to cause pain for the older child/adult when hanging out washing at above shoulder height, painting ceilings and the walls that are above shoulder height. Spring cleaning top shelves can also be a pretty painful experience!

Cognition (*Learning Behaviours*)

These include behaviours such as Concentration, Problem solving, Sequencing, Memory, Listening skills, Planning & organisation, Initiation (being able to start a task), Motivation, Perseveration (not being able to stop the task/train of thought) and Generalisation (being able to take a learned behaviour/skill and use it in a different setting).

The above behaviours are determined by clinical observation based upon medical/paramedical training and clinical experience and the use of checklists. (Some authorities have their own checklists whilst other assessments include them as part of the scoring criteria.) This may lead to the therapist referring the individual to another professional for diagnosis and/or the introduction of strategies to overcome the difficulties.

Sensory
Visual perception
Different aspects of this area will be assessed depending upon the age of the individual and the assessment tool used e.g. visual discrimination, visual memory, visual figure-ground, visual closure and depth perception. The latter includes the individual's ability to judge the trajectories of moving objects and relative speeds. This is a vital skill for drivers and cyclists and individuals with difficulties in this area may take longer to learn to drive and are likely to tire more easily when driving/riding a bike. Such children will need support when learning to judge the trajectories of balls, bikes and cars and it will take them longer to learn to cross roads safely. A referral may be necessary to eliminate the need for glasses as a cause of visual problems prior to diagnosing visual perceptual difficulties. (Also see Chapter 7 near-vision dysfunctioning)
Body spatial awareness
The ability to work out the position of oneself in relation to the rest of the world, and the relationship of the body's limbs to each other i.e. right from left and directional confusion.
Listening skills
This is looking at how the individual copes with listening tasks within the classroom. This is achieved by talking to the teacher, parent and individual and by observation during assessment.
Touch, smell and taste sensitivity
Within the classroom situation the most important one of these is touch. (Teachers need to note that smell sensitivity can cause difficulties in home economics. Taste/touch sensitivity can result in faddy eaters.) Touch sensitivity may be evident in individuals who do not like such activities as contact sports or being jostled in a

queue. Such individuals may find such things as the teacher's/work colleague's pat on the back or the teacher's hand guiding his hand when writing uncomfortable. *(Also see Chapter 10)* Some individuals may dislike the feel of certain writing implements e.g. wax crayons. Other individuals crave being touched.

Proprioception
This is the sense of knowing where your body's limbs are andwhere the limbs are moving in space. The latter is also known as kinaesthesia. This will be assessed in discussion with a teacher or individual about their performance in physical education and sport. It also concerns the very fine movements that are carried out automatically during writing (e.g. the eye is not controlling all the movements of the hand but the muscles of the hand remember what to do - kinaesthetic memory). All of these factors are also assessed through clinical observation of the individual carrying out various tasks.

Balance (vestibular) skills
Vestibular skills refer to the sense of awareness of the speed, orientation and direction of movement. Problems in this area may lead to travel sickness, poor saving reactions during a fall, poor balance reactions when walking on a beam and in serious cases difficulty in getting down onto the floor and feeling comfortable lying on their back.

————————— **TABLE 5** —————————
Referrals & Assessments
A "multidisciplinary assessment" will include a variety of the following assessments all of which may also take place separately at different stages of the individual's life. Each specialist uses different assessment tools e.g clinical observation of the individual, the use of checklists and standardised assessments. *(A list of standardised tests/ assessment procedures used by paediatric occupational therapists is on page 20 of 'Praxis makes Perfect'.)*

Assessments for dyspraxia
Either the school or the parents can ask the school doctor/GP to refer the child for dyspraxia. He may refer the child to a paediatrician or directly to *paediatric physio/occupational therapists* for an assessment of fine & gross motor difficulties (including writing skills) and sensory and cognitive (thinking) skills. (See Table 3).

Assessment may include the use of various standardised tests and/or the use of checklists either available nationally or developed by individual centres. As *speech and language difficulties* are commonly associated with dyspraxia an assessment for this is usually recommended. This can be made by either the parent or the school making a referral to her local NHS hospital's Speech and Language unit for a language assessment on her behalf or by making a direct referral to the unit herself by telephoning/writing to the unit and asking for a referral form. Such assessments are free under the national health. *Vision* should always be checked but near-vision dysfunction is so specialised a field that even non-behavioural optometrists/school nurses with an interest in this field may miss the signs of visual delay/ occulomotor dyspraxia. *(See Chapter 7)* Doctors will make referrals to orthoptists (based in hospitals) and/or optometrists to assess different areas of visual function. Teachers may refer the child to their local Visual Impairment Services.

At present *Behavioural optometrists* are only available privately *(see chapter 15 for contacts)*.

Assessments for medical conditions that can be seen alongside dyspraxia

Various professionals may assess the individual at various stages of her life. The child with severe/moderate dyspraxia is likely to receive assessments at an earlier age and from a wider variety of professionals. Any of the following: Health Visitors, School doctors/nurses, GP's, community paediatricians and child and adolescent psychiatrists are likely to be involved in the referral and assessment process of the moderate/severe child. If signs are found which could indicate a neurological disease of a specific nature then the child may also be referred to one of the few paediatric neurologists in the UK. An educational psychologist may assess for Moderate Learning Difficulties (which can occur alongside dyspraxia) and/or for behavioural difficulties. The latter may also be assessed by a paediatrician or child and adolescent psychiatrist. Various medical professionals may be involved in assessing one or more of a range of medical conditions which are associated with dyspraxia e.g. epilepsy, neurofibromation, hydrocephalus, fragile X, head injury and Asperger's Syndrome.

The latter comes within *Autistic Spectrum Disorder* where individuals have difficulties in communication *(e.g. semantic-pragmatic disorder see Chapter 2)*, social interactions and restricted, repetitive and stereotyped patterns of behaviour, interests or activity *(see Chapter 10)*.

Other assessments

Specific Learning Difficulty in literacy: If the individual has difficulties in learning to read and/or spell then a literacy assessment may be necessary *(see Chapter 3)*.

Mathematical assessment: As difficulties in numeracy/mathematics are common amongst the dyspraxic population a mathematical assessment should be carried out if the parent/teacher has concerns in this area *(see Chapter 4)*.

Educationalists/educational psychologist assessment - for an assessment of intellectual function. contact your local school, Local Educational Authority's Psychological service or Special Educational Needs Support Team. You can also find a private one with a special interest in this field by contacting your specialist agency co-ordinator e.g. local dyspraxia foundation co-ordinator and local dyslexia support group. (The British Dyslexia Association has lists of accredited teachers) (see chapter 15 for contacts.)

© Jan Poustie

Chapter 6

IDENTIFYING WRITING DIFFICULTIES

The field of writing difficulties is one in which there appears to be many strongly held views as to its various causes, valid types of assessment and the means by which the difficulties can be overcome. This is because it is a very complex field where many, if not all, of the conditions found within the SpLD Profile meet and/or are reflected. It is further complicated because our knowledge of many of its aspects is still minimal due to the limited amount of research in this field as compared with that of literacy research.

As a result of the above plus other conditions/circumstances which can affect writing skills we have a situation in the UK where by Year 3 many children need extra handwriting tuition[1] and by secondary school far too many children are in pain when they write.[2] Once into adulthood the unrecognised need for tuition (and the pain when writing) may lead to individuals failing to fulfil their potential and the pain in the more severe cases may affect the manual control of objects.[3]

Few of us escape the need to write. Despite modern technology "handwriting is still an essential skill..... People present themselves to the world through their handwriting, and are inevitably judged by it."[4] There are many different 'ways' of writing. Each 'way' will make different demands upon the individual's body and his cognitive processes. Some will make considerable demands on motor skills and require good posture e.g. writing information by hand (handwriting) and the art of calligraphy. Others are less demanding (e.g. typing, especially with an ergonomic keyboard) and dictation (though the latter does need good control of the organs of speech and the ability to think/process information whilst speaking). Of all these tasks handwriting is the one that the majority of us do the most. Writing is used for a great variety of purposes some of which can be performed slowly (e.g. writing one's signature, filling in forms) whilst others such as answering examination questions require speed.

Have we been writing more - and faster throughout the twentieth century?

Yes! In the 19th century one of the main requirements of handwriting was a very neat script that could easily be read by others e.g. copperplate (in which accuracy was more important than speed).[5] With the huge upsurge in information during the twentieth century there has come a need to both read and write more and therefore increase speed. Consequently new equipment has appeared e.g. the word processor, new writing styles and pens. Thus the old fashioned sloping desk which kept the writing hand at a good angle for writing has been replaced by modern desks/tables which are flat. Copperplate and the quill kept writing speed slow whilst modern styles and pens allow one to write faster. Therefore it would seem likely that the needs of the individual may have been sacrificed in order to meet society's need for speed and quantity. In the past many people may well have been able to easily process information whilst writing at their fastest possible speed. Now when writing creatively one has to quickly both process information and write. For many individuals that can be hard work, tiring and in many cases painful but for those with writing difficulties it can be an extremely hard, or, even impossible task.

The sheer volume of writing in both work and school can be overwhelming. In schools one of the requirements of the National Curriculum of England and Wales for English at Keystage 2 is that in writing "pupils should be given opportunity to plan, draft and improve their work on paper and on screen".[6] (This puts even more demands upon weak handwriting skills and has resulted in some teachers having concerns about providing enough *evidence of attainment*). Thus some children are being required to write most tasks two or three times rather than using less handwriting intensive ways of planning/writing (e.g. mindmapping/word-processing etc.)

Are there any easy writing tasks?

Not really, some may appear to be exceptionally easy but in reality are the opposite. **"Copying from the blackboard - that's the easiest task I give my pupils" (Year 3 teacher).** Blackboard copying is actually a very complex task. It requires memory, mechanical writing, visual and perceptual skills (including the ability to scan text over a very large area to see where you are on the board) plus the ability to stay on task. Individuals with near-vision dysfunctioning and/or perceptual difficulties are likely to have considerable problems e.g. those who have problems with releasing focus will be in a situation where the whole world is looking out of focus for a great deal of the time. This is because their eyes are failing to adapt to the changed focus of repeatedly looking up (long distance) and looking down (short distance). (See *Chapters 7 & 12*.) Individuals who have severe Attention Deficit Disorder (see *Chapter 9*), severe memory difficulties (see *Chapters 3 & 9*) or severe near-vision and/or perceptual difficulties (or a milder combination of two, or three, of them) are likely to find the task to be too hard and alternatives will need to be found.[7]

How do specialists regard difficulties in handwriting?
The difficulties appear to be regarded in four main ways at present:

1. As usually being indicators of other problems e.g. insecure spellings, stress, short sightedness, incorrect posture.[8]

2. The teacher lacking the knowledge base to: teach handwriting well, to recognise an individual's difficulties and to remediate them as they occur. *(There are some teachers in schools now who received very little instruction as to the teaching of handwriting during their teacher training course.)* There is also evidence that each teacher will interpret the school model in slightly different ways and so this can create confusion in the child.[9]

3. As being a motor planning and organisational difficulty which can be present as part of dyspraxia *(see Chapter 5)*.

4. As commonly being an indicator of any or all of several conditions that come within the SpLD Profile.

Stress often accompanies the conditions found within the SpLD Profile[10] and a person can have more than one of the conditions. Writing requires a combination of skills, the acquisition of which could be affected by various factors (including those conditions found within the SpLD Profile). Therefore all four of the above views are valid though all four may not be represented in each individual.

What term could we use when a motor planning and organisational difficulty is the cause of writing problems?

The term which is used for this difficulty in some countries e.g. Holland is dysgraphia but this term is not currently in use in the UK and is disliked by many.[11] It is also a slightly ambiguous term as it can be used as a general term to describe a condition where there are difficulties within the writing process due to slowed or delayed development of any of the skills needed for writing e.g. verbal skills, spelling, writing etc..) [12] As a result professionals will use all sorts of terms for this difficulty with perhaps dyspraxia and/or a specific learning difficulty in fine motor planning and organisation being the more common ones. Neither of these terms really define the problem - dyspraxia is too wide a term as gross motor function may only be minimally affected. Also just because there is a difficulty in fine motor control of the hand it does not mean that other fine motor skills are affected.

Certain other fine-motor based subgroups of dyspraxia have already been more accurately named by placing an identifier before the word dyspraxia e.g. occulomotor dyspraxia and articulatory dyspraxia. As the word graphomotor can be used to describe the creation of an image/letter on a surface e.g. paper, it would seem appropriate to use the term 'graphomotor dyspraxia'. This term both describes the difficulty and the condition of which it is a part and could be used to more closely define a writing difficulty where:

1. there are difficulties in fine motor planning and organisation and control relating to the hand which may range from barely noticeable to severe. Similar difficulties in gross motor skills relating to the arm/shoulder and postural movements are also likely to be present but will also range from barely noticeable to severe.

2. there may also be 'constructional dyspraxia' present which shows itself as a difficulty in accurately representing the spatial relations of letters/words (e.g. words too close to each other, letters misaligned).

3. difficulties in gross motor control

4. the causes of the difficulties mentioned at 1., 2. & 3. have been present since birth
(The use of this term throughout the rest of this chapter does not imply that

83

the writer feels that the adoption of this term is desirable by all, or any, professionals. Its use by the writer is merely a 'shorthand' way of enabling the reader to know exactly which form of writing difficulty is under discussion.)

The underlying causes of graphomotor dyspraxia can affect so many activities that it can have a considerable affect not just on the individual's writing but on the life of the individual both at school/work and at home. Research indicates that 10% of children are affected by it and that there are no significant differences in its incidence between left and right handers.[13]

What is the relationship between skills needed for writing and the conditions found within the SpLD Profile?

The conditions found within the Profile can affect the skills which are needed to achieve motor planning which is a three stage process involving mechanical, cognitive, visual and perceptual skills. (The individual has to come up with the idea, develop the plan of action and execute the movement for it.)

1. The mechanics of writing
i.e. the integration of muscle movements and sensory feedback.
When the cause of an individual's writing difficulty is a difficulty in motor planning and organisation he may be described as being dyspraxic. In such cases gross motor co-ordination problems will not always be present. Some individuals may only have graphomotor dyspraxia and some of the more subtle perceptual problems that can be seen alongside other fine and/or gross motor based forms of **dyspraxia** e.g. touch and auditory sensitivity *(see Chapter 5)*. Sometimes although the individual's writing is poor it is not graphomotor dyspraxia but is the result of a severe near-vision dysfunctioning and/or perceptual difficulties which can cause various difficulties e.g. 'glare', the writing to be out of focus, be distorted, move around as the individual writes it etc.. (See *Chapters 7 & 12*).

2. Cognitive skills
e.g. planning and organisation, problem solving, sequencing and memory.
Each type of writing task makes different demands upon the individual.[14] As has already been mentioned memory is needed in copying tasks. Other writing tasks require that the individual is

simultaneously planning and organising his thoughts, working out what he is going to write and remember how to spell each word, use punctuation and grammar plus construct and join each letter. In examinations he also has to remember what he knows about the topic. As memory plays such an important part in writing tasks and as memory difficulties are associated with dyslexia the individual may often be diagnosed as having a combination of graphomotor dyspraxia and dyslexia in cases where spelling difficulties are also likely to be present (Dyslexia - *see Chapter 3*.) As memory dificulties are also found as part of Attention Deficit Disorder this condition can be present too (*See Chapter 9*).

3. Expressive language and concentration difficulties
"*Disorganised content* often occurs and this is a written extension of associated **expressive language problems.**"[15] (*See Chapter 2.*)
Concentration difficulties may affect the quality of the work. These can be caused by various factors e.g. **Attention Deficit Disorder** (*see Chapter 9*). Tiredness and/or stress (which may be caused by the individual's brain having to think of too many things at once) can also cause concentration difficulties. *(One can then become locked into a vicious circle e.g. tiredness and stress leading to concentration difficulties leading to tiredness and stress and so on....)*

Are writing difficulties always associated with the conditions found within the SpLD Profile?
Some problems such as an inability to see the text because of short-sightedness are not associated with the conditions; whilst others might, or might not be, connected e.g.:

◆ **Paper position** - All sorts of factors relate to the way that the paper should be positioned for a particular person. If it is not in the right position for the writer it "can lead to writers adopting such an uncomfortable posture that backache, headache or cramps of all kinds can result". [16] (However, unusual paper positioning can also be because the individual has perceptual and/or visual difficulties *see Chapters 7 & 12*).
◆ **An awkward posture** or **"floppy posture** can cause backache or visual problems"[17] because the individual is too close to the text etc. but it may also indicate dyspraxia. (*See Chapter 5*).
◆ **Extremes of height, unusual body proportions or long fingers**

will also affect writing skills through the desk and/or chair being of incorrect height and pen holds having to accommodate fingers.[18]

What are the indicators of graphomotor dyspraxia?

Various indicators of dyspraxia will always be present *(see Chapter 5)* including many of the following:

Pre-school indicators can be seen as difficulties with:
1. Hand/eye tasks
2. General fine motor co-ordination tasks e.g. jigsaws, construction toys, doing up buttons/zips, colouring in (e.g. difficulties in staying between the lines), painting/drawing, use of scissors, using eating utensils.
3. An inability to control the pressure of one's fingers (a tickle from such children can hurt!
(Note: some of the difficulties at numbers 1 & 2 above could also be indicators of visual, perceptual and/or concentration difficulties. See Chapters 2, 7, 9 and 12.)

Primary school indicators. Most of the pre-school indicators will still be present at the beginning of primary school. Depending upon the severity of the condition some, or all, will still be present at the end of primary school. The following characteristics are likely to be seen in writing: *(those that are underlined are also likely to be present in secondary school and adulthood)*:

◆ difficulties in doing up shoe laces and/or an inability to consistently do them up tight enough so that they do not come undone during the day (The greater the difficulty the more likely that they will: have to tie their shoe laces frequently during the day, go around with their shoe laces undone, wear only Velcro or buckle fastening shoes.) This difficulty may well continue into secondary school but only those with the most severe difficulties are likely to continue into adulthood.

◆ difficulties in manipulating tools e.g. pen, compass, ruler, saw, comb and toothbrush. The latter along with other difficulties that can be present in dyspraxia can cause the child to rarely brush his hair and/or clean his teeth. (Also *see Chapter 5* : "Some of the associated features that can be spotted early are" section.)

◆ Presentation of self. *(Both fine and gross motor skills are needed for this so this indicator is common to both those affected by graphomotor dyspraxia and those who have another form of dyspraxia.)* 'Final touches' to dressing are not done e.g. shirts/blouses are not tucked in. Clothes may appear to have been 'thrown on' rather than 'put on' e.g. garments do not rest on the shoulders correctly, pocket flaps may be left half in, half out of the pocket. Adults may resort to wearing loose clothes that require few final touches. *(This can also be an indicator of Autistic Spectrum Disorder - See Chapter 10)*

◆ Presentation of written work. It takes so much control to just do the writing that the extra effort, concentration and control needed to present work well such as underlining using a ruler etc. cannot be faced. *If constructional dyspraxia is also present then there might be difficulties in knowing whether they can fit in a word at the end of a line. Traditional letter layouts with the address on the right hand side of the page are also likely to be a problem. (Poor presentation can also be present in those individuals who have difficulties with writing because of causes other than graphomotor dyspraxia e.g. those who have not been taught the basics well enough and those who are under stress due to spelling difficulties. For both groups writing is stressful. Good presentation on top of the stress of writing may be an unrealistic expectation until appropriate teaching/provision have been provided and easy and quick strategies for presentation taught.*

◆ Inconsistent letter size (of x-height letters) when using lined paper

◆ Small writing which can be a sign of problems in pen control - the writing will look untidy (Many of the indicators mentioned in this chapter can been seen when the child is asked to write larger or if the writing is enlarged on a photocopier).

◆ Widening of left-hand margin

◆ May find it painful to write (there is evidence that this is unlikely to occur until the age of eleven years) [19]

◆ Acute turns in connecting joins to letters when it is inappropriate in the writing model which is being used by the child e.g. a rounded cursive style

◆ Absence of joins

◆ Irregularities in joins, break in the trace of 4-5 letter words (by the end of primary school most children should be able to join each letter of words of this length.)

◆ Collisions of letters

◆ <u>There is likely to be no change in style once the child no longer has to conform to the school model taught in the early years</u>

◆ May be able to copy a writing model but may not be able to reproduce it accurately from memory and/or at speed

◆ May dislike using a computer and prefer to use manual writing skills instead even though such skills may be very weak. (Alternatively the individual may take to computers like a 'duck to water'.)

Indicators of graphomotor dyspraxia which could also indicate visual difficulties such as long sightedness or more complex visual and/or perceptual difficulties - see Chapters 7 and 12).
◆ Writing is too large

◆ <u>Unsteady writing trace</u>

◆ Bad letter or word alignment

◆ Insufficient word spacing

◆ Incorrect relative height of the various kinds of letters when using lined paper

◆ Letter distortion

◆ <u>Reversals, inversions of letters</u> . Confusion as to how to write the letter occurs within groups of letters which if they are inverted and/or reversed will be the same as another letter e.g. b/d/q/p confusion is common and i/j is much less so. Some people end up writing such letters as capitals no matter where they occur in the text as then the confusion does not occur. *This can also be present as part of Dyslexia (See Chapter 3), Autistic Spectrum Disorder (Chapter 10) and when it occurs with numbers it can be seen as part of Dycalculia (Chapter 4)*

Indicators of graphomotor dyspraxia which could also be the result of any of the above visual and perceptual difficulties and/or spelling difficulties see Chapter 3).

◆ Ambiguous letter forms

◆ Correction of letter forms

Indicators of graphomotor dyspraxia which could also be the result of any of the above visual and perceptual difficulties, spelling difficulties and/or expressive language difficulties see Chapters 3 and 2).

◆ May write slowly

◆ May only write a small amount of text

Various of the above indicators will result in the individual producing poor letter forms and these are likely to continue into adulthood.
(Poor letter forms can result in the individual having spelling difficulties, or worsening those already present, due to the inaccurate remembering of the visual aspect of words. Sometimes letters are written poorly because the individual is not sure just what letter should be written. The same can occur in speech when the individual is not certain as to what sound he/she should be making in the middle of the word and so the sounds are mumbled at this point.)

<u>**Secondary school/adulthood indicators**</u>. There are likely to be difficulties in many subjects/areas. *(The higher the intellectual ability of the individual the more likely he will have developed strategies to mask his difficulties at this stage and so others may be unaware of his problems.)* Generally the difficulties may be seen as an uncoordinated use of tools e.g. pen, fork etc. and/or much slower speed than his peer group (of similar intellectual ability) in achieving the task. The individual may also use task avoidance strategies including those of misbehaviour:

Difficulties may be seen any of the following areas:
◆ Fastenings e.g. open-ended zips such as those found on anoraks and the individual may still have problems with doing up shoe laces. *If dressing dyspraxia is also present then any activity where changing clothes is required will be stressful e.g. PE and Drama. (See Chapter 5)*

◆ Domestic science: e.g. preparation of food, control of the needle and sewing machine

◆ Science: e.g. control of science equipment. Individuals may need to exert so much pressure to hold the item that they break the test tube

◆ CDT: e.g. control of the tools. Work is likely to be slow and/or inaccurate. There may be many corrections in drawings.

◆ Computers: e.g. may have difficulties in controlling the mouse, hold it in non-efficient ways, difficulties in learning to type.

◆ Geography: e.g. drawing maps and diagrams

◆ Mathematics: e.g. control of the tools in Geometry lessons and when drawing diagrams, graphs etc.

◆ Art: e.g. drawing an accurate representation. Individuals are often unhappy with what they produce because they are aware it does not match what they see and what they feel they should be able to achieve.

◆ All subjects: e.g. drawing of charts, tables etc..

Is it easy to spot individuals with graphomotor dyspraxia as teenagers and adults via their writing?

No, except in the severe cases. This is because writing changes with maturity in both those affected by graphomotor dyspraxia and by those who are not. Some Dutch research has shown that both groups will increase the size of their writing, omit joins (in some words and in whole sentences) and the letters within words may become so close that letters collide.[20] These changes and deteriorations result in there being less difference in the letter form quality between those with graphomotor dyspraxia and those without it. However, those indicators which were underlined in the Primary School section above are still likely to be present. It is these indicators plus those which are present in secondary school/adulthood which can be used to identify the difficulty at this stage.

How are writing difficulties assessed?

Various aspects of writing can be assessed using a variety of assessment tools including observation, standardised/non-standardised tests and checklists. A comprehensive assessment by teachers and educational psychologists would include the following:

◆ error rate :

Spelling- The more errors made, the more time that will be needed to be spent on corrections. Whilst many primary school pupils can cope with having to do three or four corrections for each page of work, most will find it a loss to self-esteem and time-consuming if more than double than that are needed on a regular basis. This is likely to result in them using only the words they can spell and so masking their true intellectual ability.

Overall errors (e.g. grammar, spelling, punctuation) - Most individuals will be able to cope with correcting 10-15% of their work. Many will find having to correct much more than that (on a regular basis) so daunting that they are unlikely to be motivated to write in any quantity as the number of corrections that they will have to make is just too great.

◆ posture & penhold

◆ letter forms, their construction, spacing and alignment etc.

(<u>Writing speed</u> may also be assessed. The complexity and variety of writing tasks has caused there to be debate amongst professionals regarding the validity of such an assessment. There is also debate as to what task should be used as the basis of assessment and how long the task should take.)[21]

The use of the indicators found in the various chapters of this book plus appropriate assessment tools will enable the assessor to make the necessary referrals to other specialists as appropriate e.g.
◆ The use of the indicators in *Chapters 7 & 12* of this book (on how to recognise **visual** and **perceptual** difficulties) will help to determine whether there is also a visual and/or perceptual aspect to the difficulty and therefore whether <u>referral to the Focal Visual</u>

Impairment service, an optometrist, orthoptist, behavioural optometrist and/or a specialist in Scotopic Sensitivity Irlen Syndrome is needed.[22]

◆ The Aston Index sub-test 11 plus the use of the indicators in *Chapters 2 and 10* will determine whether a referral to a speech and language therapist for an assessment of expressive language is needed and/or a referral to a doctor for further referral for autistic spectrum disorder is needed. (Miscue analysis could be used here i.e. looking at the types of errors made such as use of prepositions, difficulties in expressing abstract concepts, grammar, word meanings and syntax.)

◆ Attention deficits can be noted during assessment and these observations plus the use of the indicators in *Chapter 9* will help the assessor determine whether a referral to a specialist such as a paediatric neurologist/educational psychiatrist is necessary.

◆ Any of the following may be used to determine whether difficulties with the mechanics of handwriting are causing problems. Those that are based on the teacher/therapist observing examples of handwriting are: *Helping with Handwriting* by Sasson, *Handwriting Checklist* by Alston & Taylor, *The diagnosis and Remediation of Handwriting Difficulties* by Stott, Moyes & Henderson and *Handwriting Helpline* [23] by Alston & Taylor. These tools also provide background information on writing and remediation strategies with the information differing according to the background of the writers. Alternatively, an assessor can use the fine motor co-ordination tasks and observation of handwriting sub-tests which are part of *Aston Index* e.g. sub-tests 3, 4, 10, 11 and 17 of these assessment tools.[24]

Referral to a doctor e.g. the individual's local GP, school doctor or paediatrician is needed for a more thorough assessment if:

◆ difficulties with the mechanics of writing are noted plus indicators of graphomotor dyspraxia are present (as outlined in this chapter) or
◆ mechanical difficulties are noted and there is cause for concern e.g. although it appears that graphomotor dyspraxia is not likely the individual has not responded to appropriate intervention.
(This is to rule out the possibility of any underlying medical condition and to make further referral to a paediatric occupational therapist to

assess whether dyspraxia is present.) The present shortage of such paediatric occupational therapists may mean a long delay before such an assessment can be made.[25]

The paediatric occupational therapist will, as part of a holistic assessment, assess a variety of Cognitive, Motor, Language and Sensory (e.g. visual) skills. There are a variety of assessment tools which the therapist can use among them are the *Movement ABC* by Henderson & Sugden and the *Bruininks-Oseretsky Test of Motor Proficiency*. They both contain sub-tests which involve the individual carrying out a variety of tasks some of which can be used to measure the foundation skills of fine motor speed and dexterity which are necessary for handwriting. (*For full details of assessment see Table 4, Chapter 5*).

If graphomotor dyspraxia or other difficulties with the mechanics of writing (e.g. letter construction) are found what can the teacher/parent to do help the individual overcome the difficulties?

Difficulties not associated with graphomotor dyspraxia

Some difficulties such as cramped writing/poor layout may be due to the individual still obeying an instruction that is long out-of-date e.g. being told in primary school to fit more onto a page so as to use less paper. The identification and solving of this sort of difficulty plus teaching strategies to overcome difficulties in the mechanics of writing may require some 1:1 tuition. For this group and (especially for those who also have literacy difficulties) Alston and Taylor's Handwriting Helpline may be suitable as some of the strategies within it integrate literacy and writing skills. Some of the information from Sassoon's Helping your Handwriting e.g. penholds [26], strategies for overcoming pain, left-handedness and tips on achieving faster writing etc. is also likely to be needed.

Difficulties due to graphomotor dyspraxia

Individuals affected by dyspraxia are likely to have difficulties in learning new motor based skills/movements. Although they may appear to have learnt them in a teaching session they are often unable to transfer this knowledge to the classroom/workplace. So for this group strategies based against a writing model that is not their own are unlikely to work. Sassoon's Helping with Handwriting is useful here as it provides details about how to adjust the individual's own handwriting. The information on penhold (especially alternative penholds that can reduce pain for some individuals e.g. Callewaert's), hand position etc. is also likely to be essential if the teacher is to provide effective help.

If graphomotor dyspraxia is suspected what can be done if a paediatric occupational therapist's assessment is either unavailable or delayed?

There are various books which give the details of simple and fun exercises that are a starting point in dealing with many of the underlying difficulties that are found as part of dyspraxia.[27] These activities require very little in the way of equipment. If you are not sure which ones to do a 'rule of thumb' method would be to try each of the tasks that are recommended (for the appropriate age group). Only practise those activities which the individual does not find very easy. If a task is particularly difficult only expect the individual to do it initially for a very short time (for some this may only be one or two minutes or less) until they have built up some skill in the activity.

How does graphomotor dyspraxia affect everyday skills?

It affects a wide number of everyday tasks some of which may be seen mainly in the school environment whilst others may be seen mainly in the home environment. An example of the latter is the difficulties that occur as a result of graphomotor dyspraxia plus sensitivities that can be associated with dyspraxia which are often noticeable in the area of hair care. A reluctance to comb one's hair can thus be due to difficulties with controlling the comb/brush due to poor fine motor control and/or poor spatial relationship skills. If the individual also uses incorrect pressure, has scalp sensitivity (which makes the 'feel' of the comb/brush unpleasant then it is not surprising that they both avoid the task and do not wish the parent to do it either. Scalp sensitivity can make it particularly difficult for girls who can find any means of tying back long hair e.g. bunches, pony tails painful. A different textured brush and short hair can help in school, difficulties in dressing e.g. at the end of PE and for swimming lessons are likely to cause the students a great deal of stress. The use of the various 'tools' used in school are often a major problem and some will need 1:1 tuition in the use of such basic apparatus as a ruler and a protractor. Any teacher of a subject which has a practical element (with skills based on the use of any type of tool) may need to devote time to teaching the pupil easy ways to use and control them. Thus the home economics teacher may have to provide specialist tuition in the use of knives, potato peelers and tin openers and the use of special tools may be necessary in some cases. Individuals will also need to be taught the presentation skills that are needed in most lessons e.g. drawing charts, underlining using a ruler and presenting maths work neatly. Such provision will reduce the stress felt by the pupil and enable them to have the opportunity to reach their potential in adulthood. If this provision is not given, the individuals difficulties (especially with the use of tools) may continue into adulthood with the consequent loss of self esteem when they may not even be able to put up a shelf or sew on a button that looks either satisfactory and/or does not fall apart.

An overview of writing difficulties

There is no doubt that moderate to severe writing difficulties (whatever their underlying reason) are a cause for concern. For many of us working in this field the writing of someone with severe graphomotor dyspraxia leaves little doubt as to the fact that a specific writing difficulty does exist:

"My handwriting looks as if a swarm of ants, escaping from an ink bottle, had walked over a sheet of paper without wiping their legs."
(Sydney Smith 1772-1845)

It is those who have low to moderate levels of writing difficulties that are likely to be unrecognised. It takes much more control to join letters and so the habit of not joining (which is becoming quite common at secondary school level in many countries [28]) can hide some of the signs of writing difficulties. If both reading and writing are poor the pupil may be regarded as being less able. (This being more likely if he only uses a very small vocabulary in written work because that is all that he has a chance of spelling.) The individual may be criticised for being lazy and/or careless and for not finishing his work fast enough. It is not realised that he is in fact affected by several conditions that come within the Specific Learning Difficulty Profile. Writing difficulties become more difficult to recognise if the individual writes very little which he may achieve by avoiding writing tasks. The child may misbehave/volunteer for tasks to get out of the classroom, write hardly anything at all whilst going into a daydream to escape from the problem, or write very neatly but very slowly (often pressing very hard). The adult, of course, can conveniently forget his glasses, pen etc. and be forced to take a job that requires very little writing.

The increased demands on handwriting skills as individuals progress through their education may highlight motor planning and control difficulties which were manageable when there were less demands being made upon them. A slow writing speed usually becomes a noticeable problem for school children when they are seven years old as this is when the emphasis starts to change from practical to written work. Often these are the children who have to stay in at breaks to complete their work. At this level the classroom walls may have many examples of 'neat' versions of writing based tasks. In some schools such work may have been handwritten three times e.g. plan, draft, neat and then typed onto the computer. Such a process is extremely time consuming and puts tremendous pressure on the child's writing skills.

By the time individuals reach secondary school writing can be a major problem. In some schools there is still a concentration on using handwriting intensively for copying, proving knowledge, note taking and creative writing. The individual may just about be able to survive the amount of written work during the day but cannot face homework requirements. So, he will either fail to bring in the work on time, submit incomplete work, or, just not hand it in at all. By the age of thirteen some may no longer be able to read their own writing all of the time (especially when they are trying to take down rushed homework instructions that are given at the end of a lesson). If this situation is not resolved by the GSCE years these individuals may not be able to show their true ability in either the assignments and/or the examinations.

If the difficulties remain unrecognised and unsupported into adulthood the individual may find filling in forms such an obstacle to employment that a job is difficult to obtain. Those who gain work may have to refuse promotion because they know that they will not be able to cope with the writing requirement that a higher post entails.

Criticism of a person's work achieves little. The individual does not need anyone to tell him how messy his work is, he already knows - but what he does not know are the strategies by which it can be improved. The only result of criticism is loss of self-esteem and the deterioration of the relationship between the educator, or manager, and the individual.

Instead of criticism individuals need both an accurate diagnosis of their difficulties plus an appropriate programme to enable the difficulties to be overcome. (This will solve the writing problem for many and reduce it's severity for others.) Such a programme will need to include ways in which they can show their knowledge and ability (without the need for writing all of the time). It will also include activities that will improve the standard of writing e.g. exercises that help to strengthen weak muscles, activities to

improve motor planning and teaching better letter construction etc.).
Other problems which could be causing (or contributing towards the
difficulty) will also need to be recognised and resolved e.g. spelling,
language, visual difficulties, stress etc.. Finally, the adoption of
alternative strategies to writing e.g. mindmaps.[TM] will be needed to
reduce the quantity, whilst improving the quality, of the individual's
written output.[29] (In schools and colleges this will benefit both the
teacher and his students as the former will have much less marking to
do and the latter will have more time for learning and less strain on the
writing arm etc..) By these means we can help individuals to gain
qualifications and jobs which reflect their true abilities and so enable
them to reach their potential in adulthood.

The high incidence of pain experienced by children when writing
(especially that which is found in high achievers)[30] is evidence that our
youth is not able to cope with the writing demands placed upon them.
Soon we may all be in the same position - too much to write and not
enough time to write it in. If we, as a society, are going to continue to
make ever-increasing demands upon our writing skills then we may
need to adjust our attitude to handwriting. This may involve changing
the way in which we teach handwriting (including writing models and
implements) and a re-evaluation of the tasks for which a handwritten
script is required. It is also likely that we will need to look more, and
more, at alternative strategies to handwriting including those of word
processing.

It is already noticeable that there has arisen a wide divide between the
school and the workplace with regards to both the quality of
information technology equipment and it's use. As a result of little, or
no, money being available to buy modern stock this divide is increasing.
Educational establishments are becoming the dumping ground for
out-of-date equipment which companies have given away (or sold
cheap) and museums for machines bought in the seventies which are
fast passing their 'use by' dates. Much of this hardware has antiquated
systems which are not simple to use and so do little to boost the
confidence of teachers/trainers who may already feel inadequate in
their use of computers. Such hardware is unable to operate the superb
modern word processing programs, text readers, predictive lexicons,
typing tutors and voice dictation systems which are now available and
make it so much simpler for students with writing difficulties to cope.[31]
The lack of experience at secondary level of modern programs that are

commonly found both in the workplace (and on the home computer) creates yet more problems. It does not enable the work started at school to be finished at home and vice versa. Neither does it enable the individual to effect a smooth transition of computer based skills from the educational environment into that of the workplace.

Conclusion

There is little doubt that the increasing need to produce large amounts of well-presented text at speed without causing pain and stress to the body will continue into the next decade. There is also a need to help those with handwriting difficulties reach their potential and so enrich our society. Both these needs can be met if there is adequate training of our teachers and workplace trainers. Such training has to cover not only the recognition of, and provision for, those with handwriting difficulties but also appropriate alternative strategies to writing. The use of computers for all writing intensive tasks is common practice in many workplaces. Such practice cannot occur in our educational establishments until teachers and trainers are enabled to feel confident in the use of their hardware and their computer (and software stock) are brought up-to-date.

Society's high demand for writing output is becoming a strain on all of us but for those with writing difficulties it is much worse. Their difficulties can place them at a severe disadvantage in both school and the workplace. The 'problem' may lie in their hands .... but the solution to it is in ours!

References

1. Cato et. al. NFER quoted in 'Handwriting Helpline' by Jean Alston & Jane Taylor (pub. Dextral Books).

2. Rosemary Sassoon, Handwriting: a new perspective (pub. Leopard Learning). "40% of girls and 25% of boys reported that they suffered pain when writing." Also see The Art and Science of Handwriting by Rosemary Sassoon.

3. The Art and Science of Handwriting by Rosemary Sassoon.

4. & 5. Rosemary Sassoon, Handwriting: a new perspective (pub. Leopard Learning).

6. English in the National Curriculum , Jan 1995. Prepared by the Department for Education (pub. Her Majesty's Stationery Office, London)

7.For further information on skills needed for different writing tasks and strategies to overcome difficulties see Solutions for Specific Learning Difficulties: Resources Guide

and Solutions Forum which are both published by Next Generation, Taunton.
8. & 9. Handwriting: a new perspective by Rosemary Sassoon (pub. Leopard Learning).

10. Dyslexia and Stress edited by Prof. Tim Miles & Ved Varma (Whurr Publishing)
11. The BHK Concise Evaluation Scale for Children's Handwriting is a test of dysgraphia (based on the Dutch model of writing) that is used in Holland and Belgium. (Further information on this test is available from: Swets & Zeitlinger, P.O. Box 820, 2160 SZ Lisse, The Netherlands.)
12. Encyclopaedia of special education edited by Reynolds & Fletcher-Janzen (pub. Wiley Interscience)

13. Dysgraphic Handwriting Compared with Normal Handwriting by Dr Lisa Hamstra-Bletz (Research psychologist) published in the Handwriting Review 1994 (pub. The Handwriting Interest Group) ISBN 1 872832 03 2

14. For further information see Solutions for Specific Learning Difficulties: Resources Guide and Solutions Forum (pub. Next Generation)

15. Dr Ian McKinlay

16., 17., 18. Handwriting: a new perspective by Rosemary Sassoon (pub. Leopard Learning).

19. The Art and Science of Handwriting by Rosemary Sassoon.

20. Dysgraphic Handwriting Compared with Normal Handwriting by Dr Lisa Hamstra-Bletz (Research psychologist) published in the Handwriting Review 1994 (pub. The Handwriting Interest Group) ISBN 1 872832 03 2
21. For further information on this see:

◆ Solutions for Specific Learning Difficulties: Resources Guide

◆ 'Writing output and writing speeds' by Jean Alston published in 'Dyslexia Review' -The Journal of the Dyslexia Institute Guild Vol.6, No.2, Autumn 1994 (pub. by The Dyslexia Institute.)

◆ The Art and Science of Handwriting by Rosemary Sassoon

22. A doctor (local GP etc.) can refer you to an optometrist (either at an NHS hospital) or one of the many who do both private and NHS work in any town. He can also refer you to an orthoptist (available in your local NHS hospital). There are very few behavioural optometrists in the UK. See Chapter 15 for the relevant address.

23. This was originally designed as an 'experimental instrument' and so its scoring system is not as easy to use as those of some other assessment tools and the reliability levels for it are very modest. (It is regarded by its authors as a training resource, both in initial teacher education and for use by those who are involved in helping individuals overcome writing difficulties.)
24. Further details on how to assess, and the usage of these assessment tools and what they contain, can be found in Solutions for Specific Learning Difficulties: Resources Guide.

25. Different health authorities place different priorities on individuals whose handwriting difficulties are based in dyspraxia and the problems that this causes. In some areas there is provision to assess and treat such individuals e.g. handwriting groups, co-ordination classes and sensory awareness groups whilst in other areas there may be only limited provision with long waiting lists.

26. Research has shown that alternative penholds can be faster than the 'dynamic tripod' which is commonly used in UK schools. See 'An analysis of children's penholds by Sassoon, Nimmo-Smith & Wing in Graphonomics: Contemporary Research in Handwriting, H S R Kao, G P van Galen, R Hoosain (eds) pub. B V (North Holland), 1986.

27. e.g. Skipping not tripping by Neralie Cocks (pub. Simon & Schuster.)

28. The Art and Science of Handwriting by Rosemary Sassoon

29. For further information on such resources see - Solutions for Specific Learning Difficulties: Resources Guide.

30. Rosemary Sassoon: Handwriting a new perspective (pub. Leopard Learning

31. For further information see Solutions for Specific Learning Difficulties: Resources Guide and Solutions Forum (pub. Next Generation)

Further information

📄 For information on how to refer to specialists see Table 5, Chapter 5.

📄 Dr. E. Hamstra-Bletz may be contacted at: Harmoniehof 12 hs, 1071 TC Amsterdam, The Netherlands.

📄 Mind Map is the registered Trade Mark of the Buzan Organisation. (*See Solutions for SpLD - Resources Guide for books which teach Mind Mapping.*)

Recommended Reading

📖 *Handwriting review* (pub. yearly by the Handwriting Interest Group *see Chapter 15 for details*)

📖 *Handwriting Helpline* by Alston & Taylor (pub. Dextral books)

📖 *Skipping not Tripping* by Neralie Cocks (pub. Simon & Schuster)

📖 *Praxis makes Perfect* (pub. The Dyspraxia Foundation)

📖 *Handwriting Helpline* by Alston & Taylor (pub. Dextral Books)

📖 *Handwriting - a new perspective* by Rosemary Sassoon (pub. Leopard Learning)

📖 *Helping your handwriting* by Rosemary Sassoon (there are two books- one for teachers and one for pupils) (pub. John Murray)

📖 *The Art and Science of Handwriting* by Rosemary Sassoon (pub. Intellect)

📖 *Solutions Forum* and *Solutions for Specific Learning Difficulties Resources Guide* (pub. Next Generation). These provide information plus details of books/equipment that can help with handwriting difficulties.

Written by Jan Poustie. Acknowledgements: Dr Lisa Hamstra-Bletz, Dr Rosemary Sassoon, Dr Ian McKinlay, Christine Stache, Hugh Bellamy and The Dyslexia Institute.

Chapter 7

NEAR VISION DYSFUNCTIONING
by Jan Poustie with acknowledgements to Keith Holland

Introduction

Two causes of near-vision dysfunctioning are occulomotor dyspraxia and occulomotor delay.(Some difficulties in reading text are also believed to be due to perceptual dysfunction *(see Chapter 12).)*

Occulomotor dyspraxia: "This is a neurological difficulty in ordering, sequencing and acquiring visual information due to a dysfunction in the control and use of the visual motor system."(1)

Occulomotor delay: This is a developmental delay in the control and use of the visual motor system.

The specialist will diagnose the cause of the problem based upon assessment, clinical observation and his own experience. Initially a developmental delay may be diagnosed but the diagnosis may change when the child is about eight years of age to that of occulomotor dyspraxia. This is because by approximately age eight the individual has developed the brain function needed for most visual skills to be mature.

Some skills continue to refine until the age of twelve years e.g. saccadic (tracking) eye movements. Saccadic functioning is dependent upon the sort of reading experience that the child has. If the child has a wide range of experience he will mature earlier therefore children need to be exposed to as much occular activity as possible. With the increased use of television, computers and handheld games in so many homes there is now concern in some quarters that some children are having less occular experience than in the past and that this is delaying maturation.

Both in Europe and in the USA it is common to start school at a later date than in the UK and so there is likely to be less pressure for children to be taught to read early. Thus these children are less likely to experience reading failure due to delayed maturation. It is important that we do not ignore signs of visual difficulties in children under the age of eight on the grounds that there could be delay as both occulomotor delay and occulomotor dyspraxia can cause considerable problems to children in primary school as the following article by Keith Holland demonstrates.

VISUAL SKILLS FOR LEARNING
By Keith Holland

Research has shown that in every class there are at least five children with visually related learning difficulties. Keith Holland sheds light on the possible causes of such problems, explains how to recognise their symptoms, and outlines the means to overcome them. The classroom teacher, standing before a room of bright, young children assumes for the most part that those children are fully equipped with the tools needed to help them learn. The child with a broken arm stands out from the rest, and receives the sympathy that is their due; the deaf child is more likely to be seen and helped; and the child with partial sight is also likely to be noted, and helped.

There is, however, a group of children thought to be far larger than any of the preceding groups who are rarely noticed, yet who are likely to be penalised for their very real but unrecognised handicaps; they are the children with visually related learning difficulties.

Extrapolation of population studies suggests that in every class across the land there are at least five children with such difficulties[1]

Unless their difficulties are recognised and addressed, they may eventually exit from the educational system having seriously underachieved relative to their potential, and may have suffered much distress as a result. This blow to confidence may remain with them throughout their adult life, affecting many apparently unrelated areas of their lives. As teachers, you have the opportunity and responsibility to recognise such individuals, and try to guide them towards appropriate help and relief.

This short article is aimed at helping the classroom teacher understand the possible visual causes of such problems, together with their symptoms, and the means available to overcome them.

Before looking at the visual skills needed for learning, it is worth understanding something of the terminology used

TERMINOLOGY

Vision refers to the total system that allows an individual to see, and to experience objects and images in space. A small part of this system is the eye, the rest includes all of the complex neurological processes that go to convert a light impulse reaching the eye into a meaningful mental image of the world we are in. Many make the mistake of saying a child's vision is all right when they really mean that the child's eyes have normal optics, and can receive a sharply focused image.

Refractive error refers to the lens power required to produce a perfectly focused image on the retina of the eye. This is normally what is assessed in a routine eyesight test, and corrected by means of spectacles.

There are three components to stable vision that together produce a mental 'space map' of the world we see, whether it be the world of the sports pitch or the world of the novel. Those three processes are: vergence, focus and eye movement (sometimes erroneously called 'tracking').

Vergence is the term referring to the movements of the eyes relative to each other, that ensure they are always looking at the same point in space. In particular, convergence refers to the turning of the eyes towards each other as they look at an object that is near to them. Difficulties may exist with the vergence system making it difficult for the eyes to converge adequately. A child with these difficulties may well experience dull headaches, become very tired with quite short periods of close work and may quickly lose concentration on the task in hand, often being easily distracted by movement around them, and looking up from the task. They may day-dream a great deal, and may have difficulty in completing work on time.

Children who over-converge may show a tendency to move in towards their work[2], perhaps laying their head on their arm, their eyes sometimes being only a few inches away from the page. These children may experience migraine, often nauseous. They may be oblivious to distractions around, preferring to plod sequentially through an activity, even though they may be doing the wrong task to begin with, having misread the question and not seen the detail of the question in relation to the whole problem. Often their handwriting will be very small and precise, although not necessarily tidy. They may well press very hard, and imprint several pages on their books.

Some children will show evidence of both problems at different times, initially starting off with poor convergence, but making so much effort to 'get things together' that they end up over-converging.

Closely linked to the vergence system is the **focus** (or accommodation) system. This serves to adjust the focus of the lens inside the eye to give a sharp picture of the subject that we are looking at. Two properties of the focus system can break down. First, the eye may simply not focus closely enough: this lack of focus amplitude means that we may be working close to the limits of our focus system, and we will have difficulty maintaining this for sustained close work without fatiguing, yawning and becoming sleepy. Second, there may be difficulty in switching focus from one distance to another the focus facility may be slow. This may lead to difficulties in copying materials off blackboards or overhead projectors. A child who additionally has short-term visual memory difficulties may be particularly vulnerable to this type of problem.

As the eye adjusts focus, it automatically adjusts convergence, and if the relationship between the two systems is not working well, there may be increasing stress, leading to difficulties in keeping clear focus at any distance. The child with these difficulties will again have problems with concentration, will be distractible and may suffer from fatigue and headaches.

There are three aspects to **eye movements** skills to be considered. First, can the child keep its eyes still long enough to take in information; in other words, can he or she **fixate** properly? Problems here can lead to distractible behaviour, inattentiveness to near tasks and hyperactive-like behaviour (although this behaviour should not be confused with true attention deficit disorders, which have a quite separate pathogenesis).

In developmental terms, once a child can fixate, s/he learns to maintain fixation on a moving target - to track or to pursue it. These pursuit movements are essential for keeping control of our hand whilst writing, and are a prerequisite for developing the **saccadic eye** movements needed for reading. During the reading process, the eyes move along a line in a series of separate jumps, or saccades, pausing on average every nine letters in an adult reader to take in information. These separate fixation fields overlap, and should be received sequentially to provide a coherent and orderly representation of the material being read.

Where problems exist with the saccadic movements, the eyes are likely to move erratically, and show a higher than normal frequency of regressive, or backward, eye movements - sometimes as many as 30 per cent of the eye movements made when reading can be regressive. In this situation, the child may have difficulty in keeping his/her place or line, finding it essential to use a finger or card as a marker. Comprehension may well suffer, so much energy going on place-keeping that little cognitive effort goes into understanding the text itself. Needles to say, the individual with these difficulties will find reading a chore that is reluctantly engaged in, and produces little personal reward.

Not only do problems with these physical visual skills affect reading, but they may also affect the development of a child's visual imagery abilities (or **visualisation skills**). The late Professor Elliot Forrest has described four basic systems used for spelling[3]:

    1 Rote learning.
    2 Rules of the language.
    3 Phonetic images.
    4 Visual images.

When a child is engaged in free writing, s/he will find it difficult to relate to lists of words learnt by rote. S/he may use language rules or mnemonics, but will often be so engrossed in the 'plot' that they fail to register. S/he will always have an auditory or phonetic impression of the word s/he is trying to spell, but s/he may not have a visual image available, and in this situation is likely to rely on the phonetic spelling, even though when held up and asked to spell the word, s/he may correctly recall the true non-phonetic spelling.

An individual child may show more than one problem area, even though s/he may have normal visual acuity, and be able to 'pass' a simple eye test. The classroom teacher is the most likely individual to spot these difficulties, since these children are often reluctant readers at home, and not seen by parents engaged in sustained near-point activities. The teacher should be able to spot the basic symptoms of visual difficulties (as, for example, outlined below). Understanding on the part of the teacher, with simple modifications to teaching techniques, may go some way to reducing the difficulties experienced by the child. Furthermore, the teacher should be able to recommend to parents referral on to appropriate agencies for further investigation.

Signs and Symptoms

Focus and convergence difficulties
◆ Transient blurring (or double vision) of print.

Figure 1. Illustration of the possible appearance of a printed page to a child with visual difficulties

This is a sample of print such as might be found in a typical school book and which children often complain is dancing, moving, or in some other way appearing unstable. This often leads to confusion and to fatigue, with concentration loss as well.

◆ Fatigue and tiredness after quite short periods of close work.
◆ Short concentration spans.
◆ Variable working distance - often very short.
◆ Observations of rubbing of the eyes, excessive blinking, grimacing or other facial strain.
◆ Headaches, usually associated with periods of close work and study, and therefore often towards the end of the school day.

Eye movement difficulties
◆ Difficulty in keeping place and/or line whilst reading.
◆ Improvement in reading fluency if a marker is used (either a finger or card, or both).
◆ A particular dislike of reading aloud individuals feeling that they read better silently.
◆ Poor handwriting (may have other causes).

Visualisation
◆ Probably the most common sign of visualisation difficulties is a strongly phonetic approach to spelling, with an absence of clear visual thinking (for further information, see Wachs and Furth [4]).
◆ Sometimes difficulties in recalling detail of past events is evident affecting the acquisition of general knowledge.

The teacher's role

As already mentioned, the teacher is a key member of the team responsible for recognising children with visual difficulties, and use of the symptoms lists above will aid in spotting children who need further investigation.

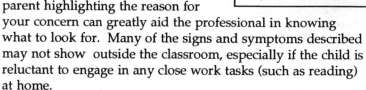

But what then? Teachers should be aware of the appropriate referral channels in their locality. This may be through the school eye service, to a local optometrist or to the child's GP. In either case, a short note to the parent highlighting the reason for your concern can greatly aid the professional in knowing what to look for. Many of the signs and symptoms described may not show outside the classroom, especially if the child is reluctant to engage in any close work tasks (such as reading) at home.

Within my practise a checklist is used, as outlined in **Figure 2.** This allows teachers to communicate rapidly their observations to others - without offence! Although this is a highly subjective approach, it does allow parents and teachers to 'focus' their thoughts on this area of function, and is a screening technique in widespread use by behavioural optometrists around the world. Most of the observations asked for have been shown to correlate to indefinable visual dysfunctions [5].

Practical suggestions

But what can be done to help theses children in the classroom? It has been suggested by several authorities that simple modification of the daily routine may help children cope better, increase concentration span and allow for greater teachability, by reducing the aggravating factors that precipitate binocular vision breakdown (for a more detailed argument, see Wachs and Furth [4]).

Research has shown that children have an optimal working distance, correlating with the distance between the middle knuckle of the third finger and the elbow ([2] and [10]). This distance is quite critical, and a shortening of this distance has been shown significantly to increase the muscular effort applied to close work. It follows, then, that the maintenance of good posture in the classroom is more than a reactionary throwback to Victorian behaviour! It is likely to improve individual efficiency. It is also important to encourage the student to maintain an erect posture, working straight on and not leaning the head too far to one side; this is often a sign that attempts are being made to suppress one eye, usually to minimise symptoms of visual difficulty. A particularly weak area in modern classroom design is seen where children are working in groups around a table. Two difficulties arise from this. First, for children with difficulties in integrating central and peripheral information there is likely to be an undue problem with distractibility; and second, three sides around a table are going to have to turn around in order to be able to see material written up on the board. The child with visually related learning difficulties may well be the one with his or her back to the board, increasing the likelihood of difficulties with this copying task and negating the positive effects of copying as an aid to learning!

Where possible lighting should be natural, and not contain a
predominance of fluorescent; children are often unduly
sensitive to flicker, particularly if it is in their mid-periphery
and, again, this can cause difficulties with
peripheral/central integration.

The work of Helen Irlen and others has suggested the use of
coloured overlays or spectacles as an aid for children with
visual perceptual difficulties. Research into Scotopic
Sensitivity Syndrome is controversial, and at the present
time no clear explanation for the efficacy of these aids has
emerged (for a fuller analysis of the situation, see [5]).
Research carried out by myself[6] has shown that children
who benefit from such aids are very likely to show clear
patterns of binocular vision difficulties, such as described in
this article, and it is my own view that they are better
helped by referral to an optometric practitioner who is
skilled in these areas.

Many optometrists incorporate visual and perceptual training
into their care regimes, and a considerable body of evidence
exists that this vision therapy can be of considerable benefit
to many children suffering from visually related learning
difficulties[7]. Programming of **vision therapy** activities is a
professional function, best left to suitably trained personnel;
but none the less, there are numerous simple exercises that
can safely be incorporated into classroom routines, or
physical activity sessions, that can benefit children with
such difficulties. Figure 3 shows simple activities that can be
safely carried out by teachers within the classroom setting
as part of routine physical movement sessions:

Finally...

Children with visually related learning difficulties are in
perhaps the worst position in the class: theirs is truly a
hidden handicap. Empathy, understanding and
accommodation are all crucial if they are to achieve their
true potential.

Figure 2. Checklist of visual signs

CONFIDENTIAL

TEACHER'S CHECKLIST FOR VISUAL SIGNS

Child's name... Form/Teacher Reference...............................

1. *Please circle the special areas (if any) of difficulty this child has with reading.*

Vocabulary	Word recognition	Oral reading	Silent reading	Rate
Interpretation	Attention	Comprehension		

2. Four classifications of frequency of performance traits are given:
    A   Meaning very often observed (many times/day)
    B   Meaning regularly observed (daily)
    C   Meaning sometimes observed
    D   Meaning seldom observed
Please ring the letter you best consider indicates the child's performance
Does the child show any of the following?

a.	Skipping or rereading lines or words	A	B	C	D
b.	Reads too slowly	A	B	C	D
c.	Uses finger or marker as pointer when reading	A	B	C	D
d.	Lacks ability to remember to read what he has read	A	B	C	D
e.	Shows fatigue or listlessness when reading	A	B	C	D
f.	Complains of print 'running together' or 'jumping'	A	B	C	D
g.	Gets too close to reading and writing tasks	A	B	C	D
h.	Loss of attention to task at hand	A	B	C	D
i.	Distracted by other activities	A	B	C	D
j.	Assumes an improper or awkward sitting posture	A	B	C	D
k.	Writes crookedly, poorly spaced letters, cannot stay on ruled lines, excessive pressure used	A	B	C	D
l.	Orients drawings poorly on paper	A	B	C	D
m.	Is seen to blink frequently	A	B	C	D
n.	Rubs eyes excessively	A	B	C	D

General Observations

o.	Clumsiness and difficulty manipulating own body and other objects in space available, including problems with ball control	A	B	C	D
p.	Awareness of things around him in the classroom to point where he turns to look at stimulus	A	B	C	D
q.	Is this child able to maintain his involvement with your instruction?	A	B	C	D

Scoring
Any scores of 'A', more than two scores of 'B', and more then three or four of 'C' suggests that prompt referral to an optometrist specialising in children's eye care is indicated.
A copy of this checklist would also be helpful to the optometrist.

Figure 3

◆ Looking up, down, left and right with the eyes only, and no head movement - possibly to the four corners of a room, and in time to a beat, may help stimulate tracking skills. Repeat this ten times at the start of a lesson.

◆ Drawing numbers at random over a blackboard and having a child draw a continuous line to connect them, again trying to avoid head movements. This can also be used to help develop sequencing skills.

◆ Reading the first and last letters on every line down a page of text, without using fingers to keep place or reading the first letter of every word, can help develop better saccadic eye movements.

◆ Having two people throwing partially inflated balloons across the line of sight of a third, who has to track the balloon, possibly shining a torch on to it as it arcs through the air.

◆ Drawing a maze on to thin card, placing a small metal object at the start, and trying to pull along the course from underneath with a magnet assist in the development of hand/eye skills.

◆ Having a child read (if not a fluent reader, reading single letters) whilst moving the material in and out, and in circles, can help develop stable focus skills. It also encourages near/far refocusing between targets placed three inches away and targets at a distance. This should only be performed for short periods as fatigue can result.

◆ Encourage pattern-copying, using increasingly complex shapes as an aid in the development of visual analysis skills. Numerous programmes exist based on the early work of Marianne Frostig; whilst the transfer of these skills was first thought to be limited, more recent research has proven the value of these techniques [8].

◆ Wordsearches are useful ways of helping children learn to spot embedded detail (commercial computer software is available to allow rapid generation of 'tailor-made' wordsearches directly applicable to current topic work).

◆ Pattern games such as 'Battleships' are excellent ways of encouraging visual analysis - and they may help with National Curriculum mapwork as well!

Figure 3 Continued:

◆ When teaching spelling, do *not* rely on simple look-and-say approaches. Try to encourage visualisation by looking, covering, closed-eye picturing, saying or writing down, re-covering, re-drawing and looking again. It sounds a mouthful, but it works!
◆ Encourage day dreaming! But only if followed by exercises in describing the dreams with as much sensory detail as possible.
◆ Listening to music with closed eyes, trying to picture the scenes the composer is trying to portray. Good pieces for this include: *Carnival of the Animals, Peter and the Wolf, Pictures at an Exhibition, Beethoven's Pastoral Symphony*, etc.

Further reading

Very little has been published within the educational journals about these areas in this country; the most useful text available is:

Thinking Goes to School, *by Harry Wachs and Hans Furth,* published by Oxford University Press, New York, 1975. This work contains a great deal of background theory, together with many practical activities for the classroom teacher.

For a full review of the current state of research in these fields, a useful text is:
Visual Processes in Reading and Reading Disabilities, edited by Dale Willows, Richard Kruk and Evelyne Corcos, Lawrence Earlbaum Associates, London, 1993.

References

1 SHERMAN, A. (1973). 'Relating vision disorders to learning disability', Journal of the American Optometric Association, 44, 140-141.

2 COHEN, L.A. (1960). 'Mechanisms in body balance and coordination', Connecticut Medicine, 24, 500-503.

3 FORREST, E. (1980). Visual Imagery - an Optometric Approach. Santa Anna, Calif.: Optometric Extension Programme Foundation.

4 WACHS, H. and FURTH, H. (1975). Thinking Goes to School. New York: Oxford University Press.

5 WILLOWS, D., KRUK, R. and CORCOS, E. (Eds) (1993). Visual Processes in Reading and Reading Disabilities. London: Lawrence Earlbaum, chapter 9.

6 TYRELL, R., HOLLAND, K., DENNIS, D. and WILKINS, A. 'Coloured overlays, visual discomfort, visual search and classroom reading', Journal of Research in Reading.

7 'The efficacy of optometric vision therapy', Special review issue: Journal of the American Optometric Association, 59, 95-105.

8 ROSNER, J. (1986). 'Management of perceptual skills disorders in a primary care practice', Journal of the American Optometric Association, 57, 56-59.

9 SOLAN, H.A. and GROFFMAN, S. (1982). 'Understanding and treating developmental and perceptual motor disabilities'. IN: SOLAN, H.A.(Ed) The Treatment and Management of Children with Learning Disabilities. Springfield, I11.: C.S. Thomas.

10 'Harmon Vision-Environment-Body Mechanics: their role on the learning disability'. In: Vision and Learning Disability. American Optometric Association, 1976.

Address for correspondence

Keith Holland is an optometrist running a specialist practise in Cheltenham, working with children suffering from vision-related learning difficulties.

All correspondence regarding this article should be addressed to the author at 27 St George's Road, Cheltenham, Gloucestershire GL50 3DT.

Originally published by NFER as an article in "Topic" Issue 13 : Spring 1995.

Chapter 8

Central Auditory Processing Disorders

(This is an extremely complex subject, although audiological terms have been kept to a minimum a certain number are necessary to understand what each of the disorders means and its assessments and causes. As this is such a complex subject the Table of Indicators is listed first so that you can quickly decide whether you need to read the rest of the chapter.)

Central Auditory Processing Disorders Indicators that would be present in individuals with normal hearing)

Individuals with this difficulty can have any of the following problems:
◆ Forget and/or confuse what people say
◆ Have difficulties in listening to the speaker if there are other noises or distractions in the environment
◆ Cannot concentrate on a listening task for a long length of time
◆ Frequently show that they have not heard e.g. say What? or ask the speaker to repeat themselves
◆ Do not react when their name is called
◆ Are easily distracted when listening
◆ Have difficulties in sounding out words when learning to read
◆ Have difficulties in spelling words
◆ Have speech problems
◆ Have problems in acquiring vocabulary
◆ Have problems with reading comprehension

In the past auditory functioning has been regarded as the necessary sub-skill for learning and using language. It has been an area in which speech and language therapists have always had an interest because of its involvement with receptive language. Since courses like the RSA Dip SpLD have come into being more and more educationalists have become interested in the various forms of auditory dysfunction as it relates to the child's ability to function in the classroom. Recently audiologists have recognised patterns of difficulties and a physical cause for them. These difficulties have now been named as Central Auditory Processing Disorders.

Language Processing Disorders

Speech and language therapists are aware that individuals with auditory dysfunctioning can have difficulties in processing language. Language processing disorder goes under many names e.g. receptive language

delay, auditory processing deficit and auditory comprehension deficit. Individuals with this difficulty may have problems with:
◆ interpreting humour
◆ understanding idioms
◆ understanding long and complicated directions
◆ understanding stories with lots of characters and events
◆ group conversations
Difficulties can also occur in reading comprehension (may need to re-read passages several times), comprehending television programmes. (Also see Chapter 2- Specific Language Impairment.)

Educationalists have taken on board the concept that auditory dysfunctioning can be the root cause of receptive language weakness and recognising problems in:
◆ **auditory discrimination**- difficulties in hearing the differences between words/sounds
◆ **auditory sequencing** - sound out a word e.g. lots and then say lost or even log (by the time these individuals have reached the last letter they have forgotten the earlier sounds
◆ **auditory memory** -difficulties in learning the words to songs/nursery rhymes; learning letter names/sounds, forgetting instructions, difficulties in following stories (problems become greater as the stories become more complex).
◆ **understanding simple directions**. The auditory processing difficulties mentioned above can cause the individual to do exactly the opposite of the instruction that he has been given which can make the adult feel that the child is being deliberately disobedient. (This difficulty can be worsened by the anxiety and stress that many individuals with conditions that come within the Specific Learning Difficulties Profile feel throughout the day.) This often makes them fearful that they will do things wrong and so they are always apologising for any errors, no matter how small.)
Now that audiologists have come fully into the Specific Learning Difficulty (SpLD) Profile picture there has become a need for all of us who are non-audiologists to become familiar with some very complex terminology of which the following two are some of the easiest to understand:
right ear advantage. The auditory system develops as the child matures so the auditory function of the child does improve with age. Up until a child is nine/ten years old his right ear usually receives language based auditory input better than the left. This is called

Right Ear Advantage (REA). The imbalance in the ears is very noticeable at seven and eight years, markedly improves by nine years and then only improves a little more between the ages of ten years and adulthood. (It is thought that this is to do with the ability to receive information in one of the two hemispheres of the brain and transfer it to the other one.)

hyperacusis. Individuals who cannot cope with levels of sound that would be tolerated by most normal listeners e.g. dentist's drills, washing machines on a spin cycle, vacuum cleaners and high pitched voices. Can be found in various conditions within the SpLD Profile e.g. Dyslexia (see Chapter 3) and Aspergers Syndrome (see Chapter 10).

Various auditory dysfunctions are now recognised as being part of Central Auditory Processing Disorders. As Central Auditory Processing Disorders have only been recognised in the recent past as disorders in their own right there is at the moment little information on them. Also, assessment for it may not always be available and specialists in it are not common.

What is the reason for these disorders?

Within the brain stem there is an ascending auditory pathway (stretching from the low brainstem upward to the auditory cortex). There is also a descending pathway which is involved in enabling the brain to select acoustic information. These pathways make up the Central Auditory Nervous System (CANS). Areas of dysfunction along this pathway can result in a number of auditory symptoms that can be identified by diagnostic tests of auditory function. Correct functioning of the CANS allows the individual to recognise and discriminate various acoustic stimuli including that of speech. The location of each dysfunction on the CANS (and the degree of dysfunctioning) will cause different auditory processing difficulties. Each area of the CANS develops at its own rate as the child gets older with the final area of the CANS to reach full development being the 'corpus callosum'. It is this area which is responsible for the interaction between the two cerebral hemispheres.

To understand what we hear we need an auditory input (voice, music etc.) and to use our cognitive (thinking) skills to process (decode) what we hear. Thus:

auditory input + cognitive skills = Central Auditory Processing (CAP).

Much of the processing occurs without us being aware of it (lower level cognitive skills). In order to accurately decode complex auditory stimuli we need to use higher level cognitive skills. These include memory and attention. The dyslexic often has short-term memory difficulties which among other things may make it difficult for him to accurately repeat what he has just heard and will affect his ability to sound blend. The individual with Attention Deficit Disorder (see Chapter 9) may have difficulties in concentrating his attention on the auditory stimuli. He may have difficulties in ignoring low-level auditory stimuli (the background noise in the classroom/office) and therefore has difficulties in paying attention to the high-level auditory stimuli (the teacher/person on the other end of the phone).

What does Central Auditory Processing involve?

This is the means by the which the auditory system's mechanisms and processes (in conjunction with higher order functioning e.g. memory and attention) interact to enable the following to occur and be processed accurately:
• Ability to determine the direction that the sound is coming from (sound localization and lateralization)
• Ability to discriminate between sounds (auditory discrimination)
• Ability to recognise patterns in acoustic signal, 'rime' etc. (auditory pattern recognition)
• Time-related aspects of the acoustic signal (the amount of time that the auditory signal is present)
• Ability to hear sounds such as voice against background noise
• Ability to process imperfectly heard auditory input

What is the importance of Temporal processing ?

This is very important for a wide range of common listening tasks. It is needed to understand both speech and music. If there is a dysfunctioning of temporal processing then words are imperfectly processed in different ways e.g.
• the last two letters may be reversed e.g. 'lots' for 'lost'
• initial similar sounding letters which are voiced (e.g. 'd' as in dime) are confused for those which are not (e.g. 't' as in time).
By about the age of twelve years the development of temporal processing skills should be complete. (However, temporal processing is also dependent upon the development of attention skills so a child

with any of the Attention Deficit Disorders is likely to have imperfect Temporal Processing skills.)

Who Assesses for Central Auditory Processing Disorder?
In the UK it may be diagnosed by an audiologist with an interest in this area e.g. a paediatric or an educational audiologist or a hearing therapist. There are not many of these therapists at present so CAPD may be recognised by a speech & language therapist or another professional who has an interest in this area e.g. an educational psychologist.

What areas of difficulty are assessed by the audiologist?
Binaural separation & Binaural integration
Binaural separation is the ability to process an auditory message coming in one ear whilst ignoring the auditory signal coming in from the other ear. Binaural integration is the ability to process information when different information is being presented to each ear simultaneously. These are assessed via Tests of Dichotic Listening. Both these skills require that the individual can process speech input from one person whilst ignoring the speech input of others and of processing speech against background noise. These skills are commonly needed by all individuals in busy classrooms where small group work is taking place. For adults it will be a necessary ability in an open plan office or during leisure activities e.g. going to the pub. Individuals with Attention Deficit Disorders who have difficulties in focusing their attention amid distractions may find such tasks particularly difficult to do.

Temporal Patterning
Speech is made up of bands of energy which change over time. When an individual is listening to a word he hears each part of it (the auditory signal) for a given amount of time. The length of time for which a signal occurs (timing information) is important for identifying the speech sound that the signal represents e.g. in distinguishing a 'p' from a 'b'. Temporal patterning refers to the ability of the individual to process this timing information in speech. Temporal (or time) processing is therefore assessed using Tests of Frequency Patterning. Individuals with this disorder have problems in recognising and using the prosodic aspects of speech e.g. rhythm, stress and intonation. Alterations in the stress in words can change

the words meaning e.g. project (Have you finished your project yet?) and project (The sales projections for next week are poor.) The speech of individuals can often sound monotonous and they will read out loud in a very boring way e.g. without intonation

Auditory Closure (decoding).
This is assessed by Monaural Low-Redundancy Speech Tests. Auditory closure is the ability of the listener to fill in the missing spaces in what he hears to work out the words/sounds which make up the sentences. (Visual closure works in a similar way only in this case the individual sees a picture of e.g. a rabbit with one ear missing and knows that it must be an ear that he has to draw in to complete the shape.) The listener has a greater chance of achieving auditory closure if the topic and the vocabulary/grammar used are familiar to him. It can cause problems in decoding words phonically e.g. will have difficulties in discriminating vowels and consonants. Some individuals will be able to understand speech in an ideal listening environment but will have major problems when listening to unfamiliar speakers and listening through background noise. Such individuals may well find initial attendance at playgroup/school very stressful, confusing and traumatic.

Binaural Interaction
This is the ability to recognise the direction from which the auditory signal is coming. It will cause the individual to have difficulties in listening to the sound they want amongst background noise. In order to understand speech against a background of sound/s both Binaural Interaction and Auditory Closure skills have to be present.

Delayed neuromaturation
(This can be identified by the left ear being suppressed on dichotic speech tests with poor performance on temporal patterning.) This is related to delayed development of the corpus callosum which controls the processing of information between the two hemispheres of the brain. It will produce a wide range of auditory difficulties. Some activities which help to speed the maturation of the corpus callosum are singing and playing a musical instrument.

How is Central Auditory Processing Disorder assessed?
Besides the use of tests such as those mentioned above (which are detailed in Chapter 12) a questionnaire that includes questions on the

child's medical and educational history, auditory symptoms and general behaviour is also advisable. The professional will be looking for a history of auditory difficulties in the family and difficulties in auditory based activities such as music and motor based subjects e.g. PE, art and CDT. An interview with both parent and child will further clarify any of the details in the questionnaire. Quite often in an interview key points will come to light that the parents did not regard as important enough to mention on the questionnaire.

How is a diagnosis of Central Auditory Processing made?

Each audiological test assesses a different central auditory process. Some of the processes may be dysfunctioning others may not. Bellis[1] recommends that a diagnosis is made if one or more of these processes is imperfect or delayed to such an extent that it is affecting the individual's ability to function (e.g. behaviour) and/or learn. As professionals in this field are aware that there is a great deal of variability in children below the age of seven years they may not be prepared to make a diagnosis of CAPD before that age.

How is the diagnosis interpreted?

As the tests are so specialised it is necessary for the assessor to explain the auditory dysfunctioning in terms that the Parents/teachers can understand and use. Various professionals in this field have come up with different sub-categories of CAPD. There are four categories which go under various names. Bellis and Ferre use terms in which a variety of data besides that of the audiological testing are used to arrive at a diagnosis. These terms are: Auditory Decoding Deficit, Integration Deficit, Associative Deficit and Organisation-Output Deficit.

◆ Auditory Decoding Deficit

The individual will have poor auditory closure skills. This will show as difficulties in phonics, sound blending, discrimination and remembering the phonemes (sound patterns e.g. br). This individual is likely to have a difficulty in reading (especially if an auditory phonics approach is used). There is likely to be poor writing/spelling and plus some areas of expressive language are likely to be weak e.g. understanding grammar and vocabulary. They will have difficulties in understanding speech against background noise. (May need the television/radio volume played at a higher level than the rest of the family when people are chatting in the background.)

◆ Integration Deficit

The individual has poor interaction between the two hemispheres of the brain. Delayed neuromaturation is a main cause of this deficit. They do not naturally use both auditory and visual cues together and therefore may struggle initially when taught in a multisensory manner where all the senses are being used. They may need a gradual introduction to multisensory techniques whereby movement and visual memory are trained first e.g. by them mouthing the sounds rather than saying them as they write the words. Once they are used to this combination then they can be encouraged to speak the words (or the teacher speak the sounds and then progress to the individual saying the sounds).

They are likely to have poor sight vocabulary in reading. They may have difficulties in any areas where symbols are involved e.g. mathematics, geography and science. They may use little or no intonation, rhythm or appropriate stresses when speaking and may have great difficulties in understanding the task/information that the speaker is giving them. They are likely to have difficulties in taking dictation and in playing musical instruments, singing and dancing etc..

◆ **Associative Deficit**

With the present body of knowledge available it appears that inefficient interactions between the two hemispheres is a main cause of this deficit. [2] This is shown by receptive language difficulties where the individual has problems in processing complex speech with vocabulary, semantics and syntax being weak. [3] Auditory word recognition skills may be poor. They may cope linguistically in their early years but as they develop and the language around them becomes more complex they start to have difficulties. These difficulties are likely to affect social communication skills and any learning tasks that require them to monitor their behaviour themselves e.g working independently. They can often repeat 'word for word' an instruction that they have been given but may not understand it.

◆ **Output-Organisation Deficit**

The individual receives auditory information correctly but has difficulties in acting upon the information. They lack sequencing, planning and organisational skills and are likely to have difficulties in sound blending. Often they will have great difficulty in processing speech against background noises. They are likely to make reversals, have difficulties in following instructions, poor recall and poor 'word finding' skills. They may also perseverate in expressive speech whereby they replace the word that they are trying to say with one that they have heard moments previously. They may be good readers but are likely to be poor spellers and writers. They may also be affected by dyspraxia (having both gross and fine motor planning difficulties). (See Chapter 5.)

Solutions for Central Auditory Processing Disorders

The individual auditory skills can be improved by therapy provided by various professionals working together e.g. an audiologist, a speech/language therapist and teachers. The latter can use specialised teaching programmes to improve auditory skills and general school performance. At present there is a need in the UK for more audiologists trained in the assessment of CAPD. At the time of going to print we have just begun to see lectures and conferences in the UK on CAPD. The more of these that are run, especially those aimed at teachers, the sooner adequate and appropriate provision will be available.

Recommended Reading

Assessment and Management of Central Auditory Processing Disorders in the educational setting *by Terri James Bellis* (pub. Singular Publishing Group Inc.) ISBN 1-56593-628-0
This is an excellent (but very complex) book aimed at educators and other professionals. It has a very good chapter on management of the disorders.
Childhood speech, Language & Listening problems -What every parent should know *by Patricia McAleer Hamaguchi* (pub. John Wiley & Sons, Inc.) ISBN 0-471-03413-4
This book has an excellent chapter on listening problems (plus an appendix which includes Help & Support agencies in the USA and in Canada. It is much easier to read than the above book but contains much less information on CAPD
Next Generation publications which included information on CAPD:
Solutions for Specific Learning Difficulties Resources Guide
Provides information on materials and books relating to CAPD.
Solutions Forum
Provides information plus events e.g. lectures, conferences on CAPD
The Internet
At present this is one of the best sources of information. As each internet search engine works differently you may need to enter inverted commas as part of the title e.g. "Central Auditory Processing

Disorders" or you may be able to enter CAPD. If in doubt try each of these methods. Some public libraries now have access to the internet for a small charge.

References

1. Assessment and Management of Central Auditory Processing Disorders in the educational setting by Terri James Bellis (pub. Singular Publishing Group Inc.)
2. The left hemisphere of the brain deals with items that are sequential e.g. lists, logic, words, numbers and order. The right hemisphere of the brain is the creative side and it deals with areas such as rhythm, daydreaming, space , imagination, colour. Many tasks require that both sides of the brain work together e.g. to write a story the individual uses the creative side to think of the plot etc. and the sequential side to remember the spellings for the words in the story.
3. Semantics = meaning of words, syntax = grammar

Acknowledgements

Many thanks to the following people and organisations for their assistance in writing this section:
Josephine Marriage (Paediatric audiological scientist based at Addenbrooks Hospital, Cambridge), Denise Caferelli-Dees (Audiological Scientist based at Southampton Audiology Dept.)
AFASIC
The views expressed by the author are her own and do not necessarily represent the views of those who have contributed to, or assisted with this chapter.

© Jan Poustie

Chapter 9
ATTENTION DEFICIT HYPERACTIVITY DISORDER

Edited by Jan Poustie

This article includes extracts from the AD/HD Family Support Group UK pack.[1]

At the time of going to press there was a move to regard this condition as a 'difference' rather than a 'disorder'. Thus although at present in the UK the correct term is Attention Deficit Hyperactivity Disorder (which can be abbreviated to ADHD) it is possible that the new term 'Attention Deficits' will be used in the future. At the moment the term Attention Deficit Disorder and its abbreviation ADD are also in use in the UK. Various of these terms are used in different places in this book but to avoid confusion in this chapter the abbreviation ADHD has been used throughout including quotes from authors who have previously used the abbreviation ADD. Although both females and males have ADHD 'he' has been used for convenience.

What is ADHD?

It is a condition "where the child/*adult* (in comparison to most children/*adults* of the same age and sex) has a markedly reduced ability to:

1 maintain attention (i.e. poor concentration)[2]
2 control doing, or saying something by thinking first (i.e. acting on impulse too often)
3 regulate the amount of physical activity according to the situation (i.e. hyperactive)[3]
4 be motivated to listen to those in authority and to act on what he/she has been told." [4]

(For indicators see Tables1 - 6).

"A school class of 20-30 children might expect to have one ADHD sufferer. It is three times more common in boys than in girls. There is increasing evidence that adults also can have their lives disrupted by ADHD."[5] It is now believed that "ADHD may be a lifelong disorder requiring lifelong assistance. The child, the family and the ADHD adult need continued support and understanding."[6]

Do all individuals with ADHD appear the same?

No, as the individual may have Attention Deficit Disorder (ADHD) where hyperactivity is present (see Table 1) or Undifferentiated Attenton Deficit Disorder (UADD) where hyperactivity is not present (see part 2 of Table 1).

The history of ADHD

Although the condition has been recognised for some time in other countries e.g. the USA and in Australia, professionals in the UK have been slow to recognise ADHD. "In the 1960's, British child psychiatry assumed that this condition was rare and only occurred in children with obvious brain damage (e.g. meningitis, birth trauma, infection and epilepsy) subsequent research has shown that this assumption was a serious error. Only recently in the 1980's have university-based child psychiatrists in Britain accepted that the American view is correct. Unfortunately, hundreds of British child psychiatrists and general practitioners have passed through medical and postgraduate training without learning about the existence of ADHD and its treatment."[7]

CAUSES OF ADHD

"There are still many unanswered questions as to the cause of ADHD. Over the years the presence of ADHD has been weakly associated with a variety of conditions including:

◆ prenatal and/or perinatal trauma
◆ maturational delay
◆ environmentally caused toxicity such as fetal alcohol syndrome, or lead toxicity
◆ food allergies.

A history of such conditions may be found in some individuals with ADHD, however in most cases there is no history of any of the above." [8]"Certain foods, such as chocolate and Coca-Cola, can significantly worsen the ADHD symptoms but they do not cause the disorder. It is well worthwhile a mother discovering what foods worsen the ADHD and make her life even more difficult".[9]

Brain chemistry

"Recently, researchers have turned their attention to altered brain biochemistry as a cause of ADHD and presume differences in biochemistry as a cause of poor regulation of attention, impulsivity and motor activity. A recent landmark study by Dr Alan Zametkin and researchers at NIMH have traced ADHD for the first time to a specific metabolic abnormality in the brain. Thus it is now believed that ADHD is caused by a brain dysfunction. The brain relies on a number of chemicals which it manufactures itself to:-

◆ enable any of us to think clearly
◆ feel reasonably stable in our mood
◆ keep our fantasies and impulses under control
◆ be satisfactorily motivated in life
◆ regulate our energy output in proportion to the situation in which we find ourselves.

If a brain chemical is too much, or too little in an area of the brain, then brain dysfunction develops and the child (or adult) behaves in an abnormal way."[10] An area of the frontal lobe which controls the ability to control oneself has now been implicated in ADHD. Two chemicals are thought to be responsible for this brain dysfunction - noradrenaline (which excites cells and dopamine (which dampens unwanted responses). "In ADHD children there appears to be both a reduction and imbalance of these brain chemicals."[11]

Heredity

"The manufacture of the brain chemicals is controlled by the genes. There is considerable evidence that ADHD is a genetic disorder.[12] There is likelihood that parents, siblings and other relatives of ADHD children will also have ADHD. Both identical twins (i.e. having identical genes) are more likely to have ADHD if one of them has ADHD than non-identical twins (i.e. do not have identical genes). A person's environment and/or life events may worsen or lessen the manifestations of ADHD, but environmental manipulations do not cure the disorder nor remove the symptoms."[13] [14]

How is ADHD diagnosed?

The biggest problem with the recognition of ADHD has been that of accurate diagnosis. Many professionals are cautious about identifying a child as having ADHD because there is as yet no diagnostic test capable of recognising this condition. Other professionals doubt a diagnosis of ADHD because of the difficulties of making objective assessment. Many parents fear that any child who misbehaves will be inaccurately labelled as having this condition. For parents this fear is increased once they realise that certainly in the USA and Australia medication in the form of drugs like Ritalin is the favoured treatment. Often the child's behaviour is incorrectly attributed to poor parenting but in fact ADHD children can make good parents appear to be lacking in parenting skills. Coping with an ADHD child can be quite exhausting and the more members of the family who have the condition the more difficult it can be for the family to function properly.

Although there are no set tests of ADHD there are various criteria which are used to diagnose it. Professionals commonly use the DSM-IV criteria or their ICD 10 equivalents There are also the criteria designed by the AD/HD Family Support Group UK.[15] *(See Table 1)* A diagnosis can be obtained by the parent asking their GP to refer their child to a community paediatrician, a child psychiatrist, a clinical psychologist or an educational psychologist.

Reliable Identification of ADHD

"The identification and diagnosis of children with ADHD is made easier by the provision of objective assessment provided by such professionals as, Teachers, Social Workers, Health Visitors etc.."[16] However, as there is a small subgroup of ADHD children whose signs of ADHD are mainly apparent at home[17] the parents assessment also needs to be taken into consideration. "The more domains assessed the greater certainty there can be of a comprehensive, valid and reliable diagnosis."[18]

At what age will you see signs of ADHD?

Although "ADHD usually begins between the ages of 3 & 4"[19] years signs can be seen from birth onwards. "If signs are noted before the child is two years old then the child is likely to have a more severe form of the condition."[20] It can be VERY apparent by the time the child is two years old and for parents of such children the 'Terrible Twos' has a whole new meaning. For parents of severe ADHD children acute social embarrassment starts here!

Overview of the Treatment of ADHD

Most experts agree that a multi-modality approach to treatment of the disorder aimed at assisting the child medically, psychologically, educationally and behaviourally is often needed. This can require the efforts of a team of professionals i.e. Psychiatrist, Educational Psychiatrist, Teacher and/or Support Worker, a Social Worker, and Parents, who can work together to ensure that the child/adolescent reaches his/her full potential and leads as normal life as possible.

Best results are obtained when medication, behavioural management programmes, educational interventions, parent training, and counselling, **(when needed**), are used together to help the ADHD child. Parents of ADHD children and adolescents play the key role of co-ordinating these services. Ideally, treatment should also include consideration of the individual's psychological adjustment targeting problems involving self-esteem, anxiety and difficulties with family and peer interaction.

Social Workers are trained to address and adjust interpersonal relationships and skills in the family. It is not an admission of failure to ask for their help, nor should parents be penalised for doing so.

Teachers play an essential role in helping the ADHD child in the classroom (see Table 6 at the end of this chapter & the Solutions for SpLD Resources Guide). Adjustments in the classroom procedures and work demands, sensitivity to self-esteem issues, and **frequent parent teacher contact** can help a great deal. Educational interventions such as compensatory educational instruction or placement in special education may also be required depending upon the particular child's needs."[21]

All professionals need to be aware that **parents** have an important role to play in the management of ADHD (see

Solutions for SpLD Resources Guide). The child (unless placed in a special school) is at home longer each day than he is at school. Therefore, it is the parents who have to cope with their child's ADHD the most. They are unlikely to have any respite as who will willingly take on their ADHD child for them? Baby sitting circles are out as babysitters expect to look after sleeping children not ones who can be building bird tables at 9 o'clock at night and who do not normally go to sleep until past 11pm![22] Most parents will need advice (and some will need counselling) from professionals on how to deal with specific behaviours and habits so that a home management plan can be designed. Professionals must have a good understanding of ADHD: otherwise, the parents are likely to be blamed or at least to feel blamed, leading to needless guilt or accusation.[23]

Specific treatments

There are two main areas of treatment available in the UK Behavioural Modification and medication[24] to restore the brain's chemical balance via drugs such as Ritalin (see Solutions for SpLD Resources Guide). As medication is not popular among UK professionals it tends to be the parents of the more severe ADHD child who favour medication as a solution in the UK. Parents of children with low-level ADHD can sometimes cope by using alternative medicine such as homeopathy.[25] In the USA coaching/counselling are also available[26]. There are as yet few practitioners of ADHD coaching in the UK.

Outcome of ADHD

"Unfortunately, ADHD does not often occur in isolation from other psychiatric disorders[27] and many ADHD children have co-existing oppositional and conduct disorders *(see Tables 2 & 3)* with a smaller number (probably less than 25 percent) having a learning disability."[28] Various of the conditions which come within the Specific Learning Difficulty Profile can also be present *(See Table 5.)* In America studies indicate that ADHD students have a far greater likelihood of grade retention, school drop out, academic under achievement and social and emotional adjustment difficulties.

Most experts agree, however that the risk for poor outcome of ADHD children and adolescents can be reduced through early identification and treatment. By recognising the disorder early and taking the appropriate steps to assist the ADHD child and family, many of the negatives commonly experienced by the child can be avoided or minimised so as to protect self-esteem and avoid a chronic pattern of frustration, discouragement and failure."[29]

Adulthood

"Compensation by the mature brain of adulthood and possibly the weakening influence of the ADHD genes do mean that only about 50% of ADHD children will have symptoms in adulthood. Work and lifestyle choices can help the ADHD adult get on in life with minimal difficulties. However it is possible that adults who are still experiencing their ADHD may be more prone to depression and anxiety. Adults with a childhood history of ADHD have more contact with the police and courts than those with no such history. Nevertheless, the vast majority of ADHD adults are not antisocial." [30]

Conclusion

ADHD does not generally have a good press. Many only see the poor behaviour that the individual may exhibit and do not realise that like many of the other conditions within the SpLD Profile ADHD gives to the individual both strengths and weaknesses.

The advantages of ADHD may not be seen until the end of the school years or adulthood. Thus the inaccurate /inappropriate focusing of attention of the young child and the teenager can be harnessed in later life to a depth and length of focus which leaves their peer group far behind. True, eating, drinking and the rest of the world may not exist whilst the mind focuses totally on the task in hand. Fortunately, this exclusion of the rest of the world can be prevented by the use of an alarm to remind the person to eat when necessary and to break off work to communicate with their family.

Added to the above some individuals are able to exist on two to four hours of sleep a night for several days/weeks and even months. The end result of such focusing for such exceptional lengths of time can be a huge amount of work achieved in a short time with adults capable of working long hours (maybe as many as five or six without stopping).

Some individuals possess the ability to think on many planes simultaneously (and all at speed). Once this ability is harnessed the mind is enabled to process information exceptionally quickly and make connections between different strands of thought that others may not easily be able to achieve.

This combination of unusual thinking skills and depth of focussing can be quite formidable both in school and in the workplace. ADHD individuals may be like runaway, wild horses but with the right support and the use of appropriate coaching and intervention strategies they can easily outdistance the rest of the field.

TABLE 1

Part 1 consists of the DSM-IV diagnostic criteria which are used by many professionals. Part 2 consists of the criteria used by the AD/HD Family Support Group UK. Use the information in __either__ part 1 & 2 as the basis for your referral. If the individual has less than the stated number of criteria e.g. only 4 or 5 in part 1 or 6 or 7 in Part 2 then

Part 1:

DIAGNOSTIC CRITERIA FOR ATTENTION DEFICIT/HYPERACTIVITY DISORDER

A. Either (1) or (2)

(1) *Six (or more) of the following symptoms of inattention have persisted for at least six months to a degree that is maladaptive and inconsistent with developmental level*

INATTENTION

(A) Often fails to give close attention to details or makes careless mistakes in schoolwork, work or other activities

(B) Often has difficulty sustaining attention in tasks or play activities

(C) Often does not seem to listen when spoken to directly

(D) Often does not follow through on instructions and fails to finish schoolwork, chores or duties in the workplace (not due to oppositional behaviour or failure to understand instructions)

(E) Often has difficulty organising tasks and activities

(F) Often avoids, dislikes or is reluctant to engage in tasks that require sustained mental effort (such as schoolwork or homework)

(G) Often loses things necessary for tasks or activities (e.g. toys, school assisnments, pencils, books or tools)

(H) Is often easily distracted by extraneous stimuli

(I) Is often forgetful in daily activities

(2) *Six (or more) of the following symptoms of hyperactivity-impulsivity have persisted for at least six months to a degree that is maladaptive and inconsistent with developmental level*

HYPERACTIVITY

(A) Often fidgets with hands or feet or squirms in seat

(B) Often leaves seat in classroom or in other situations in which remaining seated is expected

(C) Often runs about or climbs excessively in situations in which it is inappropriate (in adolescents or adults, may be limited to subjective feelings of restlessness)

(D) Often has difficulty playing or engaging in leisure activities quietly

(E) Is often 'on the go' or often acts as if 'driven by a motor'

(F) Often talks excessively

IMPULSIVITY

(G) Often blurts out answers before questions have been completed

(H) Often has difficulty awaiting turn

(I) Often interrupts or intrudes on others (e.g. butts into conversations or games

> **B.** Some hyperactive-impulsive or inattentive symptoms that caused impairment were present before age 7 years
> **C.** Some impairment from the symptoms is present in two or more settings (e.g. at school (or work) and at home)
> **D.** There must be clear evidence of clinically significant impairment in social academic or occupational functioning
> **E.** The symptoms do not occur exclusively during the course of a Pervasive Developmental Disorder, Schizophrenia, or other Psychotic Disorder and are not better accounted for by another mental disorder (e.g. Mood Disorder, Anxiety Disorder, Dissociative Disorder or a Personality Disorder)

(Reprinted with permission from the Diagnostic and Statistical Manual of Mental Disorders, Fourth Edition. Copyright 1994 American Psychiatric Association. (pages 83-85)

<u>Editor's notes:</u>

Extraneous stimuli: things outside of himself that he hears, sees, smells and touches etc.

Tasks involving mental effort: individual is likely to work better in a quiet environment. He may leave homework until the last minute and may need a parent to keep him company.

Loses things: Adults lose their keys, glasses, pen etc. (This is also associated with dyslexia - *Chapter 3 & dyspraxia - Chapter 5.*)

Often forgetful: Forgets what he should be doing, where he should be going, what it is he has gone upstairs for etc..

Difficulties in organising tasks and activities e.g. cannot get himself organised in the morning for going to school. There are also various medical conditions where this difficulty can be present including autistic spectrum disorder *(see Chapter 10).1*

Appears not to listen when spoken to: This can be present as part of several other conditions see: *specific language impairment - Chapter 2, Central Auditory Processing Disorder - Chapter 9 and autistic spectrum disorder - Chapter 10.)*

Not see the finer details of a task/activity: so will make careless errors when doing academic tasks e.g. reading, writing, spelling and numeracy. The same can occur in non-academic tasks and activities. This behaviour can occur because the individual deals with a task as a 'whole' and so does not see the 'parts' of the task clearly.

Difficulties in sustaining attention: The longer the task/activity the greater the chance of losing concentration though more severe cases may have considerable difficulties in maintaining attention for even a few minutes. However, the individual may be able to concentrate for a very long time on a task/activity which is of interest to him and may become frustrated/angry if he has to leave the task/activity.

Frequently fidgets. Some individuals control it by making very small quiet movements which are not so noticeable to the teacher/parent.

Often 'on the go': This behaviour is very exhausting for the adult who has to cope with it. There are also various medical conditions which can cause this behaviour including autistic spectrum disorder

Has difficulties in waiting for his turn: Adults may hate waiting at the supermarket checkout.

Interrupts or intrudes on others: Is also associated with specific language impairment, see Chapter 2).

The presence of 1c, 1e, 1g & 1i can put a great strain on the other family members. If more than one member is affected getting ready to go anywhere e.g. go to school in the morning/go on holiday can be very stressful.

If 1a is present it can result in the individual working very hard on an assignment/ examination question but due to misreading the instructions/question and/or failing to realise that the work is

incomplete he will gain a lower grade than is expected for his intelligence.

Footnote:

1. Another medical condition that can be seen alongside ADHD is that of 'Gilles de la Tourette Syndrome' which is characterised by the individual making repetitive and involuntary movements. Involuntary movements are ones over which he has no control. The person can also make involuntary vocal sounds. Further information on this condition can be obtained from: Tourette Syndrome (UK) Association, 27 Monkton Street, Ryde, Isle of Wight. P033 2BY Tel: 01983 5868866 Fax: 01983 565760

Part 2:
Prevalence and characteristics of ADHD.
(Information supplied by the AD/HD Family Support Group UK.)

Children with ADHD are characterised by symptoms of inattention, impulsivity, and sometimes, hyperactivity. Boys significantly outnumber girls with this disorder. In order to receive diagnosis of ADHD a child must exhibit at least EIGHT of the following fourteen characteristics for a duration of at least six months with onset before the age seven:

Characteristics of ADHD
1. Often shifts from one uncompleted activity to another.
2. Often engages in physically dangerous activities without considering possible consequences (not for the purpose of thrill seeking) e.g. runs into the street without looking.
3-14 Are the following characteristics mentioned in Part 1. - 1b, 1c, 1d, 1g, 1h, 2a, 2b, 2d, 2f, 2g, 2h, 2i,

Table 2
Undifferentiated Attention Deficit Disorder
(Supplied by AD/HD Family Support Group UK)

This term refers to those children who exhibit disturbances in which the primary characteristic is significant inattentiveness *[see DSM-IV criteria]* without signs of hyperactivity. Recent studies of this group of ADHD children without

hyperactivity indicates that they tend to show:without
hyperactivity indicates that they tend to show:

◆ more signs of anxiety and learning problems
◆ qualitatively different inattention.

These children may have different outcomes to that of the hyperactive group.

Table 3
DIAGNOSTIC CRITERIA FOR 313.81 OPPOSITIONAL DEFIANT DISORDER

(A) A pattern of negativistic, hostile and defiant behaviour lasting at least 6 months, during which 4 (or more) of the following are present:

1. Often loses his temper
2. Often argues with adults
3. Often actively defies or refuses to comply with adult's requests or rules
4. Often deliberately annoys people
5. Often blames others for his or her mistakes or misbehaviour
6. Is often touchy or easily annoyed by others
7. Is often angry and resentful
8. Is often spiteful or vindictive

Note: Consider a criterion met only if the behaviour occurs more frequently than is typically observed in individuals of comparable age and developmental level

(B) The disturbance in behaviour causes clinically significant impairment in social, academic, or occupational functioning.

(C) The behaviours do not occur exclusively during the course of a psychotic or mood disorder

(D) Criteria are not met for conduct disorder, and, if the individual is age 18 years or older, criteria are not met for anti-scoial personality disorder

(Reprinted with permission from the Diagnostic and Statistical Manual of Mental Disorders, Fourth Edition. Copyright 1994 American Psychiatric Association. (pages 93-94)

Refuses/resists rules: Such children can cause conflict in the home as either a major confrontation has to take place to get them to do their share of household chores or else they can be seen as 'getting away with it' by their brothers and sisters. This behaviour can be overcome to a certain extent if they have the adult with them when doing the task/obeying the rule.

Blames others: e.g. when the child knocks a drink off the table that he placed there it is the parent's fault for bringing him the drink in the first place.

Individuals with this disorder are exceptionally difficult to live with and the whole family can be under stress. Such children may be rarely invited away for a night let alone a weekend and so the parents often have very little respite from them. At least 5 of these indicators should be present to a degree beyond what would normally be expected for his age group. Some children show few if any signs of this disorder at school but show severe signs of this at home. Such children can become very resentful of school and teachers.

Table 4
OTHER INDICATORS OF ATTENTION DEFICIT DISORDER

Any or all of the following indicators may be present and many may still be present in adulthood though they may be less apparent:-

- easily bored
- fails to complete routine jobs unless supervised
- has difficulties in restraining his behaviour to fit the situation
- unable to work for bigger more lasting rewards instead he prefers to work for immediate but smaller ones. Thus modifications in behaviour need to be rewarded on a very frequent basis, for some this may mean every few minutes. (This can become a big problem when external examinations are being taken as the individual can find it very difficult to put in some work now for an exam grade that will come later.)
- not submit to rules and requirements. However, some of those who do not show noticeable behaviour signs of ADHD in the classroom are fearful of disobeying any school rules. These children may panic if their uniform/work is not perfect etc. They worry about breaking a school rule by accident and are

fearful that they will not follow the teacher's instructions accurately. Such children find school highly stressful and their behaviour once in the car/at home can be horrendous to deal with.

- has an inappropriate response to praise, may react to it in a negative or angry way. Can regard it as being patronising or even sarcastic.
- may be inflexible and may not be willing to compromise. Such children are very difficult to negotiate with, though if such a technique is used from toddlerhood it is possible for some of them to learn this skill by about ten years of age. Some individuals carry this behaviour on into adulthood which can make it very difficult to form lasting relationships.
- may daydream
- may think on several different planes at once
- may see unusual connections between different items of information
- there is some evidence that some individuals may have continence difficulties with bladder and/or bowel. (This appears to affect boys more than girls.) In such cases it is likely to occur when under stress and soiling and smearing of the faeces have been known to occur.
- can be highly critical of others and verbally/ physically bully them
- may have severe temper tantrums. Can have a very quick temper that is lost over the slightest thing that annoys them. (In non-ADHD children temper tantrums are common in two year olds and this stage of development can be called the 'terrible twos' for this reason. Often these tantrums re-occur when the child is four years old (the 'ferocious fours'). In the ADHD child these temper tantrums can be particularly severe and carry on for many years. Normal measures to avoid/reduce such tantrums such as distraction etc. may be ineffective. It is thought by some that these may evolve into panic attacks in the late teens/adulthood.
- too frequently not doing what has been requested. Can be difficult to control. Can either be very aggressive or can get their own way by passively refusing and/or avoiding doing things.
- may not regret their behaviour (and/or accept that their behaviour was inappropriate/incorrect for the situation).

- may not respond to punishments of any kind
- may lie to get what he/she wants or more commonly to get out of trouble. *(The latter can be a sign of low self-esteem.)* Such individuals may seem to be extremely manipulative to others. The individual may have an extremely poor short-term memory difficulty which makes it difficult for them to remember instructions for very long. If the parent/teacher demands a reason for failure to do the task/disobeying an instruction the child may have little alternative but to lie to get out of the situation.
- needs a high level of stimulation
- usually we learn new skills through methods which involve visual/auditory and movement skills however some ADHD people seem to 'learn through their emotions'. Such individuals seem to need an 'emotional high' from themselves (or others around them) before they can calm down, settle down to a task or achieve a task.

Unfortunately, this 'emotional high' seems all too often to involve the ADHD person unwittingly stretching the patience of the teacher/parent so far that they lose their temper. The ADHD person will then achieve the task etc. e.g. fall asleep immediately leaving an emotionally exhausted parent who may take hours to recover from the experience.

Table 5:
Indicators which can be present in ADHD and/or other conditions which come within the SpLD Profile.

- fear of failure, being teased and/or ignored by their peers can cause the child to avoid school. This can occur via deliberate actions e.g. playing truant, refusing to leave home and/or as a result of stress related illness e.g. stomach pains, irritable bowel syndrome, headaches and feeling sick. *(Can also occur with many of the other conditions found within the Profile e.g. specific language impairment - Chapter 2, dyslexia - Chapter 3 and dyspraxia - Chapter 5.)*
- may have low self-esteem and may become severely depressed because they blame themselves for failing to achieve in behavioural and/or academic tasks. *(See dyslexia - Chapter 3,*

dyspraxia - Chapter 5 & Asperger's syndrome - Chapter 10.)
- may play the part of the 'class clown'. If this occurs at a low level it may be accepted by the primary school teacher but by the time the child reaches secondary school it can easily become behaviour for which detentions are given. Such children can be 'egged on' by their peer group (because the resultant conflict between the child and the teacher provides entertainment for them). They can also become the focus of teasing/ bullying by their classmates. *(See dyslexia - Chapter 3.)*
- not remembering instructions *(See specific language impairment - Chapter 2)*
- is likely to underachieve academically (unless appropriate provision is given). *(See dyslexia - Chapter 3 & numeracy difficulties - Chapter 4.)*
- may have difficulties in starting tasks even if he wants to do something very much and/or may give up easily (e.g. may give up playing a musical instrument very soon after starting to learn it.) This behaviour can be because the individual has poor planning and organisational skills and so does not know where to start the task and/or fear failure. *(See dyslexia - Chapter 3 & dyspraxia - Chapter 5.)*
- may dislike being touched *(see dyspraxia - Chapter 5 & autistic spectrum disorder - Chapter 10.)*
- may like to watch a great deal of television others may never sit still long enough to watch it! Watching television seems to help some individuals relax and escape their stress. Some will watch the television no matter what programme is on. This trait can be used to an advantage in children by encouraging them to watch educational programmes and/or play good quality educational computer games. (For such children it may be best not to have any of the usual games on the computer as these are always likely to be the preferred choice.) *(Individuals with certain types of near-vision dysfunctioning/occulomotor dyspraxia can find looking at a television screen/VDU less stressful than looking at anything else around them especially if they are affected by difficulties in the ability to change focus. In severe cases the child may need to learn to read using a computer-based method. See Chapter 7.)*
- may have very noticeable food fads and may eat only a few foods. The person can be very resistant to trying new foods. Some people seem to have difficulties in recognising the body's signals

that they are hungry and/or are able to ignore such signs until
they become severe when even then they may not realise what the
stomach pains mean. *(See autistic spectrum disorder - Chapter 10.)*
- may be clumsy *(see dyspraxia - Chapter 5 & autistic spectrum disorder - Chapter 10.)*
- writing difficulties may be present *(see Chapter 6)*
- DAMP syndrome may be present *(see dyspraxia - Table 1 Chapter 5 & autistic spectrum disorder - Chapter 10.)*
- social and communication skills may be affected e.g. individuals may:
1. be tactless
2. appear self-centred (and may not realise how other people view them)
3. appear eccentric to their peer group
4. talk too much
5. have difficulties in understanding certain aspects of language such as puns, riddles and jokes.
6. play better with a partner than in a group
7. have difficulties in understanding 'facial expressions'.
8. difficulties in using the 'tone of voice' as an aid to understanding the emotional state of the talker. (When this is combined with not understanding 'facial expressions' they may not realise when someone is becoming angry. Thus when the person loses their temper it can come as a complete surprise to the individual.) They may be unable to tell when somebody is joking with them as they take whatever the person says literally and ignore the tone of voice used. Therefore, the individual may not always know when someone is being pleasant/unpleasant to them. Once they start to 'read' the tone of voice they may rely upon that as their guide to a person's emotional state. Such individuals can find it particularly disturbing if the teacher/parent shouts at another child because they are always worried that they might be shouted at next. *(See specific language impairment - Chapter 2 & autistic spectrum disorder - Chapter 10.)*

Table 6
Indicators of ADHD in the classroom
by AD/HD Family Support Group UK

1. The young child with ADHD is often an **underachiever** who seems to have more potential than they are actually using.
2. The child's achievements often seem uneven, and seem to vary with the **type** of learning activity, rather than the **skills** involved in the activity.
3. The child with ADHD may have learning problems similar to other children with Specific Learning Difficulties e.g. dyslexia.
4. The child seems disorganised, forgetful, and messy with his or her materials.
5. At times the child with ADHD may persevere at an activity, or be very rigid in his/her approach to problem solving.
6. The young child with ADHD is frequently fidgety when at their seats and impulsive in their behaviour. They jump to respond without thinking through their answer. Their hands (and their bodies) are always waving in the air.
7. This type of child is very distractible and may have a short attention span compared to other children of the same age. Any little sound or minor movement nearby can be distracting to the child.
8. Relationships with other peers may be quite poor, and the child with ADHD often has few, if any friends. Other children do not like the disruptive, fidgety, impulsive behaviour and tantruming of this child, and therefore they often avoid him/her.
9. Although this child is often unaware of the effect he/she has on others, he/she may avoid joining in group activities. The child with ADHD may appear socially withdrawn, shy, and immature compared to peers.
10. Teachers often describe the child with ADHD as one who needs or benefits from one to one instruction.
11. Ultimately, the child with ADHD often has problems with self-esteem, with a negative attitude towards education, in spite of apparent good intellectual potential and an emotionally healthy family situation.

others, he/she may avoid joining in group activities. The child with ADHD may appear socially withdrawn, shy, and immature compared to peers.
10. Teachers often describe the child with ADHD as one who needs or benefits from one to one instruction.

11. Ultimately, the child with ADHD often has problems with
    self-esteem, with a negative attitude towards education, in
    spite of apparent good intellectual potential and an
    emotionally healthy family situation.

Recommended publications

Attention Deficit Hyperactivity Disorder by Dr. P.V.F. Cosgrove
    (Consultant Child & Adolescent Psychiatrist)

ADHD Information Pack by AD/HD Family Support Group UK
    (This includes the DSM 111-R criteria for recognition of the
    different forms of attention deficit disorder.)

Understanding Attention Deficit Disorder by Dr. Christopher
    Green and Dr Kit Chee (Specialist paediatricians)

The Hidden Handicap by Dr Gordon Serfontein (Paediatric
    neurologist)

All about ADD - understanding Attention Deficit Disorder by
    Mark Selikowitz. pub. Oxford University Press.

Footnotes

1. *This pack is free. If you want the full pack contact The AD/HD Family Support Group UK (address at front of Chapter 15 -Help & Support).*
2. *Editor: or maintains concentration inappropriately e.g. the person focuses on the task to the exclusion of the needs of those around him. (The person can become so focused that he ignores body signals like hunger until the task is finished.)*
3. *Editor: Hyperactivity does not always accompany ADHD e.g. Undifferentiated Attention Deficit Disorder (Table 4).*
4. *Dr. P.V.F. Cosgrove: Attention Deficit Hyperactivity Disorder The editor has added in the words 'adult' and 'adults' as ADHD can carry on into adulthood.*
5. *Dr. P.V.F. Cosgrove: Attention Deficit Hyperactivity Disorder*
6. *The AD/HD Family Support Group UK*
7. *Dr. P.V.F. Cosgrove: Attention Deficit Hyperactive Disorder*
8. *The AD/HD Family Support Group UK*
9. *Dr. P.V.F. Cosgrove: Attention Deficit Hyperactivity Disorder*
10. *The AD/HD Family Support Group UK*
11. *Dr. Christopher Green and Dr. Kit Chee: Understanding Attention Deficit Disorder*
12. *"Most children with ADD seem to have a close relative with a similar problem": Understanding Attention Deficit Disorder (Dr Christopher Green and Dr Kit Chee)*
13. *Dr. P.V.F. Cosgrove: Attention Deficit Hyperactivity Disorder*
14. *Editor:The genetic inheritance factor also means that the child may have one or both parents affected. It can be very hard for ADHD parents to cope with their own emotions whilst trying to cope with their childs. Meanwhile their partner can find both spouse and child exhausting!*
15. *Editor: The criteria used in Table 1 Parts 1 &2 are similar so usually an individual will meet both sets of criteria however if the requisite number of indicators are only met in one of these tables then a referral should still be made.*
16. *The AD/HD Family Support Group UK*
17. *Dr Christopher Green in his Exeter lecture during his UK lecture tour 1996.*
18. *The ADHD Family Support Group UK*
19. *Dr. P.V.F. Cosgrove: Attention Deficit Hyperactivity Disorder*
20. *Dr Christopher Green in his Exeter lecture during his UK lecture tour 1996.*
21. *The AD/HD Family Support Group UK*
22. *Editor: Getting these children to sleep can be an art in itself and by the time it has been achieved with an ADHD baby the parent can be so exhausted that it takes all the 45 minutes of the baby's nap to recover from the exertion. These babies do not happily lie in their cots and look at the mobiles!*
23. *The AD/HD Family Support Group UK*
24. *Understanding Attention Deficit Disorder by Drs Green and Chee has a great deal of information on medication.*
25. *Editor:See Chapter 15 Health Help & Support section for the address of The Society of Homeopaths if you wish to go along this route.*
26. *Editor:The AD/HD Family Support Group UK produce a very interesting introduction to ADHD coaching.*

27. *Editor: the idea that their child (or they themselves as an adult) have a psychiatric disorder can be particularly threatening in the UK where psychiatrists are seen by some to be a threat and an American fad rather than highly trained and helpful professionals. As a society we will need to come to terms with the psychiatric side of ADHD if we are to achieve full recognition and treatment of this disorder.*
28. & 29. *The AD/HD Family Support Group UK*
30. *Dr. P.V.F. Cosgrove: Attention Deficit Hyperactivity Disorder.*

Acknowledgements: Dr Christopher Green and the AD/HD Family Support Group UK

Chapter 10
AUTISTIC SPECTRUM DISORDER

At present in the UK two terms are used for this condition Autistic continuum disorder and Autistic spectrum disorder. In some countries the term Pervasisve developmental disorder is used for this condition.

(The word 'continuum' refers to an imaginary line which connects the two opposite ends (extremes) of a condition to each other. Thus an individual will be diagnosed as being at some point on this line dependent upon the severity/difficulties/characteristics etc. that are present.)

Autism is a rare and very complex condition which occurs in all classes, creeds and races and which is generally believed to affect four times as many boys as girls (though some evidence shows that the number of girls affected is greater than this.[1] It is a pattern of abnormal development which is recognised by difficulties (impairments) in social interaction, social communication and imagination. These difficulties occur in varying degrees ranging from low-level to severe. This 'triad of impairments' unfolds over time (usually appearing in the first two to three years of life with there often being indications of developmental problems in the first year). (*See Table 1*)

Autistic spectrum disorder consists of a broad spectrum of communication disorders that has many components which are sometimes referred to as sub-groups.[2] Although there appears to be an element of overlapping between these sub-groups each of them has characteristics of their own and go under separate names e.g. Asperger's Syndrome and autism.[3] Autism itself is a fairly uncommon condition affecting 1 in 1000 people with about 80,000 individuals being affected by it in the UK.[4] However, autism is only part of the autistic spectrum disorder and if we look at all those affected by the various forms of it (including those individuals who also have learning difficulties) a much greater number of people are affected. Thus, at present it is believed that approximately 1 in 100 people have a form of autistic spectrum disorder.[5]

WHAT CAUSES AUTISTIC SPECTRUM DISORDER?

There is no one standard belief as to its cause. Some believe that brain dysfunction of some kind is involved and/or that there is an over production of a certain chemical in the brain which blocks the normal transmissions within it. In approximately one quarter of those affected there is a history of normal development followed by an setback (which can sometimes be traced to a physical illness) and this marks the 'onset' of the condition. Some cases can be traced to a variety of conditions which affect brain development before, during or after birth e.g. lack of oxygen at birth, a complication of whooping cough/measles.[6] In many cases genetic factors appear to be involved. Increasingly research is showing that whatever the cause, the difficulties that autism presents are based in a 'cognitive deficit' in what has been called the 'concept of mind'. This underpins all autistic-like conditions and consists of the inability to share emotions/beliefs and to see things from somebody else's point of view. This developing ability is seen as a precondition of both appropriate social behaviour and effective sharing through communication.[7]

ARE THERE ANY MEDICAL CONDITIONS THAT ARE ASSOCIATED WITH AUTISTIC SPECTRUM DISORDER?

Yes, therefore it is essential that an individual is referred to a paediatrician if autistic spectrum disorder is suspected as he/she can then exclude any other underlying medical disorder/s that may be associated with autistic spectrum disorder e.g. Fragile X syndrome, tuberous sclerosis, neurofibromatosis, congenital rubella, PKU, epilepsy and Hypomelanosis Ito.

WHAT LEARNING DIFFICULTIES ARE ASSOCIATED WITH AUTISTIC SPECTRUM DISORDER

There appears to be a strong relationship between severe/profound learning difficulties and autistic spectrum disorder. (About half of those afffected by autistic spectrum disorder have such learning difficulties.) However, of those individuals who have mild learning difficulties less than 1% of them will also have autistic spectrum disorder.[8] Individuals who are affected by autistic spectrum disorder can also be affected by various conditions which affect learning e.g.

• hyperlexia (where the individual can read much better than they can understand written text) [9]

• specific language impairment, *(see Chapter 2)*

• dyslexia *(see Chapter 3)*

• dyspraxia *(see Chapter 5)*

• attention deficit disorder *(see Chapter 9)*

HOW IS AUTISTIC SPECTRUM DISORDER RELATED TO INTELLECTUAL ABILITY?

Autism is present across the intellectual levels thus individuals can range "from being severely learning disabled to being of normal or even superior intelligence."[10] Various skills are associated with autistic spectrum disorder e.g. individuals may have dexterity in manipulating objects and good visuo-spatial or rote memory skills. [11] "About 10% of individuals have some special skill at a much higher level than the rest of their abilities e.g. music, art, numerical calculations, jigsaw puzzles, [12] and dates etc. and a few will be 'savants' - individuals of exceptionally high skill in one narrow area.

IS RECOGNITION EASY?

No, because autistic spectrum disorder neither affects the appearance of the person nor does it present in the same way throughout the individual's life and because other conditions which can be found alongside it e.g. dyspraxia can mask the signs. Individuals usually look alert, attractive and intelligent.[13] Although the symptoms usually appear before they are three years old the changing nature of autism, with different aspects of it being more obvious at some ages than at others, may make it difficult to make a firm diagnosis.[14] This change in the dominant features may also result with the diagnosis being changed from one component of autistic spectrum disorder to that of another as the individual develops. Apart from the obvious severe cases it requires a great deal of knowledge to recognise the signs in those children/adults with moderate to low-level difficulties. Also, high intelligence can mask the signs and make it much more difficult to recognise. A stumbling block to recognition and diagnosis can be the failure of everyone to see the 'whole' picture that the child is presenting. The parents may not know which information is important to the professional and during consultation the child may not exhibit the behaviour which can enable an accurate diagnosis to be made. Diagnosis is also made difficult by the similarities of Autistic spectrum disorder to other conditions e.g.

• <u>Specific Language Impairment</u> in which language is delayed but social development is relatively normal *(see Chapter 2)*

• <u>learning disability</u> in which all skills are delayed.

The characteristics found in some individuals may only fit part of the pattern of autism and in such cases the individual may not fulfil the total criterea to diagnose classical autism itself e.g.

1. *Atypical autism (also known as other pervasive developmental disorder):*

Development is abnormal in all three key areas with the picture not quite being that of classical autism. Only one or two autistic features are present and onset usually occurs after three years of age.

2. *Asperger's Syndrome:* intelligence and early language development are fairly normal, or above average. Individuals try to be sociable and clumsiness is present *(see Table 2)*

3. *Autistic Features* (Autistic tendencies): The individual falls into the grey area where a firm diagnosis either way cannot be made. [15]

4. *Childhood disintegrative disorder:* development is normal up to two years and then there is a loss of two or more of certain skills such as play, social skills, language, motor skills and bowel/bladder control.[16]

Assessment of intellectual functioning can aid diagnosis. The higher intellectual functioning individual with autism is likely to have a markedly higher non-verbal functioning as compared with his verbal ability. The individual with Asperger's Syndrome is likely to have average (or above average) intelligence and tends to have a similar level of non-verbal and verbal functioning. [17] Wing suggests that from the individual's point of view it is not particulary relevant to closely define the sub-group to which the he or she belongs. Instead the aim of an assessment should be to decide if autistic spectrum disorder is present and then concentrate on assessing their abilities[18] for such an assessment helps decide appropriate provision.

WHAT ARE THE INDICATORS OF AUTISTIC SPECTRUM DISORDER?

The baby's behaviour can range widely. There is a very small group who are irritable and difficult to soothe, the most common group are quiet and exceptionally good and there are a few who fit neither group. The 'full picture' is not likely to emerge until he starts to walk independently as up until then the range of behaviour of a baby is limited. [19] As he gets older he may seem detached and aloof and appear to see people as 'objects to be used' rather than as people with their own set of needs and emotions. Although difficulties in social integration and the use of language are usually found "there is no single feature, that if not present, excludes autism" [20] and occasionally the individual can show behaviour which we would expect to see in non-autistic individuals e.g. make eye contact, use perfect grammer, cuddle someone. It is the usual, "overall pattern of the individual that is relevant.[21] The following indicators are likely to be present:

• inappropriate interaction with others - A wide range of behaviours can be seen e.g. complete withdrawal, passivity (the child will allow others to 'play with him' in roles that require no interaction e.g. being a baby), repeated pestering, reject/are frightened of other people, making inappropriate active social approaches. This latter group show various behaviours e.g. may talk at people (usually those in authority rather than their peers) and may have difficulties in making and breaking eye contact appropriately. In adolescence and in adulthood those individuals who are the most able and who have good language skills may become overformal in their social interactions e.g. over polite even to family members.[22]

• Some individuals never speak and for the rest delayed speech development is common. [23] Unusual language/speech patterns associated with Specific Language Impairment may be seen especially that of Semantic Pragmatic Disorder and Higher Level Language Disorder e.g. very literal in their own speech and in their understanding of other people's speech and of written information, delayed speech, echoing phrases meaninglessly that have been said by others (echolalia), using the wrong personal pronouns, talking 'at' or 'questioning' people rather than conversing with them.(see Chapter 2) (There is debate as to whether Semantic Pragmatic Disorder can exist without autistic spectrum disorder being present.[24]) Odd intonation is likely as are difficulties in understanding systems of non-verbal communication e.g. gestures.[25]

• difficulties in putting themselves in 'someone else's shoes' - being able to see the other person's viewpoint

• difficulties in relating to other people

• inflexible - a dislike of any change in routine and an insistence upon certain routines occurring e.g. following an identical route to certain places, a lengthy bedtime ritual or the repetition of a sequence of odd bodily movements."[26]

• have an unusually intense interest in a narrow area of a topic e.g. dimensions of castles

• difficulties in any tasks which require the use of the imagination

• difficulties in using 'abstract' thoughts and symbolic language

• more interested in objects than people, especially when they are young

• difficulties in judging the motivations, intentions and sensitivities of others

<u>Common pre-school indicators (some of which will carry on past this developmental stage)</u>

Babies may [27]:

• dislike being physically disturbed and handled as in nappy changing, bathing, dressing etc.

• smile at something but not smile when looking at a person's face

• be fascinated by (and/or may show inappropriate distress) to visual and auditory stimuli e.g. lights, television, music. Inappropriate response to auditory stimuli can also be alongside dyslexia (*chapter 3*), Central Auditory Processing Disorder (*chapter 8*), Attention Deficit Disorder (*chapter 9*) and dyspraxia (*chapter 5*).

• have feeding problems. Signs of articulatory dyspraxia may be present e.g. sucking, chewing and swallowing difficulties. (*See Chapter 5*) Children with a combination of severe visual and hearing impairment can also reject lumpy food.[28] (*See Chapters 7 & 8.*) [29]

Children may:

• have irrational fears of particular objects and/or situations which may continue for a long time. (This is different from the fears that very young non-autistic spectrum children can have where the fear is related to something obvious that was frightening them e.g. being frightened of a lamp because its shadow distorted on the wall. Once the explanation has been given and the lamp moved, so that the distorted shadow no longer appears, the fear goes away.)

• have difficulties in knowing the passage of time e.g. cannot 'wait' for something, unable to complete a task within a given amount of time, unable to cope with the idea of the future and that all things have a beginning and more importantly an end. Such individuals rely heavily on a timetable and cannot cope when circumstances mean that the timetable has to be changed in any way.

• able to know where they (and their possessions) are in the dark and may be able to walk/cycle etc. without appearing to look where they are going

• appear aloof. They may ignore people unless they want the person to do something for them. They also may ignore people's reactions to events so cannot respond appropriately to happiness or sadness in others.[30] They may also ignore other people's reactions to their own behaviour (so do not come when called, do not react when told off). The child may have his behaviour incorrectly interpreted as disobedience by adults e.g. emotional indifference/aloofness and the child doing what he wants to do when he wants to do it.

• be delayed in (or never show) pointing behaviour. (Normally at about 12-18 months children use pointing as a way of drawing the carer's attention to an object or an event in which he is interested.) If "pointing" is delayed, or does not occur (and this behaviour is limited to the child's own interests) then Autistic spectrum disorder should be suspected. (31)

• hand-lead. This can be used instead of pointing. The child takes the hand of the carer (but does not look at them). Then takes the hand to an object of interest e.g. a bag that he wants opened.

• make eye-contact but will not use facial expressions and 'gaze' as part of his system of non-verbal communication

• not take part in social interactions with others by smiling or making sounds.

• not try to provoke an emotional reaction from others, or show how he feels (e.g. does not point at things, vocalise at interesting items or take them to show his carer).

• be very independent at a young age, can be too independent for the parent's peace of mind e.g. most young children like to stay close to their parents especially in unfamiliar situations but the child with autistic spectrum disorder may go too far away from them. *(This can also occur as part of attention deficit disorder see Chapter 9.)*

• be uninterested in others praising his successes

• be unable to tell the difference between positive and negative emotions

• like being cuddled (but only when he wants it). He does not use this as a form of social interaction and seems unaware of the feelings of others. He does not look at his parent whilst being cuddled. (Non-autistic spectrum disorder children will indicate that they are happy through sounds/words and looking at the parent's face.)

• have delayed social behaviour (or it may not exist at all). 'Play' will be affected e.g. the child may ignore other children or play 'alongside' them long after these forms of play are normally replaced by other types (e.g. after the age of four years). Will have to be taught how to play with toys. He may not show imaginative/creative play behaviour (or such play will be very limited). In pretend play he will not pretend to paint with an object that he is pretending is a paintbrush. He may like physical play e.g. being tickled, chasing, jumping etc..

- actively avoid the parent's company
- not seek comfort from parents in stressful situations
- after being frustrated or punished the toddler suddenly stops crying without the parent intervening by calming him.
- not imitate other people's behaviour so at twelve months he is unlikely to have learnt to wave 'bye-bye'. They are unlikely to learn practical skills by being told and/or shown how to do them (difficulties in learning practical skills are also common in dyspraxia - *see Chapter 5*) but can learn if their hand etc. is physically guided by the carer.
- constantly asking questions, may ask the same series of questions and demand the same standard answers regarding topics that fascinate them (*Pre-school non-autistic children aged between 3-5 years also ask many questions but they do not become upset if the answer to the question differs slightly.*)
- great need for reassurance but do not understand/respond to common forms of it e.g. explanations, cuddles etc.
- repeatedly replay the same parts of a video or CD etc. and may repetitively act out characters from popular television series.[32]
- have an unusual 'learning curve'. Normally progress can be plotted on a graph as a curve which may have one or two straight horizontal lines (which are called plateaux) which mark a certain length of time when no progress occurred. In autistic spectrum children there are far more plateaux than usual and each one lasts for a long time. Skills can also suddenly appear without any practice of the task.[33]

In common with most of the other conditions that come within the SpLD Profile individuals can have good and bad days.

Any, or all, of the following may also be seen at various stages in development:
- inappropriate reactions to stimuli e.g. laughing at the wrong things (*this can also be a sign of embarrassment*), unreasonable fears and becoming upset, may also become overly fascinated by various objects e.g. spinning objects and particular forms of light and movement (e.g. tree branches, the effect of light and shade as the car passes under a series of motorway bridges).
- do not lie.
- unusual movements. Many young children will demonstrate occasional unusual movements as part of a phase of development and when that phase finishes so do the movements. However the individual with autistic spectrum disorder will carry on doing movements such as:

walking stiffly, walking on tiptoe, twirling their body around, rocking or head banging or flapping parts of their body especially when feeling strong emotion such as excitement or when fascinated by something. 'Hand flapping', 'finger flapping' and 'arm flapping' are very distinctive movements that once seen are never forgotten as they look so unusual. Some individuals flap their hands or fingers others may flap their arms (some do all of them.) Finger flapping is a flicking of the fingers which imitates the movement of rain falling. Hand flapping is the whole hand being flapped from the wrist with the fingers being kept loose. When hand/finger flapping occurs the arms may be held rigid with the elbows bent tightly upward (it looks a bit like a chicken flapping its wings) or the arms may be extended and the elbows locked. Arm flapping is a flapping of the whole arm (upper or lower part or both parts together).

• look at an object at very close range as though they cannot see it properly (but can spot sweets with ease)

• make collections of objects (e.g. pebbles) and arrange them in lines or patterns

• seem unaware of the sounds that are around them but are immediately aware of certain sounds/words e.g. the word 'chocolate'!

• use objects inappropriately so they do not dig with a spade but might stroke, sniff, lick or kiss it instead, might become attached to odd objects rather than to a cuddly toy

• lack of fear about realistic dangers

• uses gestures to 'ask' for what he wants rather than using speech

• when talking to others they may appear: rude, boring, pompous

• seek isolation when distressed and afraid rather than going to their carers for comfort

• expect routine in those around him e.g. expect them to always sit in the same seats in the car

• show an inappropriate response to sensory stimuli e.g. the individual may be indifferent/oversensitive to pain, temperature and hunger pangs. (See dyspraxia - Chapter 5 & attention deficit disorder - Chapter 9.) The individual may also be indifferent to sound or 'hypercusis' may be present which is an over sensitivity to sound (see Central Auditory Processing Disorder - Chapter 8).

• do not like being looked at by others

• self injurious behaviours can be shown by a few individuals e.g.

head banging, hand biting, hitting one side of the head and repetitive scratching. *(However, it should be remembered that occasional examples of the first three can also be seen as the result of severe frustration and that scratching can also be an indicator of an allergic reaction/ eczema.)*

• behaviour is worse in unstructured environment (thus it may well be worse at home than in the school or the clinic) [34]

• excessive drinking of liquids - this may lead to vomiting

Indicators which may be seen but which could also indicate Attention Deficit Disorder- see Chapter 9.

• severe temper tantrums *(can also be the result of severe frustration)*
• marked food fads (with often only very few foods being accepted) which are very difficult to change and last for a long time. (Normally food fads start at about two years of age and should have disappeared by the age of five or six years.)
• refusal to do what they are told *(also see Oppositional Defiant Disorder - Chapter 9)*
• defiant and/or aggressive behaviour e.g. running away, screaming, biting or kicking other people. *(also see Oppositional Defiant Disorder - Chapter 9).* They can also destroy and/or interfere with other people's possessions,
• sleeping difficulties e.g. cannot get to sleep with ease, wake up frequently during the night, dislike going to bed
• constantly interrupting others
• difficulties in maintaining attention appropriately. May also be able to focus attention on particular tasks for an unusually long length of time

Indicators which may be seen but which could also indicate Dyslexia- see Chapter 3

• difficulties in using gestures and body language and in understanding their use by others
• anxiety *(It is also associated with highly intelligent female dyslexics in the 8-12 year old group - see Chapter 13)*
• poor memory skills *(can also be associated with attention deficit disorder - see chapter 9)*
• difficulties in sequencing
Indicators which may be seen but which could also indicate

Dyspraxia - *see Chapter 5*
• The various forms of dyspraxia can be present with difficulties in both fine motor and/or gross motor control being seen. There is a noticeable difficulty with the playing of team games where co-ordination of their own actions with those of others plus an understanding of the rules of the game is necessary.[35] (It would seem likely that part of this problem is a difficulty in spatial relationships e.g. constructional dyspraxia and receptive language difficulties/ Central Auditory Processing Disorder - *see Chapters 2 & 8*)

• show over/under reaction to any or all of the following: touch, taste, smell[36] and temperature

• pay little attention to his appearance (*dressing dyspraxia may be present*) and he may not put the final touches to his appearance (*also see Chapter 6*)

• difficulties in turn-taking in games and in understanding the rules of games
• being a loner
• failing to understand 'social distance' - can be too close or too far away from people

• motor co-ordination difficulties (clumsiness is associated with Asperger's Syndrome)
• meaninglessly copying other people's movements (echopraxia)

HOW IS AUTISTIC SPECTRUM DISORDER DIAGNOSED

Once the indicators have been spotted "it is essential that the child is referred for specialist diagnosis and assessment as early as possible. This can be achieved through the local GP referring the child to a local paediatrician who has an interest in this field. The local paediatrician will then arrange for the child to have a multidisciplinary assessment which will include representation from the local education authority. The referral process can also be started by a teacher contacting the school doctor. At present there are few specialists in this field but professionals and parents can gain help and support from The National Autistic Society for all aspects of autism and from AFASIC for the language/communication aspects of this condition. (*See Chapter 15*)

A diagnosis depends upon obtaining a detailed history of the child's development, a careful assessment of skills and abilities[37] and consideration of all the different aspects of the child's behaviour in a systematic way. This is likely to include a lengthy interview with the parents (about two to three hours), observation of the individual's behaviour and psychological testing. It is important that such an assessment is not rushed for if it is the evidence of autism may be missed. [38] Ideally a multidisciplinary assessment is conducted to assess the child throughout his/her pre-school/school years. This can involve many people e.g. paediatric neurologist, child psychiatrist, psychologist, speech & language/physio/occupational therapists, social worker, teacher and parents.[39] It is important that the assessment is seen as the first positive step along the road to change and future success. Parents need to be made aware that through appropriate intervention their child will continue to change and grow and develop new abilities. Cultural factors will affect the parent's reaction to diagnosis and may cause parents from some ethnic groups to find it very difficult to come to terms with it. [40]

WHAT HAPPENS NEXT?

The creation of an effective working partnership of parents and professionals (with the parents being **actively involved** as much as possible) will be necessary to provide the step-by-step intervention that will enable the individual's difficulties to be addressed. At present there is considerable variation between the provision being offered by the various LEA's. Ideally input is needed from the:

Health services:
Clinical support for the problems will be needed. Intervention of a clinical psychologist and psychiatrist who are experienced in this field should occur. Medication may be recommended if behavioural difficulties such as aggression and temper tantrums are severe/prolonged/ frequent and cannot be reduced by removing the cause of them.[41]

Social services:
A service plan should be created to ensure that the child's needs are met. This will include intensive and individual therapeutic programmes that involve parents and professionals, effective family support and respite care.

Education:
Specialised teaching approaches are vital [42] and a statement of Special Educational Needs (Such a statement is referred to as a Record of

Needs in Scotland) may be necessary, *(See Chapter 11))* Approximately 1 in 24 children will be severe enough to attend a unit/school for part of their education. Most will attend a school for children with moderate/severe learning difficulties. The more able child and the child with few management problems is likely to attend mainstream primary and/or secondary school but their social difficulties can make them more vulnerable and appropriate support may be necessary.

WHAT HAPPENS WHEN THE CHILD BECOMES AN ADULT?

For some of those affected by Autistic spectrum disorder there will be opportunities to attend college and university whilst others e.g. the "savants" may reach a high level of expertise in a narrow area of interest. However, the majority do not usually develop the level of social and communication skills necessary to hold down a job equal to their knowledge base. Autistic spectrum disorder "creates a lifelong need" [43] for the individual and his family and most adults will need to live and work in environments where special provision is made for them. However, the availability of such long-term provision is so scarce that it is the parents who may have to meet the bulk of such provision at present.

CONCLUSION

Early recognition and diagnosis is vital as it enables early effective intervention and management of the condition which will result in fewer and less severe symptoms. Diagnosis enables the introduction of a 'framework' which promotes structure, routine and continuity and the possibility of very gradual changes being introduced. This 'framework' enables individuals to understand and communicate with the world around them and reduces their levels of anxiety. It provides bridging mechanisms by which they can cross from their own unique environment into our own and helps the individual to reach his potential and improves the quality of life for all.

Lack of diagnosis and intervention causes individuals (and their families and teachers) to be under immense strain as they struggle to cope with low self-esteem, difficulties with adjusting to change and problems with relating and communicating with those around them.[44] Even once diagnosed these individuals place extraordinary demands upon parenting skills, the family and their teachers. The family can find the behaviour of the individual so embarrassing that just as he is isolated in his own world so they become isolated in theirs. For some, events such as family trips and using baby-sitters (so that the parents can have time to themselves) are rare, or, do not occur. Teachers who lack knowledge of effective management techniques can find that controlling the behaviour of the child takes so much time that they feel that the rest of the class is 'losing out'.

Recognition (followed by diagnosis) is the first step along a 'road' which will enable individuals affected by Autistic spectrum disorder to gain the provision that they need. This initial step enables everyone involved to have easier and greater access to information help and support. The individual will still place great demands upon parental skills, the family and their teachers but now they will be in a position to access local support groups, branches of the National Autistic Society and respite care.

Perhaps for all of those involved in the field of autistic spectrum disorder (whether affected by it, or involved in provision for it) the old saying "divided we fall, united we stand" was never more true. The 'road' may not be a smooth one but by working together and supporting each other it can be made a lot less bumpy and much more pleasant to travel along.

Footnotes:
1. There is a possibility that the ratio is more like two boys for every girl (with girls being more difficult to recognise than boys). For further information see " The Autistic Spectrum: a guide for professionals and parents" by Lorna Wing (pub. Constable).
2. The term Autistic spectrum disorder is used in the UK/Europe, in the USA the term Pervasive Developmental Disorders is used.
3. Although it is agreed by many professionals that all these conditions share similarities it is argued that the assumption that they all represent some variant of autism is unproved and may not be useful. The reply to this argument is that research by psychologists increasingly points to a complex, broad but specific cognitive ability called 'concept of mind' underpinning all autistic-like conditions. (AFASIC Glossary sheets 8 & 16)
4. Autism - a world apart (video produced by Poseidon Film Productions, Distributed by Hopeline Videos)
5. For further information see "The Autistic Spectrum: a guide for professionals and parents" by Lorna Wing (pub. Constable).
6. & 7. Could this be Autism (pub. by The National Autistic Society).
8. For further information see "The Autistic Spectrum: a guide for professionals and parents" by Lorna Wing (pub. Constable).
9. Could this be Autism (pub. by The National Autistic Society).
10. Naomi Richmond - Autism: making an early diagnosis (pub. in The

Practitioner 23/05/1988, Vol.232)

11. For further information see "The Autistic Spectrum: a guide for professionals and parents" by Lorna Wing (pub. Constable).

12. Could this be Autism (pub. by The National Autistic Society).

13. These features are included in Kanner's original description of autism. For further information see page 19 "The Autistic Spectrum: a guide for professionals and parents" by Lorna Wing (pub. Constable).

14.. e.g. impairment of social relationships being most noticeable before the age of five years.

15. See "Autism: the facts" by Dr Simon Baron-Cohen and Dr Patrick Bolton (pub. Oxford University Press)

16. For further information see page 30 "The Autistic Spectrum: a guide for professionals and parents" by Lorna Wing (pub. Constable).

17. For further information see page 21 and pages 110-119 of The World of the Autistic Child by Bryna Siegel (pub. Oxford University Press)

18. & 19. "The Autistic Spectrum: a guide for professionals and parents" by Lorna Wing (pub. Constable).

20. & 21. Could this be Autism (pub. by The National Autistic Society)

22. - 25. "The Autistic Spectrum: a guide for professionals and parents" by Lorna Wing (pub. Constable).

26. Could this be Autism (pub. by The National Autistic Society)

27. & 28. "The Autistic Spectrum: a guide for professionals and parents" by Lorna Wing (pub. Constable).

29. The National Autistic Society produce a booklet called Managing Feeding Difficulties in Children with Autism.

30. "The Autistic Spectrum: a guide for professionals and parents" by Lorna Wing (pub. Constable).

31. Could this be Autism (pub. by The National Autistic Society)

32. "The Autistic Spectrum: a guide for professionals and parents" by Lorna Wing (pub. Constable).

33. The author has also noted this in non-autistic spectrum disorder children who have other conditions that are found within the SpLD Profile.

34. & 35. "The Autistic Spectrum: a guide for professionals and parents" by Lorna Wing (pub. Constable).

36. The World of the Autistic Child by Bryna Siegel (pub. Oxford University Press)

37. This information is collated via checklists/rating scales e.g. ABC, CARS, ADI. These correlate the information against the standardised criteria for autism as found in the DSM-1V (used in the USA) or the internationally used ICD-10.

38. "The Autistic Spectrum: a guide for professionals and parents" by Lorna Wing (pub. Constable).

Table 1

THE TRIAD OF IMPAIRMENTS

Difficulties with social interaction:
"The child will:

1. often appear aloof and indifferent to other people, especially other children, although some will enjoy certain forms of active physical contact.
2. passively accept social contact and even show some signs of pleasure in this, but will rarely make spontaneous approaches.

3. occasionally approach other people but in an odd, inappropriate, repetitive way, paying little or no attention to the responses of those they approach.

Difficulties with social communication (verbal & non-verbal)
The child will:

1. not appreciate the social uses and the pleasure of communication. This is true even of those who have a lot of speech, which they use to talk 'at' others and not 'with' them.

2. not understand that language is a tool for conveying information to others. They may be able to ask for their own needs but find it hard to talk about feelings or thoughts and will not understand the emotions , ideas and beliefs of other people.

3. not really understand the meaning of gestures, facial expressions or tone of voice. Higher functioning children do use gestures but these tend to be odd and inappropriate.
4. understand and use language very literally, with an idiosyncratic, sometimes pompous choice of words and phrases and limited content of speech. Though some children are fascinated with words, they will not use them to interact socially.

Difficulties with imagination (affects play, written work etc.)
The child will:

1. be unable to play imaginatively with objects or toys or with other children or adults.
2. tend to focus on minor or trivial things around them, for example an earring rather than the person wearing it, or a wheel instead of the whole toy train.
10. have a limited range of imaginative activities, possibly copied and pursued rigidly and repetitively.

11. miss the point of pursuits that involve words e.g. social conversation, literature, especially fiction and subtle verbal humour."[1]

Reference:

1. *Could this be autism (Pub. The National Autistic Society)*

Table 2

Asperger's Syndrome

It is only fairly recently that the following set of characteristics were given the name of Asperger's Syndrome:

General
• difficulties during birth
• dislike changes in routine (can find changes in school/work/ timetable/change of staff upsetting and difficult to cope with)
• likely to have difficulties in learning by observation
• likely to have problems in working as part of a team
• may be aware that they are 'different' from their peer group and may be distressed by it (with this awareness being heightened in their teens and early adulthood)
• anxiety and/or depression may be present

Intellect and academic skills
• average (or above average) intelligence
• similar level of non-verbal and verbal functioning
• often excel at learning facts and figures
• have difficulties in thinking in abstract ways (this causes difficulties various subjects e.g. creative writing in English, religious education and literature.)
• may have original and creative thought patterns

Social skills
• may try to be sociable (but peers tend to avoid them because of their apparently eccentric behaviour)
• may be the subject of teasing and/or bullying *(can also occur with dyslexia- chapter 3, dyspraxia- chapter 5, Central Auditory Processing Disorder- chapter 8, Attention Deficit Disorder- chapter 9 and Specific Language Impairment- chapter 2)*
• difficulties in making and maintaining relationships
• may become more isolated (and obsessional) as they get older

• difficulties in understanding how other people think
• may develop antisocial behaviour (may be violent to and/or threaten others)(*Also see Chapter 9*)

Movement
• clumsy (may have difficulties in learning certain motor skills e.g. learning to ride a bike and to swim) *(also see Chapter 5 - dyspraxia)* Individuals who also have attention deficits *(see Chapter 9)* and perception difficulties present may be defined as having DAMP syndrome *(see Chapter 5- Table 1)*
• may exhibit repetitive movements e.g. swaying and rocking
• may develop unusual postures

Language Development
• fairly normal early development
• may speak very fluently
• fail to make adjustments in their use of language to fit different social contexts, or, the needs of their listeners
• likely to have problems in expressing themselves e.g. via facial expressions, gestures or posture
• may have semantic-pragmatic disorders or higher level language disorder *(see Chapter 2)*

Interests
• have unusual interests in which the individual becomes deeply engrossed and which usually involve classifying information and exceptional memory skills e.g. lists of dates.

Each person will have the characteristics but there will be big variations between individuals as to which features will be more noticeable than others. The presence of better language skills (as compared with classical autism) may mean that the condition remains undiagnosed for a long time, possibly until their teens or adulthood. The individual may also have other conditions that are found within the Specific Learning Difficulties Profile e.g. dyspraxia which may mask the indicators of Asperger's Syndrome. This late recognition can cause considerable problems for the individual including them developing emotional and behavioural problems as a result of being bullied and teased by other children who find their 'difference' in behaviour offensive and/or upsetting. Lack of recognition results in a failure to meet their needs and their parents may blame themselves (or the child/adult) for their unusual behaviour.

Once recognised there are few facilities available for this group at present. Academic progress will depend upon the support and encouragement of parents, carers and teachers. Some children will be in mainstream school whilst others will be in specialist schools for children with autism, learning disabilities, or, a school catering solely for children with Asperger's Syndrome.[1] If adequate provision is not made they may become isolated, distressed and depressed in adulthood because they find it so hard to make friends. However, adults can go on to live fulfilling lives, can attend further education (including university) and go into employment and develop friendships. They may also be able to live independently, or, near their families.

References
1. *Contact The National Autistic Society for further information (see Chapter 15 for details).*

Acknowledgements: Dr. Pullaperuma (Consultant paediatrician with an interest in children with autistic spectrum disorder.)

Chapter 11

ASSESSMENT & PROVISION.

This chapter is divided into four parts. Part 1 - The Code of Practice, Part 2 - Assessment, Part 3 - Provision and Part 4 - Should we use labels?

Adult assessment

At the moment fewer adults than children are being assessed. Some private tutors and some organisations e.g. the Dyslexia Institutes (*see Chapter 15*) assess adults. Adults who want a referral for a speech and language assessment can either make a direct referral to their local Speech & Language Therapy service [1] or ask their GP to make the referral for them. The availability of local assessment/provision may be different across the UK as it is dependent upon what the Local Authority has contracted the service to provide. An adult's GP can also refer them to physio/occupational therapists for assessments. Adults who are looking for assessment/provision can get advice from The Dyspraxia Foundation's adult helpline Tel: 0171 4355443 and from the Adult Dyslexia Organisation Tel: 0171 7377646.

PART 1 - THE CODE OF PRACTICE

The way in which the Department for Education recommends that assessment and provision should be carried out, and provided for pupils with Special Educational Needs in UK schools, is laid out in The Code of Practice (*see Chapter 13*). It has five stages (starting with Stage 1 - identification of initial concern and progressing to Stage 5 - issuing of a Statement of Special Education Needs) but a child does not have to pass through all of them. Those who need a Statement of Special Education Needs can go directly to Stage 4 whereby a multidisciplinary assessment is made as a result of asking for a Statutory Assessment of Special Education Needs. The Code of Practice works in the same way no matter which of the conditions found within this book affects the child. Throughout the whole process there is an expectation that parents will both be kept informed at all stages and that the school will have endeavoured to gain the support of the parents by involving them in the creation, delivery and evaluation of detailed plans to help their child in and out of school.

Unless a multidisciplinary assessment is made it will often be the most noticeable area of difficulty that is assessed first and then as the 'whole picture' of the child emerges further assessments are made. The school may ask for information from various outside professionals at any point e.g. at Stage 2 they may seek informal advice from their LEA's Special Needs Support Team or other professionals who already work within the school e.g. paediatric occupational/physio/speech & language therapists etc.. As the parent can also make direct referrals via her doctor for motor and speech & language assessments these may all have been done by the time that the child reaches Stage 3. In the case of a child affected by dyspraxia the most noticeable area of learning difficulty may have already been recognised/assessed by Stage 1 but no-one may have yet made the connection with dyspraxia.

Stage 1: 'involves the initial identification and registration of a child's special educational needs, the gathering of basic information about the child, taking early action to meet the child's needs within his or her normal classroom work and monitoring and reviewing his or her progress." Developmental records may be checked as this stage via the Health Visitor.

Its triggered by: an 'expression of concern that a child is showing signs of having special educational needs, together with evidence for that concern" which can come from any professional e.g. teacher/health visitor etc. and/or the parent.

Outcome: may be a period of special attention with carefully differentiated teaching within the normal classroom work being provided.

Review: review date is set, at the first review it may be decided that the present provision should be continued, or that the child no longer requires help, or after TWO reviews the child is moved to Stage 2 because she has not made satisfactory progress.

Stage 2: "The SEN co-ordinator (SENCO) takes the lead in assessing the child's learning difficulty, and planning, monitoring and reviewing the special educational provision, working with the child's teachers and ensuring that the child's parents are consulted."

Its triggered by: decision made at Stage 1 review or (as a result of initial concern of teachers and parents) the SENCO " considers that early intensive action is necessary".

Outcome: an Individual Education Plan (IEP) is drawn up which will include the nature of the learning difficulties, action to be taken (e.g. staffing, materials, equipment, number of lessons, in classroom and/or outside of it.), help from home, targets, monitoring of the situation plus the review dates.

Review: If satisfactory progress a new IEP may be drawn up with new targets, period between reviews may be changed, individual may revert to Stage 1 or after TWO reviews (in which the parent and child should be involved) the child will move to Stage 3 as progress is not satisfactory and additional expertise needs to be sought.

Stage 3: "The school calls upon external specialist support to help the pupil to make progress."

Its triggered by: a decision at Stage 2 review, or as a result of discussions of an initial concern between the SENCO, teachers and parents the SENCO (in consultation with the head teacher) "considers that early intensive action with external support is immediately necessary.

Outcome: as in Stage 2 but now there will also be assessments conducted by outside specialists e.g. educational psychologists. A new IEP (developed with the help of the outside specialists but usually implemented in the normal classroom setting). It should ensure a "co-ordinated cross-curricular and inter-disciplinary approach which takes due account of the child's previous difficulties."

Targets:"specific target should be set for all aspects of the education plan. There should be special assessment arrangements made for those targets" ...... some of which "may be conducted by outside specialists".

Review: If satisfactory new IEP drawn up and child continues at Stage 3. If satisfactory after two reviews the time between reviews may be increased. After at least two satisfactory review periods child may go to stage 1 or 2. Or, the head teacher considers referring the child to the LEA for statutory assessment.

Stage 4: This has two elements-

1. "consideration by the LEA in co-operation with those concerned with child (parents and professionals) of whether a statutory assessment should be made". If they say no, then the parents can appeal against this decision.

2. If the decision is made to conduct an assessment then the following has to be sought in writing: parental, educational, medical, psychological, and social services advice plus any other (including that of the child) that is regarded as being desirable If no statement is made then appeal can be made against this decision. *(For information on the appeals procedure see Chapter 13)*

Stage 5: The child becomes the subject of a Statement of Special Education Needs. The Statement includes details of each of the child's special educational needs and the provision for those needs. A lot of detail may be needed, especially if equipment like computers are part of the statement e.g. the exact specification of the computer, the availability of a printer and disks for it etc.. The Statement also includes its objectives and how they will be monitored, the name and type of school which the child will attend plus the non-educational needs of the child and provision for them.

(All quotes are from the Code of Practice on the Identification and Assessment of Special Educational Needs (pub. The Department for Education ISBN 0 85522 444 4) It is a long document, the above is just core information from it. It includes information for both parents and professionals. Free copies can be obtained by ringing: 0171 5100150

PART 2 - ASSESSMENT

Most assessors use various diagnostic tools which include a mixture of formal and informal tests and, in the case of children, classroom observation. The assessment 'tools' (tests/diagnostic checklists etc.) that a professional can use are determined by his/her qualifications.

Standardised tests are scored and their results can be based against the 'average standard' of a person of a given chronological age. Theoretically standardised test results are only valid for the day of assessment and if an individual was assessed the next day (or by another assessor) the results might be slightly different. The way in which some tests are scored has been changed to allow for such variations and thus enable them to be more reliable e.g. some test results are given in age bands as in The New Reading Analysis. Some test scores are given in 'centiles' (or percentiles) which are expressed in numbers from 0-100. Centiles/percentiles are interpreted in the following way: if Tom is assessed as 95 then 94% of children (of Tom's age) would do LESS WELL than him on this task. A score of 10 indicates that only 9% of all children (of his age) would score LESS THAN him. Technically the 50th percentile is the average of such a scoring system with the *'average band'* being approximately 35-85. However, some tests may start, or end, this *band* at a slightly higher/lower score. Usually, the assessor takes the view that there is no cause for concern if an individual is within the *'average band'* of a particular test. The further the score is below *the 'average band'* then the greater the cause for concern. Scores above the *'average band'* are regarded as good to excellent depending on how far away they are from the average thus if Tom scores 98 he is of superior intellectual ability for the task.

THE EDUCATIONAL PSYCHOLOGIST'S ASSESSMENT

Many individuals are referred to an Educational Psychologist for assessment of intellectual functioning as part of a wider assessment for one or more of the conditions which come within the Specific Learning Difficulty Profile. They are the only group of professionals who can use the British Ability Scales (BAS) and the Wechsler Intelligence Scales (e.g. the WISC test). Both of these scales have sub-tests which identify different aspects of an individual's performance. Each sub-test in the WISC is scored from 1-19 (with 8-12 being an average score for each sub-test). There are special tables to convert these scores into standardised scores (of which an IQ is one example). Results can be expressed as percentiles/centiles and as age-equivalent scores with the latter often being more meaningful to the non-educational psychologist.

Using the WISC to diagnose dyslexia and dyspraxia

The WISC looks at seven factors i.e. verbal comprehension, perceptual organisation, freedom from distractibiliy, processing speed, verbal IQ, performance (non-verbal) IQ and full scale IQ. The educational psychologist will use the factor scores, the sub-test profile analysis and other diagnostic features of a child's performance to reach a diagnosis of dyslexia. A few educational psychologists still compare the average of the Arithmetic, Coding Information, and Digit Span sub-tests (commonly called the ACID profile) against the average of all the other sub-tests as part of the assessment process to diagnose dyslexia. However, this is not totally reliable for several reasons among them being that the individual may have several of the conditions found within the SpLD Profile. Madeleine Portwood has determined that the sub-test scores can reveal indicators of some forms of dyspraxia i.e. "if the scores in arithmetic, coding, block design and digit span are significantly depressed in relation to the scores in the other sub-tests." [2]

THE REPORT

After assessment the assessor should spend time with the parent/guardian/adult discussing the assessment's findings, explaining any terms that may not be understood and appropriate provision. In the case of children both the school and the pupil's parent/ guardian are entitled to a copy of the report and this should be done automatically without them having to request a copy. When discussing provision with staff parents should not assume that the school has a copy of the report even though they may have been sent one. It can be lost in the post or within the school itself especially when a number of people have access to it .

The language of reports

Although it is accepted that each discipline has its own 'language' it is important than any special terms used in a report are explained. Assessors have to be very careful in their choice of words in a report because of the dangers of litigation and this can lead to difficulties in interpretation. Phrases like the 'individual would *benefit* from using a computer.......' are regarded as safe to use whilst 'it is *essential* that the individual has the use of a computer............' might cause problems for the assessor if his findings were contested in a court of law. Unfortunately the first statement can be interpreted by the reader as meaning that it is not necessary to implement the recommendation as it is not a 'need'. Some assessors no longer use the terms IQ or Intelligence Levels with the terms changing on a fairly regular basis e.g. 'gifted' is out but 'more able' and 'superior intellectual ability' is in ....for the moment!

Help & support

Assessment and the diagnosis that goes with it is often a traumatic event for the adult, parent and child. It can be the realisation of their worst fears, long needed proof that there is indeed a problem or require a complete reassessment of their life and the reasons for failure. It is inexcusable to assess and report on an individual without providing counselling to both parent and adult/child and informing them of both the national agencies and their local support groups to whom they can turn for Help & Support.

School based Remediation Strategies

The coursework of some assessor's qualifications e.g. Prof Sharma trained, RSA Dip SpLD focuses on good report writing. Such assessors have been trained to provide comprehensive reports which can be used as working documents by the teacher/Special Needs Assistant (SNA). These reports are designed to enable the educational staff to cope effectively with the individual and meet his learning needs. Good reports include a list of WORKABLE and EFFECTIVE strategies to remediate the individual's difficulties which can be implemented by the teacher/SNA WITH THEIR PRESENT LEVEL OF KNOWLEDGE AND EQUIPMENT. It is not enough to state that the child would benefit from structured multisensory phonological training without defining EXACTLY how to do it. The educational staff should be able to sit down with the child and the report's list of recommended strategies and implement them immediately.

PART 3 - PROVISION

Qualifications of the providers

There are various professionals who are qualified to provide for the conditions found within the SpLD Profile. Local professionals with an interest/expertise in this field can be found via the local groups of the national organisations found in Chapter 15. Specialised medical staff such as occupational/physio therapists, doctors etc. have *paediatric* qualifications. Teaching staff (including Special Needs Assistants) may hold a variety of qualifications [3] (The British Dyslexia Association hold a list of Accredited teachers who have appropriate qualifications. Individuals with the highest qualifications can write AMBDA after their name.) Some medical professionals may also hold qualifications that are normally held by teachers e.g. the *RSA Dip SpLD*. Some courses leading to specialist educational qualifications concentrate on literacy difficulties and so if the individual has a condition which is non-literacy based it is important to check to see whether the professional has a good knowledge of the area that is required.

Medical
The assessor/s will recommend various activities and strategies which will help the individual, many of which can be carried out in the classroom and/or home. The individual with moderate/severe difficulties is likely to require specialist intervention which may take place in school, in a speech & language/physio/occupational therapy unit and in the home.

Educational
Dependent upon the knowledge and experience of the teachers local state schools should be able to provide for individuals with low-level forms of the conditions found within the SpLD Profile. Moderate and severe difficulties are likely to need specialist input from an LEA Special Needs Support Team, by suitably qualified specialist teachers (who may be employed by the school or paid for privately) or by provision in a school that specialises in the particular condition. In some cases there can be difficulties in gaining provision (*see Chapter 13*). The local organisers of the various national agencies may be able to advise on local private/state provision. [4] Two books which can be of help are: 'Which school for special needs' edited by Derek Bingham and the CreSTed free booklet [5] which both list specialist schools.

PART 4 - SHOULD WE USE LABELS?
There is much discussion amongst professionals, and those who are affected by the conditions within the SpLD Profile, as to whether one should 'label' the individual by stating the conditions that are present. Some parents/individuals feel relief when they can give a name to the difficulties whilst others feel that such labelling is inappropriate. Some parents/adults are very resentful if they are not told the name of the condition and feel that the professional is 'hiding' the condition from them (or has been inefficient and has failed to recognise it). Many professionals feel that too much importance is given to the label i.e. it is not the condition but the provision for it that matters. Some may be reluctant to name the condition for fear of misdiagnosing or because they cannot, at this stage, make a clear-cut diagnosis. Still other professionals are aware that some parents may not be ready to face the implications of the condition

being named and the future it holds for both them and their child e.g. Autistic Spectrum Disorder.

There are several good reasons for giving the individual/parent a name for a condition. Individuals are unlikely to find a book about it in a library unless they know what the condition is called and it also makes it easier to which of the specialist agencies e.g. The Dyspraxia Foundation could help them. Labels can also help us know what a particular individual needs not just academically but in the wider social context. They help us understand, tolerate and make allowances for the behaviours that can be found as part of the condition e.g. the clinging/'personal space invading behaviour' of some children affected by dyspraxia and the dyslexic child who always lays the table incorrectly.

The arguments over the labelling issue no doubt will always be with us - perhaps this is where we have to say that in this case there is unlikely to be a Solution!

Acknowledgements:

Hugh Bellamy, The College of Speech and Language Therapists and Dr. Peter Gardner.

© Jan Poustie

References

1. The address of your local Speech & Language therapy service can be found by contacting the Information Office of The College of Speech & Language Therapists, 7 Bath Place, Rivington Street, London EC2A 3DR. Tel: 0171 6133855 Fax: 0171 6136413.

2. Developmental dyspraxia by Madeleine Portwood (pub. Durham County Council)

3. See the Solutions Resources Guide

4. & 5. See Chapter 15

Chapter 12

SCOTOPIC SENSITIVITY IRLEN ⓁⒾ
SYNDROME

by Patricia Clayton (Irlen diagnostician)
and edited by Jan Poustie

Scotopic Sensitivity Irlen Syndrome is a perceptual dysfunction affecting reading and writing based activities as well as depth perception. Individuals with Irlen syndrome need to put more energy and effort into the reading process because they are inefficient readers who see the page differently from the 'good' reader. Constant adaptation to distortions from print or from the white background causes fatigue and discomfort and, more importantly, limits the length of time these individuals can read and maintain comprehension. If the syndrome is undetected affected people, although often appearing bright, may be viewed as underachievers with poor behavioural attitudes or motivational problems. and/or incorrectly labelled as being of low ability.

one of the common distortions

The syndrome causes a variety of problems among them being:

▲ Reading: it deteriorates, is slow & hesitant, poor reading comprehension, unable to sustain reading for any length of time (difficult to spot using conventional reading tests as they may do well for ten minutes and then begin to fade), skips words/lines, misreads words, slow reading rate, avoids reading, trouble in tracking, background too bright (glare), print indistinct, needs to read in dim lighting.
▲ Writing: writes up or downhill, unequal spacing, makes errors when copying.
▲ Maths: criticised for sloppy/careless maths errors, misaligns numbers.

▲ Music: difficulties in reading music, plays better by ear.
▲ General: general strain or fatigue, falling asleep, headaches or nausea, watery eyes, eye strain, hot/dry eyes.

Irlen Syndrome can aggravate other learning disorders and physical disabilities which may be shown in the following ways:

▼ Physical: clumsy and uncoordinated, difficulties in catching balls, drives extremely cautiously, cannot judge distances, inability to sit still, motion sickness.
▼ Academic: inability to concentrate, finds difficulty starting work, difficulties in organising thoughts, searches for words, difficulties in expressing ideas clearly, hesitancy & jumbled expression when explaining ideas, diverts attention to avoid completing tasks, needs frequent repetition of instructions.
▼ General: low self-esteem, withdrawn, sensitivity to noise, faulty perception of colour, difficulties in looking at a computer screen.

<u>Treatment of Irlen Syndrome</u>

It is a perceptual dysfunction caused by sensitivity to light rather than a visual problem of a refractive nature. Neurological research suggests that the Irlen filter technique allows receptor cells in the visual cortex to analyse visual information more efficiently by selectively filtering the input of specific wavelengths of light . The Irlen filters are specially modified filters in a very wide range of different colour combinations.   They will reduce eye-strain, headaches, migraine in individuals who are affected by these difficulties due to Irlen Syndrome. Assessment is by consultation with a specialist at an Irlen Centre (see Chapter 15 for address) who will carry out an intensive diagnostic interview in order to determine which combination of the different Irlen filters will be most beneficial. Individuals with problems which cannot be rectified by the use of the filters will be referred to other specialists.

© Jan Poustie

Chapter 13

GAINING PROVISION ———

*The gaining of provision
for a child can either be
very quick and easy, or
very slow and may not be
achieved at all. There are
pockets of excellent
practice within the schools
of Britain. In some cases a
parent can express her
concern, it is acted upon,
assessments are made and
appropriate provision is
made. Unfortunately this
is not always the case,
because the child's form of
Specific Learning
Difficulty is so deeply
hidden.*

**There are several factors
which can hide the various
conditions that are found
within the SpLD Profile
among them are:**

❏ Superior intellectual
ability which masks the
difficulties. (Thus the child is
seen to be working at the
average level of ability, his
superior intellectual ability is
not apparent and therefore
teaching staff feel there is no
cause for concern.)

❏ Frequent absences from
school due to ill health.
Asthma, eczema, and other
allergic conditions are
common amongst those
affected by the conditions
which come within the SpLD
Profile. Stress caused by
trying to cope with their
learning difficulties can also
cause the child to have more
illness than is the norm.
(This causes the teaching
staff to believe that the
reason for the child's
standard of work to be
behind his level of apparent
ability is because he has not
attended school enough.)

❏ Difficulties within the
family situation, such as a
divorce, can mask the
learning difficulty. (The
teaching staff believe that
emotional problems to do
with home are causing the
child to react in an
emotional way e.g. anxiety,
misbehave, daydream etc.)

The child could be affected by one of the less known conditions that come within the Profile e.g.

Attention Deficit Disorder

The teaching staff may have little or no knowledge of these specific learning difficulties. They therefore are unable to recognise them.

The child shows signs of apprehension, insecurity, pessimism, anxiety and stress. The child may become anxious because he feels that he is failing, because he does not find it easy to follow instructions, because his mind feels so confused and muddled (some even wonder whether they are going mad). Gerald Hales' research (see Dyslexia Matters Published by Whurr.) has found that girls aged 8 -12 years of above high intelligence (IQ 115 and above) are particularly prone to being apprehensive and insecure. His research also shows that Specific Learning Difficulty children have a pessimistic patch between the ages of 8 -12 years with girls being affected by it more than boys. (The child's stress and anxiety may be very apparent. The parent believes the cause of the anxiety and stress is because

her child has a specific learning difficulty which is preventing him from reaching his potential. However, the teacher may see the cause as being 'an over-anxious' and pressurising mum who is making the child anxious; and that the parent has an incorrect understanding of the child's ability.)

The result of the conditions within the Profile being hidden can be horrendous for the child, the parents and the teachers.

All of them have beliefs which are in conflict with each other, all firmly believe that they know the truth. The parent may well have been concerned for some time that her child has difficulties but has only just told the school of her concerns. She expects immediate action not to be told "We will observe the situation this term, to see if we can see any difficulties." If, after several meetings, provision is still not being offered and the difficulties are still not being recognized, she may well become an anxious parent. This will affect the relationship between the parent and the teacher.

The teacher can feel that the parent is being unreasonable, that she is expecting special treatment for a child that does not need it. As the situation progresses the relationship between parent and teacher worsens until the trust, which is essential for progress to be made, no longer exists.

The child is the piggy in the middle. Children are aware when they do not fit in. They are aware when they are different, they do not have to be told. Those with Dyspraxia may frequently knock things flying, those with literacy difficulties are aware that their friends can read and spell with greater ease than they can. The child with near vision dysfunction is aware that they often feel sick, have headaches and feel exhausted by the end of the day, while their friends do not. The child with language difficulties is aware that they easily misunderstand instructions and feel foolish when they get them wrong. Children with mathematical difficulties feel stupid when they get low marks in the table test and the child with behavioural difficulties feels at war with itself.

The lack of recognition of the difficulty, and therefore the lack of provision, is caused by all the parties seeing the situation from vastly different viewpoints based upon their own experience and knowledge.
It is like the story of The Six Wise Men And The Elephant. Each man felt a different part of the elephant and so described it as a completely different beast e.g. the one who touched the tail described it like a rope:

The teacher is seeing the tail - the anxiety. Every time there is dispute between the parent and the teacher over provision the tail is twisted. When the child is expected to cope with tasks which his difficulties make difficult for him, he becomes anxious and the tail is twisted again. The tail is twisted when the child becomes stressed and anxious and comes home exhausted at the end of the school day. He may be bullied because of his specific learning difficulties or is depressed because of his lack of success. At its worst he is racked by stomach pains, headaches, feelings of nausea from the moment he wakes up until the moment he goes to sleep. Eventually even the shorter Easter and Christmas holidays are not long enough to allow him to recover from it. The parent seeing this becomes stressed, parental anxiety sets in, she talks with the teacher who perceives her as an 'anxious' parent and the tail is twisted again.

The parent is seeing the tusks.

If she herself has Specific Learning Difficulties she knows the problems it causes throughout life and the effect it can have on career choices. If adequate provision is not made quickly she feels that she is fighting for her child's rights. She can see the difficulty but does not wish to upset the 'apple cart' too much by frequently drawing the teacher's attention to the child's difficulties as she fears creating a poor relationship with the teacher. The parent is also trying to keep a balance between these concerns whilst trying to enable her child, and her family, to cope with the emotional and social effects that the difficulties cause. As Dyslexia is 80% inherited she may also be trying to cope with more than one child's difficulties.

The child is the body of the elephant.

He is being pulled in two directions by the tail and the tusks. He may be aware of his parent's concern, especially if the provision is not granted quickly (it can take several years to obtain provision). He may be embarrassed, not only by his difficulties, but also by the fact that the parent is mentioning them to the teacher as he may not wish for his peers to know that he has problems. He may also fear that anything that the teacher does to help him may make him noticeable within the classroom. If he is aware that his parent has concerns he may be worried that his difficulties are causing her problems. He may then not tell his parent the problems that are occurring at school. He may be trying to please everyone. In school he will do whatever he needs to do to cope. So any of the following can happen - work is

179

unfinished, he completes written tasks by writing the minimum amount and only uses the words he can spell. He can push himself to the limit and as a consequence feel ill. He can misbehave /daydream to remove himself from an impossible situation or he removes himself completely by truanting from school.

How can this situation be improved?
Imagine that you are in a chemistry lesson. The instructor has asked you (the teacher) to conduct an experiment. You are given the equipment (the child). You then go and attempt to conduct the experiment to achieve the result the instructor said you should expect. If you do not get the right result first time then he will give you tips on how to perfect your experiment. However, if by the end of the lesson you still do not have the expected result he will ask you to take it 'on trust' that he is right because of all the research that has been conducted in the past that has proven it to be so. He will explain to you that you did not have the right

environment (heat, proportions of chemicals etc.) to enable you to show the correct result.

When a parent expresses concern she is like the chemistry instructor advising on how to conduct the experiment, she has given the teacher tips on how to recognise the child's problems. The reports that she obtains proving the difficulties are the further tips that the chemistry instructor gives his students. However, if the environment (the teacher's knowledge and experience) is not right then the teacher cannot see the learning difficulties, they therefore do not exist and so he will make no provision. The teacher is unable to make the leap of faith that the student chemist has to make, and accept 'on trust' the specialist's advice.

The road to gaining provision can be very stony and very isolating for the parent and stressful for the child, parent and school.
Besides the parent's 'tips' the government also provides tips on how to meet the needs of Special Needs children via the Code of Practice. All too often when the child's Sp.LD's are

 hidden neither of these systems work effectively which results in the child's needs not being met and the parent and the teacher becoming estranged and the following events can occur:

The SENCO and the Special Educational Needs register.

Initially, the parent may say that she is worried about the child's progress. (The Special Educational Needs Co-ordinator, usually known as the SENCO, then enters the child's name onto the Special Educational Needs register as defined by Stage 1 of the Code of Practice). If the SENCO and the class teacher cannot see a cause for concern then the child's name will be kept on the register with no provision being made, though they both should continue to observe him. The child's name should then stay on the register until both the school and the parent agree that the child has no special needs.

Involving your local contacts for help and support

By now hopefully the parent will have approached the appropriate local support groups of the various national agencies. (*See chapter 15.*) The support provided by these organisations enables the parent to cope with an increasingly stressful situation. Many teachers do not realise that they too can receive help and support from these agencies.

Private specialist assessment

The parent may become so concerned that she wants an assessment of the child's intelligence and/or confirmation of the child's learning difficulties. At this point she may take advice from her local help and support groups regarding availability of local specialists within the appropriate field. At asesment the specialist will diagnose which conditions are present and will provide her with a report of his findings. Recommendations will also be made regarding appropriate intervention.

Direct parental referrals

By making such referrals (which are often made much

faster than referrals made by the school) she can gain some free assessments of her child. Some local authorities allow you to make a direct parental referral to their Psychological Service). She would need to insist on a full assessment of the child as otherwise her suspicions might not be confirmed - a full assessment takes about one and half hours. If she suspects that there is a language difficulty she could make a direct parental referral to her local Speech and Language unit. If movement difficulties are suspected then the parent will have to make a direct referral to her local Paediatric Physiotherapist and Paediatric Occupational Therapist. (These are all based at local NHS Trust hospitals and referrals are made via the child's GP.)

The parent may decide to pay privately for an assessment of her child e.g. via an Educational Psychologist or specialist school assessment (these can be expensive) or via a Behavioural Optometrist if they suspect that the learning difficulties relate in part to a visual problem.

However, the school may not accept the findings of these reports if they still cannot see evidence in the classroom that the difficulties exist and so could continue to make no provision.

Private specialist tuition

The parent may, by now, be so concerned that she arranges for her child to receive specialist lessons after school by a suitably qualified private tutor to help the child overcome the main areas of difficulty. The parent is now in a 'catch 22' situation. All specialists in this field agree that the earlier the child receives the correct intervention the less severe will be his problems in later life. By providing the intervention she will be reducing the social, academic and emotional affects of the condition but the non-specialist class teacher will have even less chance of being able to see the child's difficulties within the classroom. The family is also now under greater pressure as they are having to fund the cost of the lessons.

The OFSTED inspection

If the school is due for an OFSTED inspection the parent may voice her concerns at the parent's meeting held by the OFSTED inspectors prior to the inspection of the school, mention her concerns via the confidential questionnaire which they have sent her plus provide them with written documentation of the difficulty she is having in gaining provision for her child.

If the teacher is still unable to see the child's learning difficulties, they do not exist and therefore no provision is made

Superior intellectual ability and the SpLD Profile

This problem of recognition of learning difficulties can be worsened if the child has both superior intellectual ability, a condition that comes within the Profile and is of primary school age as few children come into this category and therefore primary school teachers are unlikely to meet them very often. How can they recognise what they have never seen before? Such individuals are often only spotted in late secondary school or adulthood. (Superior intellectual ability is defined by the British Psychological Society as covering those 2% of children who have an IQ of 130 and above. The chartered educational psychologist Dr. Peter Gardner states: "Though research studies and experts differ in their attributions of the incidence of severity, there does appear to be agreement that approximately one child in twenty-five shows evidence of severe Specific Learning Difficulties and one child in six shows evidence of milder difficulties which are still causing problems in the classroom.)

If teachers do accept the diagnosis but see that the child is performing at chronological age they may feel that the child does not have "a significantly greater difficulty in learning than the majority of children of the same age" [Code of Practice 2:1] and so feel that no intervention is needed. However, as Peter Gardner says: "All teachers consider it their duty to maximise the potential of each child. It is unlikely that a teacher would expect a pupil of more limited potential to achieve their chronological age level. Therefore, it should also be the case that (all things being equal) the teacher should expect the very intellectually able pupil to attain a level above his chronological age appropriate to his intellect." By now the teacher may well be as frustrated as the parent and the child. The parent and the reports say that the difficulties exist and are causing problems for the child at school. At this point the teacher may decide that a condition exists but since they cannot see any evidence of them in the classroom they cannot be causing the child any difficulties and therefore no provision is necessary.

The parent's concerns increase.
The child's behaviour may deteriorate, he may become aggressive, more demanding, have stomach aches, headaches and feel sick. He may have poor sleeping habits with difficulties going to sleep and frequent waking during the night, so now both child and parent are tired from the moment they wake up. The child may be receiving private intervention but many of the events of the child's school day are causing him stress e.g. the amount of copying, writing and reading that he has to do without the use of a spellchecker or computer. (Many schools have so few computers that there is no way that the child could do most of his work on a computer unless the parent provides it, or he is provided with one via a Local Educational Authority Statement.) She may discuss

with, or make a complaint, to the School's governors but they may agree with, and support, the school's actions because they still are unable to see the difficulties and therefore are unable to respond to them.

The school can feel harassed
By this stage the school may well feel that they are being harassed by a parent who has unreasonable expectations of both their child and the school. The school and parent are now in conflict and communication may have become very difficult for both. The parent realising this may ask for intervention by The Parent Partnership Officer. (His name and telephone number is available from you Local Education Authority.) He may be able to re-establish the lines of communication between the parent and the school but he has no power over what the school does.

Involving the Local Education Authority
Eventually the parent (if she lives within a Local Education Authority that allows this) may involve the Authority by making a direct parental referral to their Special Educational Needs Department. If they accept the findings of

the specialists they will make recommendations to the school which include detailing what the difficulties are and the areas in which provision needs to be made. However, the school may refuse to accept the recommendations of their Local Education Authority as they still are unable to see evidence of the child having any difficulties within the classroom.

By this stage no-one is happy.
The parent and child and the rest of the family are under great stress, as may be the school. There is no easy solution because both parents and the school each still believe that they are correct.

The parent and child now have several choices, they can:
❒ **Change L.E.A. schools**
(and hope that they will have better luck next time). The child will have to cope with making new friends, learn to trust that the teacher will meet his needs and cope with the changes in school routine, something which many SpLD Profile children find daunting. The parent may have little trust in teachers by now and can fear that her child will still not receive the provision he needs.

❒ **Move the child to a specialist private school**
but this will cost a great deal of money and the strain of funding it will affect the whole family. The best of these specialist schools have a 'whole school' policy where every teacher is aware of the difficulties that the different conditions cause in every subject - though not every teacher may have an appropriate qualification in the teaching of Specific Learning Difficulties. (A list of Specialist Schools is obtainable from CReSTeD, *see Chapter 15.*)

❒ **Take the child out of the education system and teach them at home.**
This can itself cause difficulties e.g. it may mean that the family will be deprived of the mother's income and there may be difficulties with finding other children during the school day with whom the child can relate. (**"Education Otherwise"** can advise you on teaching your child at home -look for their address in the Supplementary information at the end of this chapter.)

❒ **Make a request for a statutory assessment** under section 167 of the 1993/96 Education Act - all parents have this right under section 3:29 of it. (The parent may need to take advice from their local help and support contact *(see chapter 15)* e.g. Dypraxia Foundation co-ordinator to ensure that she does this correctly.) The Local Education Authority (LEA) only have to comply with this request if the child has Special Educational Needs and it is necessary for the LEA to make provision. Generally, the LEA will expect the school to have done everything they can to meet the child's needs before the LEA decides it needs to determine the provision. However, the Code of Practice recognises in section 3:18 that there will be times when the parent is dissatisfied with school-based provision and then turns to the LEA. When the LEA has completed a statutory assessment it may issue a Statement of the child's needs in which they may state the provision necessary. On occasion it may be that the LEA makes a monitoring statement without providing additional resources.

❏ **Make a formal complaint to the Secretary of State for education**
under sections 496 and 497 of the 1966 education act in that the governing body of the school has acted unreasonably and unlawfully. (The parent will need to take advice from their local help and support contact on the correct wording of the complaint.)

How is the teacher feeling at this point?

❏ He may feel that he is failing the child, and therefore the family, because he cannot get the parent to recognise that the school is correct in its view that the child is having no difficulties with school work and therefore no provision needs to be made.

❏ He may feel that he is dealing with a parent who will never be satisfied with anything that he does or says and therefore can become distressed by the fact that the parent will not stop making demands of him that he feels unable to meet.

❏ He may dread every conversation and meeting with the parent. Every statement made by the parent may be analysed to see if the parent is 'having a go' at him.

❏ He may feel that he is at risk of losing control of the situation so be even less ready to discuss the child's learning difficulties with the parent.

❏ He may resent the amount of time and energy that this

parent is taking when he has children in the school who he feels have far greater needs than this child.

☐ He may feel that the parent is being pushy and unreasonable, she has an overrated expectation of the child and the school and after all no child can be good at everything.

☐ He may feel intimidated by the parent's knowledge of Specific Learning Difficulties and like a doctor who resents the patient telling him the diagnosis he may feel that his experience and hard-earned qualifications are being regarded as worthless or imperfect.

The Code of Practice

(Numbers in brackets that are underlined refer to the relevant sections of the Code of Practice on the Identification and Assessment of Special Educational Needs. It is published by the Department for Education - see Chapter 11 for further details. All references to 'the OFSTED report' refer to "The Implementation of the Code of Practice for pupils with special educational needs, published by HMS) 1996 ISBN 011 35 00807 and all numbers in italics refer to its paragraphs.)

The teacher may feel intimidated by the Code of Practice itself. The Code of Practice was issued as a result of the 1993 Education Act. All schools by law have to have regard to the Code and must not ignore it. These facts alone can make a teacher feel

insecure. Implementation of the code is still in its infancy. Although all SENCO's should have had training in the use of the Code by now some may well feel that the training they have received is inadequate, that they still do not understand it well enough and therefore feel insecure about using it. Its complexity may make the teacher want to bypass it completely. The parental demands for recognition and provision for the child and/or parental knowledge of the Code may only inflame the situation and increase the insecurity.

A parent who understands the Code of Practice will know that it is not being implemented correctly, will resent that this is the case and become anxious regarding the school's knowledge base. The teacher can then feel that they are being bludgeoned with the Code of Practice by the parent and yet another area of conflict has arisen.

The Code requires that the school liaises with and accepts information from the parent and the child regarding the latter's special needs. "That there should be close consultation and partnership with the parent, that consideration should be given to the ascertainable wishes and feelings of the child." (2:64) However, the OFSTED report revealed that "pupils are often not involved in reviewing their own progress and are rarely a party to producing or reviewing their IEPs

{Individual Education Plans}.
......Only in some schools are the IEP targets shared with parents and their views occasionally sought before the IEP is finalised." (106) This seems a great pity as in fact by working with the child educational staff can make their lives much easier for "where the IEPs were produced in collaboration with the pupils themselves they were often simpler and more manageable." (107)

The Code states: "The school-based stages should therefore utilise parents' own distinctive knowledge and skills" (2:9). "Children's progress will be diminished if their parents are not seen as partners in the educational process with unique knowledge and information to impart. Professional help can seldom be wholly effective unless it builds upon the parents' capacity to be involved and unless parents consider that professionals take account of what they say and treat their views and anxieties as intrinsically important." (2:28)

Given that a teacher may already feel that the parent is trying to usurp his position and authority, may dread the appearance of the parent in the classroom door, and may feel threatened by the parent's knowledge base how can we expect him to accept and follow these guidelines?

In the past teachers have been informers - your child has this difficulty, we will do this about it. They may feel that because of their experience and qualifications that 'they know best'. Now they are expected to discuss provision. Negotiation requires compromise and agreement between the parties. It requires skills that have not been part of the teacher's training. He may feel out of his depth, or may continue to only use his 'informing skills' which to the parent may seem autocratic and part of a 'them and us' situation.

The teacher may have placed the child on one of the five Stages of the Code of Practice (see Chapter 11) but the parent may feel that more intervention is required. Some teachers still do not realise that children do not have to progress through all the stages starting with Stage 1. If the parent knows the Code of Practice this again will be an area of conflict. In other cases the teacher is trying to do his best with limited resources and may not wish to put the child at a higher stage which will involve more funding.

The parent regards the provision as being inadequate, insufficient or inappropriate whilst the teacher wonders if this parent will ever be satisfied with the provision that the school makes.

• The teacher may feel, if he has a specialist qualification in Special Needs, that his knowledge base is being slighted. He may be unaware that even a single module dedicated to SpLD of a Special Needs course is unlikely to have given him the ability to access, recognise and provide for the child who has a hidden condition that comes within the SpLD Profile.

• He may feel that he is vulnerable, that he is being personally criticised by the parent and that his work in the classroom is not appreciated.

• He may not fully understand the reports that the parent has submitted to him regarding the child's learning difficulties but is unhappy about admitting it to either the parent or other professionals/teachers for fear of appearing inadequate.

• He may feel that if he recognises that the child has learning difficulties then the parent will become more demanding and other parents will start to expect more for their children too and that there is no way in which his limited resources can cope with this.

• He may feel on the defensive all of the time, feel that the problem is not with the school but with the parent and so will look for events at home that are making the child anxious and put the child/parent relationship under severe scrutiny.

• As the standard of a child's work who comes within the Profile is often inconsistent he may observe that the child may be able to do the work sometimes and with comparative ease. He therefore may assume any or all of the following: that the child is lying about his difficulties to his parent, that the child is lazy, careless or has an attitude problem.

• He may feel very distressed, isolated and vulnerable if the parent tries to travel further along the road of gaining provision by asking the LEA for Statement or by making a formal complaint to the Secretary of State for Education on the grounds that the school is acting unlawfully and unreasonably.

The school can then be in crisis, it lacks the knowledge to move forward, it can feel that it cannot go back on what it has said in the past as that would show its lack of knowledge. A dislike for the parent, who the teaching staff feel is causing the crisis in the first place, can then be apparent. As a result of all these factors - the inability to assess, recognise and provide for the child to the satisfaction of the parent plus his awareness of the school's limited resources the teacher may decide to opt out. He may feel that the parent will never be content so there is no point in trying. He puts the child onto the Register of Children with Special Needs as the Code indicates but offers no provision at all and only communicates with the parent about the child's possible special needs when the parent insists upon a discussion.

There could also be conflict regarding the child's provision within the school.
SENCOs were appointed as a result of the Code of Practice and it suggests that in small schools the head or deputy take on this role. The result of this is that the SENCO in a primary school, especially, may not necessarily be the teacher with the most experience or interest in the conditions that come within the SpLD Profile. The SENCO may know a great deal about the general field of Special Needs but know little about the relevant conditions (or may know little about either and still be in the process of learning about them). Thus the very difficult situation can arise where a class teacher (or supply teacher) recognises the learning difficulties but the SENCO/Headteacher do not.

A part-time or supply teacher may be wary of 'rocking the boat' for fear of losing their teaching hours whilst the full-time teacher is only too aware as to who will be writing his next reference. In such a case, the teacher may well be very limited in what he can do without upsetting the SENCO and the Headteacher. He may be limited to emotionally supporting the child and make minor adjustments to the way in which he is taught. (One of the most useful things he could do is to boost the child's confidence by finding an area in which he has more than average skill and enable him to demonstrate his talents within the classroom.) Such teachers are forever in a balancing act between the 'devil and the deep blue sea' as they also have to have regular dealings with the parent whilst knowing that the correct provision is not being made.

Some parents decide never to try to gain provision via the child's school
They realise that it may never be successful and purposefully hide their child's difficulties from the teacher. They pay for private tuition from a specialist tutor to help the child overcome as many of his difficulties as possible. Sometimes these children come to light when they start their GCSE course when the teacher realises that the child is struggling or the parent voices their concern as they fear that their child's career choices

will be limited by poor grades. Sometimes individuals only find out in adulthood the reason for their struggle at school.

The parent who has travelled along the stony road of trying to gain provision may well be exhausted by now.

The affects of non-provision on the family

The attempt to gain provision may have caused serious rifts within the family as brothers and sisters become jealous of the child who gets away with aggression, climbing into mum and dad's bed and seems to have more attention than them. Sometimes one of the parents can no longer cope with the stress that the non-provision causes the family and a divorce occurs. In some, thankfully few cases, the child takes the tragic step of finally opting out by committing suicide.

Parental stress and dissatisfaction

The parent may decide to give up trying for provision because of the effect that the stress and work involved of trying to gain provision is too much. She and the child try to make the best of a very bad situation. The parent may remain dissatisfied with the child's education throughout the child's school life.

The price of non-provision

The child only fulfils his potential of he is lucky and meets a teacher that teaches him in the way that he needs to learn. If he is unlucky he will never recover from the related emotional aspects such as being bullied and teased by his peers for his difficulties. He may always feel a failure, be a 'round peg' in the 'square hole' that is his school environment. He may retreat from society as he becomes more and more convinced that society has never helped him. He may then join the large proportion of the prison population who have conditions that come within the SpLD Profile.

Hidden difficulties can create a 'no-win' situation for all the parties involved.

To go back to the original analogy of the Six Wise Men and the Elephant. From the parent's point of view each meeting, with its associated failure to gain adequate provision chips away at 'the tusks' until only the stumps are left - the parent has no more fight in her. From the teacher's point of view each meeting with its associated failure to get the parent to believe that no provision is necessary (or that the present provision is sufficient) twists 'the tail' again until it is a mass of knots and tight curls and can thus destroy the teacher/parent relationship. From the child's point of view for each week that the child does not receive adequate provision 'the body' starves until it becomes emaciated and is no longer able to function in its environment.

The teacher
He cannot recognise what he does not realise exists or what he cannot see, he therefore is unable to make provision for it. He has not seen those small signs that indicate that all is not well with the child's learning processes.

Non-recognition of the small signs.
The teacher has not seen the associated body movements when the child is working at academic tasks, the fidgeting, the hair twisting as he has to work extra hard to control his body and visual functions which can indicate dyspraxia or near-vision dyfunctioning/occulomotor dyspraxia. He does not see or understand the smile of relief on the child's face as he greets his parent at the end of an exhausting and frustrating school day. He does not see the hooked hand and distorted paper position which can indicate difficulties with writing and possible near-vision dysfunctioning/occulomotor dyspraxia. The odd sitting position favoured by the child is not seen as a possible indicator of dyspraxia. That impulsive child who leaps into tasks, often interrupts and just cannot wait his turn may well be affected by Attention Deficit Disorder (ADD) and how on earth can the daydreamer who has opted out because he has been told once too often not to dominate the classroom discussions also be affected by ADD! The signs are so small, the underlying difficulty and stress that the conditions found within the SpLD Profile can be so great. Such signs are like the mouse rustling through the hedgerow - too small to be of any significance in the general landscape except for the sharp, watchful eye of the parent/specialist teacher who knows that they can lead to the discovery of something much bigger.

The parent
She may have had concerns for several years before she even made the school aware of them. Thus from her first initial concern it may have taken five or six years to have reached this stage. Now the parent may feel the need to withdraw both herself and the child from the situation (by electing to educate him at home for a while) so that they can gradually recover from the emotional battering that this experience has given them. The parent sees the difficulties but cannot convince the teacher and thus endures years of frustration, anxiety and stress.

The child
He may never receive the provision that he needs and may well have to adjust to years of frustration and a feeling of inadequacy or failure. Whatever the parent gains for him is likely to be a compromise between

what the parent knows he needs and what she can obtain for him. However, although the school may not accept or provide for the child's needs few parents will be able to ignore that they exist.

The best she may be able to achieve is to provide the understanding, support and love that the child needs. When the child asks her "Why does not one help me, why don't they understand that I have a problem" she will need to explain rationally and unemotively why our present educational system is unable to help him. Thus she may help avoid him growing up hating 'the system' and the society that it represents and eventually elect to become an outcast from it.

The child who lacks appropriate provision always loses. Both his family and teacher are under stress, academic work is a struggle and for those with behavioural difficulties the stress can continue into the playtimes as they try to develop and maintain social relationships with their peers. His whole personality may be affected by the intolerable situation that he is in. As one parent observed "he always sang until he started school, I only realised that he had stopped singing throughout the whole of his school life when he started to sing again the day after he completed his 'A' levels". Our

children who have a condition that comes within the SpLD Profile should be able to sing, they should be enabled to be at peace with their world.

THE SOLUTION
Training the educators
There is hope, a solution is possible for this seemingly impossible situation but it will take time and commitment on the part of our educators. It is recognised, by those working in the field of Specific Learning Difficulties, that the only way to improve this situation for teacher, parent and child is for all educators (no matter what subject or age group that they teach) to have a minimum training in this field. Since our children move onto further education it is not just teachers that need this but lecturers in colleges and universities as well. Of vital importance is the training of those who train our teachers. A module that deals with Specific Learning Difficulties to an adequate depth should be a compulsory part of all teacher training courses for as Violet Brand says:
"We need to train teachers in their initial teacher training. They need to be aware of these specific problems that they will be meeting whatever subject they are teaching, whatever age group."

Our children are our greatest resource, if they do not reach

their potential then neither does the society of which they are a part.

Training the governors

(All references to 'the OFSTED report' refer to the previously mentioned report "The Implementation of the Code of Practice for pupils with special educational needs, published by HMSO. Numbers in italics relate to the relevant sections of it.)

Courses/lectures on Special Educational Needs which are arranged for school governors by national organisations such as the British Dyslexia Association and LEAs are not always well attended. This has resulted in a lack of knowledge amongst governors with regard to the Code of Practice and the implications of the 1993 Education Act. This problem was highlighted in the OFSTED report where the inspectors found that "in many schools governors are finding major difficulties in fulfilling all of their specific responsibilities under the Code." *(69)*

Comment was also made that "while some governing bodies exercise their statutory functions and accept their full responsibilities under the Code, the majority take too limited a lead and leave the staff of the school to make their own decisions" *(22)* and are "reluctant or uncertain as to how to proceed to examine critically their school's SEN provision." *(23)*

The report mentioned several factors that contributed to this situation. It revealed that while "most [of the Chairs of governing bodies and nominated governors for SEN] were aware of some but not all of their duties under the 1993 Education Act, others were ignorant of almost all the requirements." *(61)* "Often governors (Chairs and sometimes nominated governors) admitted to not having read the Code in full or the shorter introduction to the Code produced by the DfEE for parents .....On many occasions they defensively stressed the fact that their services were voluntary and unpaid." *(66)* "Governors could rarely detail the amount of SEN funds available to the school as a result of the Local Management of Schools (LMS) or how it was allocated; most were therefore unable to judge whether or not the use of the funds was effective." *(68)*

The findings of this report are of grave concern to those of us in the field of Specific Learning Difficulties. We appear to have a situation where a proportion of those who are legally responsible for managing our schools lack the knowledge to meet their commitment as far as Special Educational Needs (SEN) is concerned. As a large number (approximately 20%) of all pupils are expected to come under the SEN heading at some time in their lives it is vital that our governors are properly trained.

As more and more power is being devolved to schools (and therefore to the governors who manage them) surely it is time that they were both expected to become much better informed (by attending appropriate lectures/courses etc.) and were paid for their labour in just the same way as local councillors are.

Training priorities

Research shows that early intervention is the nearest 'cure' for the conditions that come within the SpLD Profile. So, it is essential that all of our primary school teachers are trained as quickly as possible to recognise, assess, provide for and support such children.

OFSTED inspections

Schools are inspected by OFSTED inspectors via a tender system. If a school has indicated in its form "s" that it has a specific SEN unit then it will be ensured that the inspection team will include a member with appropriate SEN experience. However, an SEN specialist inspector will not necessarily be included otherwise. During 1996 changes were made in the inspection system which meant that OFSTED reports no longer have to have a section devoted to SEN but that all subject inspectors are required to report on the SEN provision within their subject. This does of course mean that the subject inspectors themselves need to have an adequate knowledge of SEN. Up to that time such inspectors had a basic SEN training via OFSTED but OFSTED itself was aware that the 1996 changes would mean further training for its inspectors in this area. *(Further information on this can be found in the OFSTED report.)*

Availability of training

Many educators are aware of their lack of knowledge in the field of Specific Learning Difficulties and are concerned by it, as they wish to do their best for all the children and students in their care. However, they may not know where they can receive training and/or may not have the time to devote to it. Parents often seek/need to know more in their struggle to gain provision. Thus this book was written as a way of meeting the needs of both groups. (The Solutions for SpLD: Resources Guide contains a Training Section which includes a list of the agencies who offer the R.S.A.)

diploma (or certificate) in SpLD and other bodies who offer training in this field. Schools can also approach their Local Education Authority and ask for in-service training in SpLD. Some of these bodies and all of the main agencies mentioned in *Chapter 15* of this book offer courses that parents too can attend.)

Conclusion

There is no doubt that now that training is available throughout the country all schools that have a commitment to meeting the needs of their SpLD Profile children will ensure that they have at least one member of staff who is fully trained in this field. (They will also ensure that the knowledge that specialist teacher has is used by all the teachers in the school.) Perhaps the first thing a parent should ask a school is whether this is the case, and if not, why not? "Does this child have a condition that comes within the Specific Learning Difficulties Profile?" should be the first question that teachers ask when a parent has concerns. Only by training and learning about this field will our educators and inspectors be able to recognise all the different forms of these

difficulties and so enable our children to receive the support and education that they need and deserve.

SUPPLEMENTARY INFORMATION
THE CODE OF PRACTICE*:
(*Note the Code of Practice was not altered by the 1996 Education Act.)
Martin Sharpe (Head of the Department for Education and Employment's Code of Practice Team states that: "Under the 1993 Education Act schools have the responsibility to use their best endeavours on behalf of children with Special Educational Needs. The Code offers practical advice as to how schools can fulfil that duty. It is based on models of good practice that were already in operation in many schools around the country pre-1993. Schools are required to have regard to the Code.
The Department of Education and Employment expect that whilst a school was not adopting all the procedures recommended in the Code it was nevertheless achieving the same ends by different means."
The sentence above can put some parents in the invidious situation of having to rely upon a verbal agreement to provide

rather than a written Individual Education Plan (IEP)as detailed in the Code. Few people would agree to a verbal contract without having anything in writing to define specification of the goods bought and the date of delivery. Some teachers may prefer a verbal agreement as they feel that an IEP with its defined targets and the necessary negotiation between parent, child and school (*as to what the targets are, how they are to be achieved, the expected result and time frame by which they will be evaluated*) will be difficult to negotiate. What may not be realised is that a verbal agreement, with its attendant ambiguity and lack of fixed goal posts, is likely to increase the tension between the parties and thus further exacerbate the conflict that may already be present between them.

All our SpLD Profile children should be the recipients of the educational 'good practice' that Martin Sharpe advocates and with a verbal agreement that cannot be guaranteed. This situation could be avoided if all schools always put the child's provision into a written format so that all the parties know where they stand.

SpLD AND OFFENDERS.

John Stevenson, the Prison Inspectorate's Education Consultant states that he "suspects that it is likely that a significant proportion of prisoners are affected by Specific Learning Difficulties. In most prisons there is no automatic and systematic detailed diagnosis of Sp.L.D. and therefore in most prisons SpLD prisoners are unlikely to obtain the provision they need to overcome their learning difficulties."

The Channel 4 video 'Dyslexia' states that 45% of the prison population are estimated to be dyslexic. BBC 2 television's Public Eye programme stated that 52% out of a group of 110 offenders tested showed strong indications of dyslexia. A Dyspel Project leaflet states that "a study in Louisiana USA showed a 25% reduction in re-offending by addressing dyslexic problems, both literacy difficulties and also dealing with the problem of self-image." (*The Channel 4 video is in the 'Solutions for SpLD: Resources Guide.*) The Dyspel Project was a one year pilot project to work with the probation service to identify and address dyslexia as a factor in offending and to break the pattern of under achievement, frustration and low self-esteem that often characterise people with undiagnosed dyslexia and may lead to offending. The project was a partnership between the London Language and Literacy Unit, the Inner London Probation Service and the London Action Trust. Further information can be obtained from: Cynthia Klein, Dyspel Project Director, London Language and Literacy Unit, Southwark College, St. Mary's Road, London SE15 2EA. Tel: 0171 639 l9512 Fax: 0171 815 1690)

Even those who are sent to prison as juvenile offenders and have a Local Education Authority Statement of Educational Need may not receive either appropriate or adequate provision. This is because the evidence of their learning difficulties which was originally produced as a result of an assessment leading to the Statement is often not reaching the appropriate Prison Education Department. This situation is exacerbated by the fact that prisoners move from one penal institution to another with the continual reassessment which that entails.

The reassessments are conducted by education officers in the light of their own knowledge base and experience. At the moment no-one knows how many officers hold a specialist qualification such as the RSA Diploma in Specific Learning Difficulties but the figure is likely to be small. If they lack specialist qualifications they are unlikely to be able to make an accurate diagnosis of the learning difficulties, the sub-skills deficiencies which contribute to the problem and plan /implement an adequate and appropriate provision.

OFSTED:

OFSTED, Alexandra House, 29-33 Kingsway, London WC2B 6SE Tel:0171 4216800 Fax:0171 4216707 Helpline: 0171 4216673

INSPECTIONS - All parents should receive the leaflet "Making the most of Inspection" prior to the inspection.

REPORTS and ACTION PLANS - The report is issued 2 months after the inspection. All parents should be given a summary version of the report and a full copy of the School's Action plan that follows it. They are also entitled to see the full copy of the report which is held at the school. The school has to write up the Action Plan within 40 working days after receiving the full report (excluding Easter,

Christmas and Summer Holidays). It should be sent to every parent and every person who works at the school. The Code recommends that the Action Plan is reported on every year at the Annual Parent's Meeting. Generally speaking the onus is upon the parents and governors to ensure that the Action Plan is implemented as Ofsted was not established to follow-up every school Action Plan. Schools that are in Special Measures (i.e. failing or likely to fail), or, have serious and significant weaknesses are automatically followed up. Outside of these groups only a limited number of Action Plans are followed up. A full copy of the OFSTED report and the School's Action plan are kept in the local public library. Full copies of the reports can be obtained from one of the following companies.

Reports from schools in the SOUTH OF ENGLAND (including Warwickshire)
BDC Holdings Ltd, Slack Lane, Derby, DE22 3FL Tel: 01332 347123 Fax:01332 291464

Reports from schools in the NORTH OF ENGLAND
SIA Ltd., Warwickgate House, Warwick Road, Old Trafford, Manchester M16 0SY
Tel: 0161 8724077 Fax: 0161 8723997

Reports are put onto the OFSTED internet site 12 weeks from the date of inspection:
http://www.open.gov.uk/ofsted/ofsted.htlm

APPEALING TO THE SEN TRIBUNAL:

A request can be made to the Local Education Authority (LEA) by either the school or the child's parents, for an assessment leading to a Statement of Special Educational Needs under stage 4 of the Code of Practice. The LEA can refuse to make the assessment. (An assessment is expensive -it can cost over £2000 to make a full multi-disciplinary assessment so this may well make an LEA reluctant to assess a child that they feel will not require a Statement). Once an assessment is made the LEA can then refuse to issue a Statement on the grounds that the child's learning difficulties are not severe enough to warrant one. If the LEA refuses to either assess the child or provide a Statement then appeal to the tribunal can be made to reverse the decision. **A school cannot appeal to the tribunal.** An appeal can only be made by the parents. The tribunal will ask for a copy of the parent's letter in which the request for assessment was made. At present there is a grey area as to what constitutes a 'parental request' as it is unclear as to what proof is needed to show that the parent requested the school to ask for the assessment on their behalf. In 1995 an appeal to the tribunal was 'struck out' because although the parent's section on the school's request form had been filled in by them stating "we do hope that you respond to our request for help with 'x'." the request was deemed not to have been made by the parents under section 173 of the 1993 Education Act. If the school's request has been refused then the parent can make their own request for assessment of the LEA. Once this too is refused, they can then appeal to the tribunal. Such a situation can be avoided if parent's make the initial request for assessment with the school providing supporting evidence for it.

TEACHING YOUR CHILD AT HOME:

It is legal to teach your child at home even if you are not a qualified teacher. For information on this send a A5 stamped addressed envelope to: Education Otherwise, PO Box 7420, London N99 SG. This is an umbrella organisation for families who are teaching their children at home. It provides self-help, support and information. The helplines for urgent enquiries are:

England has 4 helplines: 01283 532 547 or 01359 231 890 or 01837 851 620 or 0181 924 1243 Scotland helpline:015956 94898 Wales helpline: 01978661882

(For convenience the parent has been referred to as 'she', the teacher has been made male and the child has been referred to as 'he' but the author is aware that Sp.L.D. affects both sexes, that both parents can be involved in gaining provision for their child and that teachers who have to face these difficulties are of both sexes.)

ACKNOWLEDGEMENTS:
Colin Allen (Deputy Chief Inspector for Prisons) John Stevenson (Prison Inspectorate's Education Consultant) Dr. Peter Gardner (Chartered Educational Psychologist and co-founder of Appleford School) Cynthia Klein (Dyspel Project Director) Carol Orton (Befriender Co-ordinator British Dyslexia Association) Violet Brand, Mary Coyle and Hilary Finn plus various departments at OFSTED and the Department of Education and Employment
Copyright Jan Poustie March 1996.

Chapter 14

CONCLUSION

You have read this guide - What do you do next?
This Guide has explained the problems and how to identify them. It has also provided information about the appropriate professionals to whom you will then need to make referrals for diagnosis of the condition. If you as a Professional, Parent or an Adult wish to know more about Specific Learning Difficulties then you can:

❏ read some of the books mentioned in this guide.

❏ join one or more of your local support groups (*see Chapter 15*)

❏ start to attend some of the many excellent national and local conferences and lectures that are organised by various agencies for both the professional and non-professional. (*see Chapter 15*)

A rosebud without water or light will fail to thrive. Although full of the potential to be a beautiful blossom it will wither and die. Human beings also need to thrive - they need to fulfil their potential .....to succeed! Some individuals succeed despite their difficulties, others will fail without support. One cannot support what one does not recognise. Without the recognition that a difficulty is present, inappropriate provision may be given or no provision at all.

The conditions in this book affect many individuals regardless of their race, colour or creed. For some of them the daily tasks that they have to do can be likened to climbing Mount Everest without any equipment. Some cannot maintain that sort of will power and ability for a long length of time and so they start to fail. The more they fail the lower their self-esteem, the lower their self-esteem the more anxious they become about their difficulties (and the less inclined to attempt the task because they now expect to fail). Identification (and the later diagnosis) of a difficulty can be the first step towards success. This leads to the second step - making appropriate provision to help them to gain the equipment needed to climb their mountains (*see Solutions Resources Guide*). Often the diagnosis starts the 'raising of self-esteem' which is an essential part of provision for the difficulties. Diagnosis provides an explanation for the failure - the individual no longer has to feel responsible for it - he is not lazy, careless etc..

All people have strengths and weaknesses. Thus although the difficulties exist they are only a part of a person - a part which may have great relevance in certain situations (such as school) but may have very little in others. Alongside the difficulties they may also have received 'gifts' which if they are enabled to develop may far exceed the abilities of others (though few will be an Einstein, Rodin or Leonardo Da Vinci). Many of them have managed to achieve their goals despite their difficulties. Their difficulties may not have disappeared but have just been hidden or reduced by their strengths. However, under stress some, or all, of the difficulties may return (or in later life they may see similar difficulties affecting their children) and so again they have to start looking for solutions - and so this book was named.

Chapter 15

Main sources of Help & Support

These all arrange conferences & lectures, offer telephone help and produce various publications and leaflets. Each agency has its own local groups which can provide information about local teachers/therapists plus hold lectures etc..

THE BRITISH DYSLEXIA ASSOCIATION
98 London Road, Reading, RG1 5AU United Kingdom.
Tel:0118 966 2677
e-mail:admin@bda-dyslexia.demon.co.uk
Fax: 01734 351927
Helpline: 0118 966 8271
e-mail:info@
dyslexiahelp-bda.demon.co.uk
World wide web:
http://www.
bda-dyslexia.org.uk./

SCOTTISH DYSLEXIA ASSOCIATION
Unit 3,
Stirling Business Centre,
Wellgreen Place, Stirling,
Scotland.
FK8 2DZ.
Telephone: (01786) 446650
They supply an information pack for which they charge a small fee

DYSPRAXIA FOUNDATION
8 West Alley, Hitchin, Herts.
United Kingdom. SG5 1EG
Telephone:01462 454986
Fax:01462 455052

AFASIC - Overcoming Speech Impairments.
Association for all speech impaired children
347 Central Markets,
Smithfield, London. EC1A 9NH
Tel: (0171) 2363632

THE NATIONAL AUTISTIC SOCIETY
393 City Road.
London.
EC1V 1NE
Tel: (0171) 833 2299
Fax: (0171) 833 9666

THE ADHD FAMILY SUPPORT GROUP UK
c/o Mrs G Mead
1A High St, Dilton Marsh
Westbury, Wiltshire, BA13 4DL.
Tel: (01373) 826045
Fax: (01373) 825158

Specific Learning Difficulties Support

ADULT DYSLEXIA ORGANISATION

Helpline: 336 Brixton Road, London, SW9 7AA.
Telephone: Helpline 0171 924 9559 Administration:0171 7377646 Fax:0171 2747840.
Email:dyslexia.hq@dial.pipex.com
Worldwide web address:
http:\\www.futurenet.co.uk/charity/ado/index.html

PATOSS (Professional Association of Teachers of Students with Specific Learning Difficulties.)

PO Box. 66 Cheltenham Gloucestershire GL53 9YF
Has a Newsletter. Local Groups and an Annual Conference

REAL AND EFFECTIVE ACTION FOR DYSLEXIA

Chairperson: Mrs Gillian Cloke, 21 Mylady's Mile. Hollywood,Co. Down. N. Ireland. BT18 9EW

ARTS DYSLEXIA TRUST

Lodge Cottage, Brabourne Lees, Ashford, Kent. TN25 6QZ Telephone: 01303 813221

THE HYPERACTIVE CHILDREN'S SUPPORT GROUP

71 Whyke Lane, Chichester, West Sussex. PO19 2LD
Tel & Fax:01903 725182
Provides a free Basic Introductory pack for professionals plus a Resource Professional pack (which is free at the moment). Also provides information for parents.

HANDWRITING INTEREST GROUP

Contact for information, conferences, courses, workshops, Handwriting Review annual journal andBooklets. To join the organisation:Felicity Barnes, 6 Fyfield Road, Ongar, Essex CM5 0AH

USA Help and Support

The Orton Dyslexia Society

Chester Building Suite 382
La Salle Road, Balitimore
Md. 21286-2044
Tel: 001 410 825 2881

Learning Disabilities Association of America

4156 Library Road
PITTSBURGH Pennsylvania
15228
U.S.A
Jean Patersen
National Executive Director
Tel: 001 412 341 1515
Fax: 001 412 344 0224

There have been successful candidate(s) who have completed the Hornsby Correspondence Course in this country. For further details or contacts who may be willing to help, contact:-
Michael Gardener
Hornsby
International Centre
262 Trinity Road
LONDON SW18 3SN
Tel: 0181 874 1844

IPSEA

(Independent Panel for Special Education Advice)
4 Ancient House Mews, Woodbridge, Suffolk.IP12 1DH
Tel/Fax:01394 380518
It guides parents through the assessment and tribunal procedures. Offers advice and help with understanding reports. It can represent parents at special educational needs tribunals.

CONTACT A FAMILY

170 Tottenham Court Road, London, W1P 0HA. Tel:0171 383 3555 Fax:0171 383 0259
Helpline: 0171 383 3555 (open to parents, relatives and professional workers.)
Provides support for families who care for children with disabilities and Special Needs. Produces various publications and factsheets including: "Siblings and Special Needs" and "A parent's guide to statements of Special Educational Needs in England and Wales."

SCOTTISH SOCIETY FOR AUTISTIC CHILDREN

Hilton House, Alloa Business Park, Whins Road, Alloa FK10 3SA
A multidisciplinary organisation for practitioners in speech and language difficulties. Holds an annual conference and provides information on aspects of speech and language.

THE DYSLEXIA ARCHIVE

HENSA Unix Computing Laboratory .
University of Kent
Canterbury. Kent CT2 7NF
Tel: 01227 823784 Fax: 01227 762811
e-mail dyslexia-admin@unix.hensa.ac.uk

An ever growing collection of up-to-date material covering all aspects of dyslexia. It is stored electronically and is accessed using a computer connected to the Internet. It is specifically designed to make it easy for the specialist and casual browser alike to find , read and retrieve the information held locally and at other sites throughout the world.

Computer Help and Support

Computer Information and Advice Service

98 London Road, Reading, RG1 5AU
Tel: 0118 966 2677
e-mail: admin@bda-dyslexia
An excellent source of information on software and computers suitable for Specific Learning Difficulty individuals of all ages.

National Council for Educational Technology (NCET)

Milburn Hill Road, Science Park, Coventry. CV4 7JJ Tel: 01203 416994 Fax:01203 411418 Provide information on computers and software, produce some specialist publications relating to Specific Learning Difficulties

Scottish Council for Educational Technology (SCET)

74 Victoria Crescent Road, Glasgow, Scotland. G12 9JN
Tel:0141 3375051. Provides general information.

Other Help and Support Available.

BRITISH ASSOCIATION OF BEHAVIOURAL OPTOMETRISTS (BADO)

72 High Street,
Billericay, Essex.
CM12 9BS.
Telephone:01277 624916
Behavioural Optometrists specialise in Visually related learning difficulties and use lenses and Optometric Vision training to improve and develop the effeciency of the visual system.
BABO maintains a register of accredited Optometrists throughout the UK.

THE IRLEN INSTITUTE

International Contact: Patricia Clayton,
Irlen Centre,
123 High Street,
Chard, Somerset.
TA20 1QT.
Telephone/Fax 01460 65555
Irlen Centres deal with perceptual learning problems which affect some dyslexics and non-dyslexics. This can cause many difficulties such as print blurring, background distortions, headache and reluctance to read for a sustained period. Irlen colour tinted lenses and overlays may be prescribed which can assist in overcoming the problem and learning strategies are also recommended.

Health , Help and Support

This section is included because many S.p.L.D. individuals suffer from various allergies, others are badly affected by stress and anxiety induced by the difficulties their S.p.L.D. causes them in school, or, at work.

NATIONAL ASTHMA CAMPAIGN

Providence House, Providence Place, London. N1 0NT Tel:0171 226 2260 Asthma helpline: 0345 010203 (9am-7pm Monday -Friday) Provides information. Produces a large number of very useful freeleaflets including: "Asthma at school".

NATIONAL EXZEMA SOCIETY

163 Eversholt Street, London. NW1 1BU. Tel: 0171 388 4097 Information line: 0171 388 4800 Produce a large number of very useful free leaflets.

THE SOCIETY OF HOMEOPATHS

2 Artizan Road, Northampton NN1 4HU Tel: 01604 21400 Fax: 01604 22622. Send a stamped addressed envelope (A5 size or bigger) for a list of qualified professional homeopaths and information leaflets. Some practices now run Paediatric clinics. Homeopathic treatments can be of great benefit to individuals whose Sp.L.D. causes them severe stress and anxiety.

THE BRITISH ALLERGY FOUNDATION

23 Middle St London EC1A 7JA Tel: (0171) 600 6127 Fax: (0171) 600 8459 Helpline: 0171 600 6166 A friendly, confidential service offering callers individual, up-to-date allergy advice and information. The foundation also publishes a quarterly newsletter which contains lots of helpful information and tips.To recieve this newsletter and become a member of the foundation please send a cheque for £5.00 with your details to the above address

THE BRITISH MIGRAINE ASSOCIATION

178a High Road, Byfleet, West Byfleet, Surrey. KT14 7ED Tel: 01932 352468. This charity is run by migraine sufferers and offers useful advice and information. Signs of migraine are a headache with some, or all of the following: a deep throbbing in the head, a pain on one side of the head, feel sick or vomit, feel as if you are unable to continue with normal activities, see flashes, zigzags or see things as dark patterned or strange, can only see part of your environment - as though your eyes have a shutter across part of them, you try to avoid light and noise, your sense of smell changes, you feel worse if you move, you hate being touched, you want to be alone, you find it lasts between four hours and three days, you have to go to bed.

ALLERGIES
THE BRITISH GOAT SOCIETY
34-36 Fore Street, Bovey Tracey,
Newton Abbot, Devon TQ13 9AD
Tel:01626 833168

**THE SHEEP DAIRYING
ASSOCIATION**
Wield Wood, Nr. Alresford,
Hants SO24 9RV,
Tel: 01420 631151

PILGRIMS SCHOOL
Firle Road, Seaford, East Sussex
BN25 2HX
Tel: 01323 892697

HEALTH
**BRITISH ACUPUNCTURE
ASSOCIATION**
34 Alderney Street, London SW1
Tel: 0171 834 1012 or 0171 834 6229

**REGISTER OF CHINESE
HERBAL MEDICINE**
21 Warbeck Road, London W12
8NS

**INSTITUTE OF
COMPLEMENTARY
MEDICINE**
PO Box 194, London SE16 1QZ
Tel: 0171 237 5165

**BRITISH SCHOOL OF
REFLEXOLOGY**
92 Sheering Road, Old Harlow,
Essex CM17 0JW
Tel: 01279 429060

SHIATSU SOCIETY
5 Foxcote, Wokingham, Berks,
RG11 3PG
Tel: 01734 73083

STRESS
**TRANSCENDENTAL
MEDITATION**
Freepost, London SW1P
4YY
Tel: (freephone 0800 269
303
ALSO SEE 'SHIATSU SOCIETY

RELATIONSHIPS
**BRITISH ASSOCIATION OF
PSYCHOTHERAPISTS**
37 Mapesbury Road,
London NW2 4HJ
Tel: 0181 452 9823

**BRITISH ASSOCIATION FOR
COUNSELLING**
1 Regent Place, Rugby
CV21 2PJ
Tel: 01788 578328

RELATE
Herbert Gray College, Little
Church Street, Rugby CV21 3AP
Tel: 01788 573241

**INSTITUTE FOR
TRANSACTIONAL ANALYSIS**
BM Box 4104, London WC1N 3XX
Tel:0171 404 5011

**ASSOCIATION OF CLINICAL
HYPNOTHERAPISTS**
229A Sussex Gardens,
Lancaster Gate,
London W2 2RL
Tel:0171 402 9037

General Support

It would be ideal if the telephone numbers of these organisations were displayed (and the agencies explained as appropriate) by all of us working in this field. (Many of our Sp.LD. children/teenagers (and possibly their parents) and may not be able to access information via the normal routes (e.g. leaflets)). The impact of undiagnosed or unprovided for Sp.L.D. can be tremendous. There have been tragic cases of children committing suicide because of their Sp.L.D., parents too may reach breaking point.

SAMARITANS
10 The Grove Slough,
Berks, SL1 1QP
Tel: 01753 532713 Helpline:
0345 909090 National
organisation offering support
to those in distress who feel
suicidal or despairing and need
someone to talk to.

CHILDLINE
Royal Mail Building,
Studd Street, London
N1 0QW.
Tel: 0171 239 1000
Fax: 0171 239 1001
Free national helpline for children
and young people in trouble or
danger.

DRUGLINE
9a Brockley Cross,
Brockley, London
SE4 2AB.
Tel: 0181 692 4975
Fax: 0181 692 9968.
Provides support to addicts, their
family friends and relatives,
telephone advice and counselling.

TERRENCE HIGGINS TRUST LTD
52-54 Grays Inn Road, London
WC1X 8JU.
Tel: 0171 831 0330
Provides information and
support concerning AIDS.

DEPRESSION ALLIANCE
35 Westminster Bridge Road,
London SE1 7JB
Tel: 0171 633 0557
Fax: 0171 633 0559
Publish a variety of booklets
including Depression in children
and young people, Self help and
Student Survival.

MIND
15-19 Broadway, London
E15 4BQ.
Tel: 0181 519 2122 ext:214
Produces some useful booklets
that deal with stress and
depression including
"Understanding Childhood
Distress" and "How to cope with
the stress of student life" and
"How to recognise the early signs
of Mental Distress".

General Help & Support
Continued:

ANTI-BULLYING CAMPAIGN
185, Tower Bridge Road, London SE1 2UF
Tel/Fax: 0171 378 1446
SpLD children are often more at risk from being bullied than their peers. Children with dyspraxia are especially vulnerable. This organisation provides advice, information, understanding and support to parents of bullied children and to children themselves.

CURB (Children Under Risk from Bullying)
Maureen Booth-Martin, Heath,
Cardiff CF4 3NT.
Helpline: 01222 611300
Aims to help parents to help their children. Is in the process of producing a leaflet at the moment.

RELATE (Marriage Guidance Council)
Herbert Gray College, Little Church Street, Rugby, Warwickshire CV21 3AP.
Tel: 01788 573241 / 01788 560811
Fax: 01788 535 007
Coping with family members with Sp.L.D. can put the parents under a great deal of stress which can result in a breakdown of their relationship. Relate can help by providing counselling.

SPEECH ——
NAPLIC
7, Bath Place. Witherington St. London EC2 3TR
College of Speech and Language Therapists,
Tel: 0171 613 3855